In Battle for Peace

THE OXFORD W. E. B. DU BOIS

Henry Louis Gates, Jr., Editor

The Suppression of the African Slave-Trade to the United States
of America: 1638–1870
  Introduction: Saidiya Hartman

The Philadelphia Negro: A Social Study
  Introduction: Lawrence Bobo

The Souls of Black Folk
  Introduction: Arnold Rampersad

John Brown
  Introduction: Paul Finkelman

Africa, Its Geography, People and Products
Africa—Its Place in Modern History
  Introductions: Emmanuel Akyeampong

Black Reconstruction in America
  Introduction: David Levering Lewis

Black Folk: Then and Now
  Introduction: Wilson J. Moses

Dusk of Dawn
  Introduction: Kwame Anthony Appiah

The World and Africa
Color and Democracy: Colonies and Peace
  Introductions: Mahmood Mamdani and *Gerald Horne*

In Battle for Peace: The Story of My Eighty-third Birthday
  Introduction: Manning Marable

The Black Flame Trilogy: Book One
The Ordeal of Mansart
  Introduction: Brent Edwards
  Afterword: Mark Sanders

The Black Flame Trilogy: Book Two
Mansart Builds a School
 Introduction: Brent Edwards
 Afterword: Mark Sanders

The Black Flame Trilogy: Book Three
Worlds of Color
 Introduction: Brent Edwards
 Afterword: Mark Sanders

Autobiography of W. E. B. Du Bois
 Introduction: Werner Sollors

The Quest of the Silver Fleece
 Introduction: William L. Andrews

The Negro
 Introduction: John K. Thornton

Darkwater: Voices from Within the Veil
 Introduction: Evelyn Brooks Higginbotham

Gift of Black Folk: The Negroes in the Making of America
 Introduction: Glenda Carpio

Dark Princess: A Romance
 Introduction: Homi K. Bhabha

IN BATTLE FOR PEACE
The Story of My 83rd Birthday

W. E. B. Du Bois

With Comment by Shirley Graham

Series Editor, Henry Louis Gates, Jr.

Introduction by Manning Marable

OXFORD
UNIVERSITY PRESS

For Cornel West

OXFORD
UNIVERSITY PRESS

Oxford University Press, Inc., publishes works that further
Oxford University's objective of excellence in research,
scholarship, and education.

Oxford   New York
Auckland   Cape Town   Dar es Salaam   Hong Kong   Karachi
Kuala Lumpur   Madrid   Melbourne   Mexico City   Nairobi
New Delhi   Shanghai   Taipei   Toronto

With offices in
Argentina   Austria   Brazil   Chile   Czech Republic   France   Greece
Guatemala   Hungary   Italy   Japan   Poland   Portugal   Singapore
South Korea   Switzerland   Thailand   Turkey   Ukraine   Vietnam

Published by Oxford University Press, Inc.
198 Madison Avenue, New York, NY 10016
www.oup.com

Library of Congress Cataloging-in-Publication Data is available.

ISBN: 978-0-19-938688-8

Contents

The Black Letters on the Sign:
W. E. B. Du Bois and the Canon

"... the slave master had a direct interest in discrediting the personality of those he held as property. Every man who had a thousand dollars so invested had a thousand reasons for painting the black man as fit only for slavery. Having made him the companion of horses and mules, he naturally sought to justify himself by assuming that the negro was not much better than a mule. The holders of twenty hundred million dollars' worth of property in human chattels procured the means of influencing press, pulpit, and politician, and through these instrumentalities they belittled our virtues and magnified our vices, and have made us odious in the eyes of the world. Slavery had the power at one time to make and unmake Presidents, to construe the law, and dictate the policy, set the fashion in national manners and customs, interpret the Bible, and control the church; and, naturally enough, the old masters set themselves up as much too high as they set the manhood of the negro too low. Out of the depths of slavery has come this prejudice and this color line. It is broad enough and black enough to explain all the malign influences which assail the newly emancipated millions to-day.... The office of color in the color line is a very plain and subordinate one. It simply advertises the objects of oppression, insult, and persecution. It is not the maddening liquor, but the black letters on the sign telling the world where it may be had ... Slavery, stupidity, servility, poverty, dependence, are undesirable conditions. When these shall cease to be coupled with color, there will be no color line drawn."

—FREDERICK DOUGLASS, "The Color Line," 1881.

William Edward Burghardt Du Bois (1868–1963) was the most prolific and, arguably, the most influential African American writer of his generation. The novelist and poet James Weldon Johnson (1871–1938) once noted the no single work had informed the shape of the African American literary tradition, except perhaps *Uncle Tom's Cabin*, than had Du Bois's seminal collection of essays *The Souls of Black Folk* (1903). While trained as a sociologist at Berlin and as a historian at Harvard, Du Bois was fearless in the face of genre—even when some of the genres that he sought to embrace did not fully embrace him in return. Du Bois published twenty-two single-author works, twenty-one in his lifetime (his *Autobiography*, edited by his friend and literary executor, Herbert Aptheker, would not be published until

1968). A selection of his greatest works, *An ABC of Color: Selections from over a Half Century of the Writings of W. E. B. Du Bois*, appeared in 1963, the year he died. And while these books reflect a wide variety of genres—including three widely heralded and magisterial books of essays published in 1903, 1920, and 1940 (*The Souls of Black Folk, Darkwater: Voices from within the Veil*, and *Dusk of Dawn: An Essay toward an Autobiography of a Race Concept*), one biography, five novels, a pioneering sociological study of a black community, five books devoted to the history of Africa, three historical studies of African American people, among others—Du Bois was, in the end, an essayist, an essayist of the first order, one of the masters of that protean form that so attracted Du Bois's only true antecedent, Frederick Douglass (1818–1895) as well as Du Bois's heir in the history of the form, James Baldwin (1924–1987). (Baldwin, like Du Bois, would turn repeatedly to fiction, only to render the form as an essay.)

Du Bois, clearly, saw himself as a man of action, but a man of action who luxuriated within a verdant and fecund tropical rainforest of words. It is not Du Bois's intoxication with words that marks his place in the history of great black public intellectuals—persons of letters for whom words are a vehicle for political action and their own participation in political movements. After all, one need only recall Du Bois's predecessor, Frederick Douglass, or another of his disciples, Martin Luther King Jr. for models in the African American tradition of leaders for whom acting and speaking were so inextricably intertwined as to be virtually coterminous; no, the novelty of Du Bois's place in the black tradition is that he wrote himself to a power, rather than spoke himself to power. Both Douglass and King, for all their considerable literary talents, will be remembered always for the power of their oratory, a breathtaking power exhibited by both. Du Bois, on the other hand, was not a great orator; he wrote like he talked, and he talked like an extraordinarily well-educated late Anglo-American Victorian, just as James Weldon Johnson did; no deep "black" stentorian resonances are to be found in the public speaking voices of either of these two marvelous writers. Booker T. Washington (1856–1915) spoke in a similar public voice.

First and last, W. E. B. Du Bois was a writer, a writer deeply concerned and involved with politics, just as James Baldwin was; as much as they loved to write, Douglass and King were orators, figures fundamentally endowed with a genius for the spoken word. Even Du Bois's colleague, William Ferris, commented upon this anomaly in Du Bois's place in the tradition, at a time (1913) when he had published only five books: "Du Bois," Ferris wrote, "is one of the few men in history who was hurled on the throne of leadership by the dynamic force of the written word. He is one of the few writers who leaped to the front as a leader and became the head of a popular movement through impressing his personality upon men by means of a book" ("The African Abroad," 1913). Despite the fact that Du Bois by this time had published his Harvard doctoral dissertation in history, *The Suppression of the African Slave-Trade* (1896), his sociological study, *The Philadelphia Negro* (1899), *The Souls of Black Folk* (1903), the sole biography that he would publish, *John Brown* (1909), and his first of five novels, *The Quest of the Silver Fleece* (1911), Ferris attributed Du Bois's catapult to leadership to one book and one book alone, *The Souls of Black Folk*. Indeed, it is probably true that had Du Bois published this book alone, his place in the canon of African American literature would have been secure, if perhaps not as fascinating!

The Souls of Black Folk, in other words, is the one book that Du Bois wrote which most of us have read in its entirety. It is through *The Souls of Black Folk* that we center Du Bois's place in the literary canon; it is through *Souls* that we structure the arc of his seven decade career as a man of letters. There are many good reasons for the centrality of this magical book to Du Bois's literary career, but it is also the case that the other works that comprise Du Bois's canon deserve fresh attention as a whole. And it is for this reason that my colleagues and I have embarked upon this project with Oxford University Press to reprint Du Bois's single-authored texts, and make them available to a new generation of readers in a uniform edition. The only other attempt to do so—Herbert Aptheker's pioneering edition of Du Bois's complete works, published in 1973—is, unfortunately, long out of print.

The Souls of Black Folk is such a brilliant work that it merits all of the attention that it has been given in the century since it was published. In April 1903, a thirty-five-year-old scholar and budding political activist published a 265 page book subtitled "Essays and Sketches," consisting of thirteen essays and one short story, addressing a wide range of topics, including the story of the freed slaves during Reconstruction, the political ascendancy of Booker T. Washington, the sublimity of the spirituals, the death of Du Bois's only son Burghardt, and lynching. Hailed as a classic even by his contemporaries, the book has been republished in no fewer than 120 editions since 1903. In fact, it is something of a rite of passage for younger scholars and writers to publish their take on Du Bois's book in new editions aimed at the book's considerable classroom market.

Despite its fragmentary structure, the book's disparate parts contribute to the sense of a whole, like movements in a symphony. Each chapter is pointedly "bicultural," prefaced by both an excerpt from a white poet and a bar of what Du Bois names "The Sorrow Songs" ("some echo of haunting melody from the only American music which welled up from black souls in the dark past.") Du Bois's subject was, in no small part, the largely unarticulated beliefs and practices of American Negroes, who were impatient to burst out of the cotton fields and take their rightful place as Americans. As he saw it, African American culture in 1903 was at once vibrant and disjointed, rooted in an almost medieval agrarian past and yet fiercely restive. Born in the chaos of slavery, the culture had begun to generate a richly variegated body of plots, stories, melodies, and rhythms. In *The Souls of Black Folk*, Du Bois peered closely at the culture of his kind, and saw the face of black America. Actually, he saw two faces. "One ever feels his two-ness—an American, a Negro," Du Bois wrote. "Two souls, two thoughts, two unreconciled strivings; two warring ideals in one dark body, whose dogged strength alone keeps it from being torn asunder." He described this condition as "double consciousness," and his emphasis on a fractured psyche made *Souls* a harbinger of the modernist movement that would begin to flower a decade or so later in Europe and in America.

Scholars, including Arnold Rampersad, Werner Sollors, Dickson Bruce, and David Levering Lewis, have debated the origins of Du Bois's use of the concept of "double consciousness," but what's clear is that its roots are multiple, which is appropriate enough, just as it is clear that the source of one of Du Bois's other signal metaphors—"the problem of the twentieth-century is the problem of the color line"—came to him directly from Frederick Douglass's essay of that title. Du Bois had studied in Berlin during a Hegel revival, and Hegel, famously, had written on the relationship between master and bondsman, whereby each defines himself through the recognition of the other. But the concept comes up, too, in Emerson, who wrote in 1842 of the split between our reflective self, which wanders through the realm of ideas, and the active self, which dwells in the here and how, a tension that recurs throughout the Du Bois oeuvre: "The worst feature of this double consciousness is that the two lives, of the understanding and of the soul, which we lead, really show very little relation to each other."

Even closer to hand was the term's appearance in late-nineteenth-century psychology. The French psychologist, Alfred Binet, writing in his 1896 book, *On Double Consciousness*, discusses what he calls "bipartititon," or "the duplication of consciousness": "Each of the consciousnesses occupies a more narrow and more limited field than if there existed one single consciousness containing all the ideas of the subject." William James, who taught Du Bois at Harvard, talked about a "second personality" that characterized "the hypnotic trance." When Du Bois transposed this concept from the realm of the psyche to the social predicament of the American Negro, he did not leave it unchanged. But he shared with the psychologists the notion that double consciousness was essentially an affliction. "This American world," he complained, yields the Negro "no true self-consciousness, but only lets him see himself through the revelation of the other world. It is a peculiar sensation, this double-consciousness, this sense of always looking at one's self through the eyes of others, of measuring one's soul by the tape of a world that looks on in amused contempt and pity." Sadly, "the double life every American Negro must live, as a Negro and as an American," leads inevitably to "a painful self-consciousness, an almost morbid sense of personality and a moral hesitancy which is fatal to self-confidence." The result is "a double life, with double thoughts, double duties and double social classes," and worse, "double words and double ideas," which "tempt the mind to pretense or revolt, hypocrisy or to radicalism." Accordingly, Du Bois wanted to make the American Negro whole; and he believed that only desegregation and full equality could make this psychic integration possible.

And yet for subsequent generations of writers, what Du Bois cast as a problem was taken to be the defining condition of modernity itself. The diagnosis, one might say, outlasted the disease. Although Du Bois would publish twenty-two books, and thousands of essays and reviews, no work of his has done more to shape an African American literary history than *The Souls of Black Folk*, and no metaphor in this intricately layered book has proved more enduring than that of double consciousness, including Du Bois's other powerfully resonating metaphors, that of "the veil" that separates black America from white America, and his poignant revision of Frederick Douglass's metaphor of "the color line," which Du Bois employed in that oft-repeated sentence, "The problem of the twentieth-century is the problem of the color line"—certainly his most prophetic utterance of many.

Like all powerful metaphors, Du Bois's metaphor of double consciousness came to have a life of its own. For Carl Jung, who visited the United States in the heyday of the "separate but equal" doctrine, the shocking thing wasn't that black culture was not equal, the shocking thing was that is was not separate! "The naïve European," Jung wrote, "thinks of America as a white nation. It is not wholly white, if you please; it is partly colored," and this explained, Jung continued, "the slightly Negroid mannerisms of the American." "Since the Negro lives within your cities and even within your houses," Jung continued, "he also lives within your skin, subconsciously." It wasn't just that the Negro was an American, as Du Bois would note, again and again, but that the American was, inevitably and inescapably, a Negro. The bondsman and the slave find their identity in each other's gaze: "two-ness" wasn't just a black thing any longer. As James Baldwin would put it, "Each of us, helplessly and forever, contains the other—male in female, female in male, white in black, black in white."

Today, talk about the fragmentation of culture and consciousness is a commonplace. We know all about the vigorous intermixing of black culture and white, high culture and low—from the Jazz Age freneticism of what the scholar Ann Douglass calls "mongrel Manhattan" to Hip Hop's hegemony over American youth in the late-twentieth and early-twenty-first centuries. Du Bois yearned to make the American Negro one, and lamented that he was two. Today, the ideal of wholeness has largely been retired. And cultural multiplicity is no longer seen as the problem, but as a solution—a solution to the confines of identity itself. Double consciousness, once a disorder, is now the cure. Indeed, the only complaint we moderns have is that Du Bois was too cautious in his accounting. He'd conjured "two souls, two thoughts two unreconciled strivings." Just two, Dr. Du Bois, we are forced to ask today? Keep counting.

And, in a manner of speaking, Du Bois did keep counting, throughout the twenty two books that comprise the formal canon of his most cogent thinking. The hallmark of Du Bois's literary career is that he coined the metaphors of double-consciousness and the veil—reappropriating Frederick Douglass's seminal definition of the semi-permeable barrier that separates and defines black-white racial relations in America as "the color line"—to define the place of the African American within modernity. The paradox of his career, however, is that the older Du Bois became, the more deeply he immersed himself in the struggle for Pan-Africanism and decolonization against the European colonial powers, and an emergent postcolonial "African" or "Pan-Negro" social and political identity—culminating in his own life in his assumption of Ghanaian citizenship in 1963. And the "blacker" that his stand against colonialism became, the less "black," in a very real sense, his analysis of what he famously called "The Negro Problem" simultaneously became. The more "African" Du Bois became, in other words, the more cosmopolitan his analysis of the root causes of anti-black and -brown and -yellow racism and colonialism became, seeing the status of the American Negro as part and parcel of a larger problem of international economic domination, precisely in the same way that Frederick Douglass rightly saw the construction of the American color line as a function of, and a metaphor for, deeper, structural, economic relations—"not the maddening liquor, but the black letters on the sign telling the world where it may be had," as Douglass so thoughtfully put it. The Negro's being-in-the-world, we might say, became ever more complex for Du Bois the older he grew, especially as the Cold War heated up and the anti-colonial movement took root throughout Africa and the Third World.

Ironically, Du Bois himself foretold this trajectory in a letter he wrote in 1896, reflecting on the import of his years as a graduate student at Friedrich Wilhelm University in Berlin: "Of the greatest importance was the opportunity which my *Wanderjahre* [wander years] in Europe gave of looking at the world as a man and not simply from a narrow racial and provincial outlook." How does the greatest black intellectual in the twentieth century—"America's most conspicuously educated Negro," as Werner Sollors puts it in his introduction to Du Bois's *Autobiography* in this series—make the rhetorical turn from defining the Negro American as a metaphor for modernity, at the turn of the century, to defining the Negro—at mid-century—as a metonym of a much larger historical pattern of social deviance and social dominance that had long been central to the fabric of world order, to the fabric of European and American domination of such a vast portion of the world of color? If, in other words, the Negro is America's metaphor for Du Bois in 1903, how does America's history of black-white relations become the metaphor of a nefarious pattern of economic exploitation and dominance by the end of Du Bois's life, in 1963? Make no mistake about it: either through hubris or an uncanny degree of empathy, or a mixture of both, throughout his life, W. E. B. Du Bois saw his most naked and public ambitions as well as his most private and intimate anxieties as representative of those of his countrymen, the American Negro people. Nevertheless, as he grew older, the closer he approached the end of his life, Du Bois saw the American Negro as a metaphor for class relations within the wider world order.

In order to help a new generation of readers to understand the arc of this trajectory in Du Bois's thinking, and because such a large part of this major thinker's oeuvre remains unread, Oxford University Press and I decided to publish in a uniform edition the twenty-one books that make up Du Bois's canon and invited a group of scholars to reconsider their importance as works of literature, history, sociology, and political philosophy. With the publication of this series, Du Bois's books are once again in print, with new introductions that analyze the shape of his career as a writer, scholar, and activist.

Reading the canon of Du Bois's work in chronological order, a certain allegorical pattern emerges, as Saidiya Hartman suggests in her introduction to *The Suppression of the African Slave-Trade*. Du Bois certainly responded immediately and directly to large historical events through fierce and biting essays that spoke adamantly and passionately to the occasion. But he also used the themes of his books to speak to the larger import of those events in sometimes highly mediated ways. His first book, for example, proffers as its thesis, as Hartman puts it, a certain paradox: "the slave trade flourished under the guise of its suppression," functioning legally for twenty years following the Compromise of the Federal Convention of 1787 and "illegally for another half century." Moreover, Du Bois tackles this topic at precisely the point in American history when Jim Crow segregation is becoming formalized through American law in the 1890s, culminating in 1896 (the year of the publication of his first book) with the infamous *Plessy v. Ferguson* "separate but equal" decision of the Supreme Court—exactly twenty years following the end of Reconstruction. Three years later, as Lawrence Bobo shows, Du Bois publishes *The Philadelphia Negro* in part to detail the effects of the "separate but equal" doctrine on the black community.

Similarly, Du Bois's biography of John Brown appeared in the same year as a pioneering band of blacks and whites joined together to form the National Association for the Advancement of Colored People (NAACP), the organization that would plot the demise of legal segregation through what would come to be called the Civil Rights Movement, culminating in its victory over de jure segregation in the Supreme Court's *Brown v. Board of Education* decision, which effectively reversed the *Plessy* decision, and in the Civil Rights Act of 1964 and the Voting Rights Act of 1965. John Brown, for Du Bois, would remain the emblem of this movement.

Likewise, Du Bois's first novel, *The Quest of the Silver Fleece*, published just two years following his biography of John Brown, served as a subtle critique both of an unreflective assimilationist ideology of the early NAACP through its advocacy of "a black-owned farming cooperative in the heart of the deep South," as William Andrews puts it, just as it surely serves as a critique of Booker T. Washington's apparently radical notion that economic development for the newly freed slaves could very well insure political equality in a manner both irresistible and inevitable, an argument, mind you, frequently made today under vastly different circumstances about the role of capitalism in Du Bois's beloved Communist China.

Du Bois registers his critique of the primitivism of the Harlem Renaissance in *The Gift of Black Folk*, as Glenda Carpio cogently argues, by walking "a tightrope between a patriotic embrace of an America in which African American culture has become an inextricable part and an exhortation of the rebellion and struggle out of which that culture arose." In response to the voyeurism and faddishness of Renaissance Harlem, Du Bois harshly reminds us that culture is a form of labor, too, a commodity infinitely exploitable, and that the size of America's unprecedented middle class can be traced directly to its slave past: "It was black labor that established the modern world commerce which began first as a commerce in the bodies of the slaves themselves and was the primary cause of the prosperity of the first great commercial cities of our day"—cities such as New York, the heart of the cultural movement that some black intellectuals passionately argued could very well augur the end of racial segregation throughout American society, or at least segregation between equal classes across the color line.

Paul Finkelman, in his introduction to *John Brown*, quotes the book's first line: "The mystic spell of Africa is and ever was over all America." If that is true, it was also most certainly the case for Du Bois himself, as John Thornton, Emmanuel Akyeampong, Wilson J. Moses, and Mahmood Mamdani show us in their introductions to five books that Du Bois published about Africa, in 1915, 1930, 1939, and 1947. Africa, too, was a recurring metaphor in the Duboisian canon, serving variously as an allegory of the intellectual potential of persons of African descent; as John K. Thornton puts it, "What counted was that African

history had movement and Africans were seen as historical actors and not simply as stolid recipients of foreign techniques and knowledge," carefully "inte-
grating ancient Egypt into *The Negro* as part of that race's history, without
having to go to the extreme measure of asserting that somehow the Egyptians
were biologically identical to Africans from further south or west." The history
of African civilization, in other words, was Du Bois's ultimate argument for the
equality of Americans white and black.

Similarly, establishing his scholarly mastery of the literature of African history also served Du Bois well against ideological rivals such as Marcus Garvey,
who attacked Du Bois for being "too assimilated," and "not black enough."
Du Bois's various studies of African history also served as a collective text for
the revolutions being formulated in the forties and fifties by Pan-African
nationalists such as Kwame Nkrumah and Jomo Kenyatta, who would lead
their nations to independence against the European colonial powers. Du Bois
was writing for them, first as an exemplar of the American Negro, the supposed
vanguard of the African peoples, and later, and more humbly, as a follower of
the African's lead. As Wilson J. Moses notes, Du Bois once wrote that "American
Negroes of former generations had always calculated that when Africa was
ready for freedom, American Negroes would be ready to lead them. But the
event was quite opposite." In fact, writing in 1925 in an essay entitled "Worlds
of Color," an important essay reprinted as "The Negro Mind Reaches Out" in
Alain Locke's germinal anthology *The New Negro* (as Brent Staples points out in
his introduction to Du Bois's fifth novel, *Worlds of Color*, published just two
years before he died), Du Bois had declared that "led by American Negroes, the
Negroes of the world are reaching out hands toward each other to know, to
sympathize, to inquire." And, indeed, Du Bois himself confessed at his ninety-
first birthday celebration in Beijing, as Moses notes, that "once I thought of you
Africans as children, whom we educated Afro-Americans would lead to liberty.
I was wrong." Nevertheless, Du Bois's various books on Africa, as well as his
role as an early theorist and organizer of the several Pan-African Congresses
between 1900 and 1945, increasingly underscored his role throughout the first
half of the century as the father of Pan-Africanism, precisely as his presence and
authority within such civil rights organizations as the NAACP began to wane.

Du Bois's ultimate allegory, however, is to be found in *The Black Flame Trilogy*,
the three novels that Du Bois published just before repatriating to Ghana, in
1957, 1959, and 1961. The trilogy is the ultimate allegory in Du Bois's canon
because, as Brent Edwards shows us in his introductions to the novels, it is a fictional representation of the trajectory of Du Bois's career, complete with several
characters who stand for aspects of Du Bois's personality and professional life,
including Sebastian Doyle, who "not only studied the Negro problem, he
embodied the Negro problem. It was bone of his bone and flesh of his flesh. It
made his world and filled his thought," as well as Professor James Burghardt,
trained as a historian at Yale and who taught, as Du Bois had, at Atlanta
University, and who believed that "the Negro problem must no longer be
regarded emotionally. It must be faced scientifically and solved by long, accu-
rate and intense investigation. Moreover, it was not one problem, but a series of

problems interrelated with the social problems of the world. He laid down a program of study covering a hundred years."

But even more important than these allegorical representations of himself, or early, emerging versions of himself, Du Bois used *The Black Flame* novels to underscore the economic foundation of anti-black racism. As Edwards notes, "The real villain," for Du Bois, "is not an individual Southern aristocrat or racist white laborer, but instead capitalism itself, especially in the corporate form that has dominated the economic and social landscape of the world for more than a century," which underscores Du Bois's ideological transformations from an integrationist of sorts to an emergent mode of African American, first, and then Pan-Africanist cultural nationalism, through socialism, landing squarely in the embrace of the Communist Party just two years before his death.

Despite this evolution in ideology, Mansart, Du Bois's protagonist in the triology, ends his series of intellectual transformations precisely where Du Bois himself began as he embarked upon his career as a professor just a year after receiving his Harvard PhD in 1895. In language strikingly familiar to his statement that the time he spent in Berlin enabled him to look "at the world as a man and not simply from a narrow racial and provincial outlook," Du Bois tells us in the final volume of the trilogy that Mansart "began to have a conception of the world as one unified dwelling place. He was escaping from his racial provincialism. He began to think of himself as part of humanity and not simply as an American Negro over against a white world." For all of his ideological permutations and combinations, in other words, W. E. B. Du Bois—formidable and intimidating ideologue and ferocious foe of racism and colonialism—quite probably never veered very far from the path that he charted for himself as a student, when he fell so deeply in love with the written word that he found himself, inevitably and inescapably, drawn into a life-long love affair with language, an affair of the heart to which he remained faithful throughout an eighty-year career as a student and scholar, from the time he entered Fisk University in 1885 to his death as the Editor of "The Encyclopedia Africana" in 1963. And now, with the publication of the Oxford W. E. B. Du Bois, a new generation of readers can experience his passion for words, Du Bois's love of language purely for its own sake, as well as a conduit for advocacy and debate about the topic that consumed him his entire professional life, the freedom and the dignity of the Negro.

✦ ✦ ✦

The first volume in the series is Du Bois's revised dissertation, and his first publication, entitled *The Suppression of the African Slave-Trade to the United States of America*. A model of contemporary historiography that favored empiricism over universal proclamation, *Suppression* reveals the government's slow movement toward abolition as what the literary scholar Saidiya Hartman calls in her introduction "a litany of failures, missed opportunities, and belated acts," in which a market sensibility took precedence over moral outrage, the combination of which led to the continuation of the Atlantic slave trade to the United States until it was no longer economically beneficial.

Lawrence D. Bobo, one of the foremost urban sociologists working today, argues in his introduction to *The Philadelphia Negro: A Social Study* (1899), that Du Bois was not only an innovative historian, as Hartman properly identifies him, but also a groundbreaking social scientist whose study of Philadelphia displays "the most rigorous and sophisticated social science of its era by employing a systematic community social survey method." Although it was well reviewed at its publication—which coincided with the advent of the field of urban sociology—*The Philadelphia Negro* did not become the subject of significant scholarly attention until the 1940s, and has become, since then, a model for the study of black communities.

The distinguished scholar of black literature and culture, Arnold Rampersad, calls *The Souls of Black Folk* "possibly the most important book ever penned by a black American"—an assertion with which I heartily agree. A composite of various essays, subjects, and tones, *Souls* is both very much of its time, and timeless. It contributed to the American lexicon two terms that have been crucial for more than a century in understanding the African American experience: the "color line" and "double consciousness." For Rampersad, that we have learned so much about both issues since Du Bois first wrote, but have not made either irrelevant to our twenty-first century experience is, in a real way, our scholarly blessing and burden.

Abandoning the scholarly and empirical prowess so vividly on display in *Suppression* and *Philadelphia Negro*, Du Bois meant his biography of John Brown to be not a work of scholarship but rather one "about activism, social consciousness, and the politics of race," argues the legal historian Paul Finkelman in his introduction to *John Brown* (1909). The only biography in Du Bois's vast oeuvre, the book grew out of his participation in the Niagara Movement's meeting at Harpers Ferry in 1906 (an event the centenary of which I had the good fortune to celebrate), and—with the myth of John Brown taking precedence at times over the facts of his life—marks Du Bois's transition from professional academic to full-time activist.

There was not a genre that Du Bois did not attempt in his long career as a writer. After the John Brown biography, Du Bois turned to the novel. In his introduction to *The Quest of the Silver Fleece* (1911), Du Bois's first novel, the literary historian William Andrews looks beyond the Victorian diction and sometimes purple prose to see a work that is the "most noteworthy Great *African American* Novel of its time." *Quest* is a "Southern problem" novel writ large on a national and even mythic canvas, and one that is ultimately radical in its endorsement of strong black womanhood, equality and comradeship between the sexes, and, in Du Bois's words, "a bold regeneration of the land," which for Andrews means a hitherto-unheard-of proposed economic alliance between poor blacks and poor whites in the rural South.

Moving from a national to an international canvas, Du Bois published *The Negro* (1915), more than half of which is devoted to African history. In this way, John K. Thornton argues in his introduction, Du Bois firmly grounded for an educated lay readership the history of African Americans in the history of Africa. Drawing on the emergent disciplines of anthropology and linguistics and including, even sketchily, accounts of what would now be called Diaspora communities in the Caribbean and Latin America, *The Negro* is important in that it presents, in Thornton's words, "African history [as having] movement and Africans . . . as historical actors and not simply as stolid recipients of foreign techniques and knowledge."

Dismissed by some critics and lauded by others as the "militant sequel" to *The Souls of Black Folk*, *Darkwater: Voices from Within the Veil* (1920) appeared in a world radically transformed by the ravages of World War I. In addition to these international upheavals, and to the "crossing and re-crossing" of the color line engendered by the war, the historian Evelyn Brooks Higginbotham tells us in her magisterial introduction to this volume that blacks at home in the U.S. faced major changes and relocations. The Great Migration was in full swing when Du Bois wrote *Darkwater*, and the change in the center of black life is reflected in the change of scene to the North, a far, urban cry from the rural setting of most of *Souls*. If *Souls* saw the American landscape in black and white, Higginbotham finds that *Darkwater* is like chiaroscuro, the painting technique developed by artists of the Italian Renaissance: "Du Bois, like these Renaissance painters, moves beyond the contouring line of the two-dimensional and introduces depth and volume through his representation of color—through his contrast and shading of white and various darker peoples." Higginbotham goes on to say that "Du Bois continually undermines the fixedness of racial boundaries and subverts the visual coherence of racial identities to an extent that cannot be accidental." The Du Bois who emerges in *Darkwater* is increasingly a citizen of the world, whose gaze may be fixed on his native land but whose understanding of that land is inextricably bound to the larger world around him.

The Gift of Black Folk (1924) had an odd genesis as part of the Knights of Columbus's series on "Racial Contributions to the United States." In her introduction, Glenda Carpio notes that Du Bois's celebration of black accomplishments did not turn away from the bitter history of slavery that spawned them: these were not gifts always rendered freely, Carpio points out. Though less substantial than many of his other works, and primarily a catalog of black accomplishments across different fields, *Gift* is notable for the complex ways Du Bois links African American contributions in the arenas of labor, war, church and social life, fraternal organizations, and especially the arts, by both women and men, to the bitter history of slavery.

Homi Bhabha sees *The Dark Princess* (1928) as another odd work, a "Bollywood-style Bildungsroman," in which the race-man Mathew Towns teams with Kautilya, the "dark Princess of the Tibetan Kingdom of Bwodpur," to combat international colonialism in the struggle for global emancipation. But in this somewhat messy novel, which renders the international scenes with a Zolaesque precision, Bhabha detects a serious philosophical purpose: to elaborate on the "rule of juxtaposition" (first defined in *Darkwater*), which "creat[es] an enforced intimacy, an antagonistic proximity, that defines the color-line as it runs across the uncivil society of the nation."

Du Bois moved from the esoteric exercise of *The Dark Princess* to a more accessible form for his next publications, *Africa, Its Geography, People and Products*, and

Africa—Its Place in Modern History (1930). Published as Blue Books for the edu-cated lay reader by E. Haldeman-Julius of Girard, Kansas, the two volumes are, for the African historian and African Emmanuel Akyeampong, remarkably use-ful and trenchant. The first volume is a relatively straightforward analysis of Africa's geography, climate, and environment, and the impact these physical fac-tors have had on the development of African civilization. The second volume, which seeks "to place the continent at the very center of ancient and modern his-tory," is more polemical, with economics cited as the central motivating factor behind modern colonialism and the slave trade.

The anger that was evident in the second of the two Blue Books came to full flower in *Black Reconstruction* (1935), a sweeping corrective to contemporary his-tories of the Reconstruction era, which (white) historians had shaped with the view of blacks as inadequate to the task of capitalizing on the freedom that eman-cipation had given them, and black history as "separate, unequal, and irrelevant," in the words of Du Bois's Pulitzer Prize-winning biographer, David Levering Lewis. Inspired by *The Gift of Black Folk* and from Du Bois's own withdrawal of his article on the Negro in the *Encyclopedia Britannica*, which demanded an excision of "a paragraph on the positive Reconstruction role of black people," *Black Recon-struction* provided original interpretations of black labor's relation to industrial wealth and, most radically, of the *agency* of black people in determining their lives after the Civil War. In his introduction, Lewis contends, rightly, that the books marks a progression in Du Bois's thought, from his early faith in academic knowl-edge and empiricism as a cure-all for the nation's problems, to the "more effective strategy of militant journalism informed by uncompromising principles and vital social science."

Wilson J. Moses presents *Black Folk Then and Now* (1939) as a midway point between *The Negro* (1915) and *The World and Africa* (1946). While all three volumes sought to address the entire span of black history, the special mandate of *Black Folk* was to "correct the omissions, misinterpretations, and deliberate lies that [Du Bois] detected in previous depictions of the Negro's past." In this volume, he went back to the original Herodotus and provided his own translation, which led him to affirm, with other black writers, that the Egyptians were, indeed, black (a conclusion he had resisted earlier in his career). But even in this work, with such evidence of his intellectual background on display, Du Bois is less interested in intellectual history than in social history. Even as he tracks developments in the United States, the Caribbean, Latin America, Du Bois neglects the Pan-African movement and his own involvement in it.

Du Bois's autobiography, on the other hand, shows a man far more interested in writing about his intellectual journey than his personal or social life. The philosopher Anthony Appiah, in his subtle introduction to *Dusk of Dawn*, tells us that Du Bois was famous for nothing so much as his accomplishments as an intel-lectual and a writer; his institutional affiliations (with the NAACP, with the Pan-African Congress) were fleeting, and his internal contradictions were vexing (he was both a committed Socialist and a committed elitist). The aim of this account, like so much of Du Bois's other work, was to address the problem of the color line, and he presents his distinguished, singular life as emblematic of that problem, and himself as hopeful for its solution.

At the time he rejoined the NAACP to oversee its global programming in 1944, Du Bois was prepared to dedicate himself completely to the abolition of colonialism, which he saw as the driving force behind all global conflicts. What was remarkable about his anti-colonialism was, as Gerald Horne rightly points out in his introduction to *Color and Democracy* (1946), Du Bois's inclusion of Asia, and particularly Japan, in the discussion. As fertile ground for colonial enterprises, Asia yielded still more evidence of the "inviolate link between color and democracy."

Color continued to preoccupy Du Bois, and in *The World and Africa*, he attempted to correct the ways in which color (black) had affected history. Mahmood Mamdani tells us in his introduction that Du Bois's motivation in writing this somewhat hasty volume was to tell the story of "those left out of recorded history" and to challenge, in effect, "an entire tradition of history-writing . . . modern European historiography." Du Bois was aware that this was just a beginning to a much larger project, to connect the history of Europe that dominated the academic discipline of history to events and progress in the world at large, including Africa.

In Battle for Peace: The Story of My 83rd Birthday features an embattled Du Bois enduring prosecution by (and eventually winning acquittal from) the federal government whose indictment of him as an unregistered agent for the Soviet Union was, according to Manning Marable, a trumped-up means by which to discredit the great black leader and frighten his fellow supporters of international peace into silence. It worked, at least in part: while Du Bois drew support from many international associations, the NAACP essentially abandoned him. Ten years later, in 1961, Du Bois would permanently leave the United States for Ghana.

Brent Hayes Edwards in his introduction calls the *Black Flame* trilogy of novels Du Bois's most neglected work. Written in the last few years of life, *The Ordeal of Mansart* (1957), *Mansart Builds a School* (1959), and *Worlds of Color* (1961) follow the life of Manuel Mansart from his birth in 1876 (the last year of Reconstruction) to his death in 1956, a period which spans his rise from a noted but provincial Southern educator to a self-educating citizen of the world of color. With its alternating apocalyptic and utopian tone, its depiction of real historical figures and events, and its thoughtful "animation of economic history and especially labor history," the *Black Flame* trilogy offers, according to Edwards, "the clearest articulation of Du Bois's perspective at the end of his life, and his reflections on an unparalleled career that had stretched from Reconstruction through the Cold War."

Du Bois was a largely marginalized figure in the last decade of his life, and his work published at that time, most notably the *Black Flame* trilogy, went into the critical and cultural abyss. Mark Sanders suggests that the "invisibility" of the trilogy, then and now, can be explained by an evolution in literary "taste" in the 1950s, wrought by new trends in literary criticism and magazine culture, the emergence of the Civil Rights Movement, and Du Bois's own development. Even if we have rejected in many real ways the ethos of the 1950s, for Sanders, our prescriptions for taste still owe a great deal to that decade.

Werner Sollors finds "four major narrative strains" in the posthumously published *Autobiography of W. E. B. Du Bois* (1968): the personal (including "startling" sexual revelations from the famously staid Du Bois); the academic, editorial, and organizational, in which his work is fully explored, and the political is always personal even while science and reason are held to be the solution to the race problem; the Communist, first as interested onlooker and then as Party member; and the elderly, in which an old man takes stock of contemporary youth culture with something of a jaundiced eye. Sollors suggests that far from being disjointed, the various strands of the *Autobiography* are united by Du Bois's ongoing quest for recognition. I would argue that there is nothing pathetic in this quest; it is simply the desire for respect from the society (black and white) that Du Bois spent his long life trying to understand.

Henry Louis Gates, Jr.
Cambridge, Massachusetts
December 7, 2006

Introduction

Manning Marable, Columbia University

One of the most neglected and obscure books written by the noted African American scholar W. E. B. Du Bois is *In Battle for Peace* (1952).[1] The slender volume documents Du Bois's emotionally packed experiences in the years following World War II, during his attempts to mobilize black and white Americans to resist the emerging transnational political and military confrontation between the United States and the Soviet Union. During this difficult time, Du Bois's long-standing national reputation as a major intellectual and public leader on issues of American race relations was rapidly shattered. Indeed, even as late as 1947, the author John Gunther's *Inside U.S.A.* characterized the African American scholar as having "a position almost like [George Bernard] Shaw or [Albert] Einstein, being the most venerable and distinguished of leaders in his field." But only three years later, on February 9, 1951, Du Bois and four of his political associates were indicted and arrested by the federal government for "failure to register as [an] agent of a foreign principal," the Union of Soviet Socialist Republics. Du Bois and his colleagues faced a humiliating public trial, and if they had been convicted they would have received possible fines of ten thousand dollars each and sentences of up to five years in a federal prison. Although the trial resulted in a directed acquittal on November 20, 1951, Du Bois continued to face severe political persecution for another decade.[2]

From a historical perspective, *In Battle for Peace* can be fully understood as a political statement and semibiographical narrative only within the context of the author's profound, lifelong commitments to two ideals: peace and black liberation. As early as his 1904 "Credo," Du Bois passionately declared: "I believe in the Prince of Peace. I believe that War is Murder. I believe that armies and navies are at bottom the tinsel and braggadocio of oppression and wrong, and I believe that the wicked conquest of weaker and darker nations by nations whiter and stronger but foreshadows the death of that strength."[3] The first significant text that Du Bois produced in which the quest for world peace was systematically linked to the emancipation of people of African descent, however, was "The African Roots of the War," published in the *Atlantic Monthly* in May 1915. The current global conflict between European nations, Du Bois argued, had been provoked by Western imperialism's desire to oppress Africa and Asia. Western leaders had even mobilized their nations' respective working classes "to share the spoils of exploiting 'chinks' and 'niggers.'" To preserve their political control over their own proletariats, politicians and capitalists had vied for control of the natural resources and inexpensive labor within black and brown territories. "All over the world there leaps to articulate speech and ready action that singular assumption that if white men do not throttle colored men, then China, India, and Africa will do to Europe what Europe has done and seeks to do to them."

The worldwide conflict was thus "the result of jealousies engendered by the recent rise of armed national associations of labor and capital, whose aim is the exploitation of the wealth of the world."[4] The practical implication of this analysis to Du Bois meant that the ideal of international peace and the abolition of warfare could not occur unless the colonial territories in Africa, Asia, and other non-Western populations were granted self-determination and ultimately political sovereignty. Thus the objectives of "black freedom" and "global peace" could be reconciled only under an international regime committed to social justice and the nonexploitation of working people.

However, at certain moments in his long public career Du Bois himself deviated from his own theoretical formulations. The most notorious instance of this occurred in 1918 when Du Bois astonished his followers by embracing America's entry into World War I, on the side of the Allies against Germany. In his July 1918 editorial in the National Association for the Advancement of Colored People (NAACP) journal *The Crisis*, Du Bois even urged black Americans: "Let us, while this war lasts, forget our special grievances and close ranks shoulder to shoulder with our white fellow citizens and the allied nations that are shoulder to shoulder with our own white fellow citizens and the allied nations fighting for democracy."[5] Immediately attacked for his political inconsistency, Du Bois used the pages of *The Crisis* to justify his new position. "This is our country: we have worked for it, we have suffered for it, we have fought for it," Du Bois argued in August 1918. Black Americans should not "bargain with our loyalty" during the nation's time of warfare.[6]

The consequences of Du Bois's newfound patriotism and support for the presidential administration of the segregationist Woodrow Wilson were profound and long lasting. An entire generation of black activists and militants who came to maturity during World War I, such as the trade union leader A. Philip Randolph and the black nationalist Marcus Garvey, emerged to challenge Du Bois's leadership of the African American community. Even many of Du Bois's friends and political associates found Du Bois's actions difficult to fathom. Byron Gunner, then president of the National Equal Rights League, privately wrote to Du Bois that he was "unable to conceive that said advice comes from you . . . I'm amazed beyond expression."[7]

The aftermath of World War I produced a level of political repression and racial violence that Du Bois had not anticipated. Despite the sacrifices and military service of hundreds of thousands of black Americans, a number of black troops upon their return to the United States were lynched by vigilante mobs. More than two dozen major race riots occurred in 1919, and sixty African Americans that year were victimized by public burnings and lynchings. The

Wilson administration harassed and threatened civil rights organizations; even some congressional leaders called for the suppression of *The Crisis* and the prosecution of Du Bois under the espionage act. This tidal wave of racism and political repression taught Du Bois that he had committed a grievous error by endorsing America's military involvement in the war. He was determined never to make the mistake again.

By the early 1920s Du Bois had reverted to his "African Roots of the War" posture of 1915, regarding the necessity for black Americans to pursue the dual goals of international peace and black freedom. In the October 1923 issue of *The Crisis*, for example, Du Bois observed that the basis for the recent world war had been the quest by European corporations "to 'develop' the tropics" in order to exploit local native populations. European imperialists understood, Du Bois observed, that "it pays to kill 'niggers.'"[8] Three years later, in the March 1926 issue of *The Crisis*, Du Bois called upon all nations formally to "outlaw war." To achieve such a visionary goal the colonized nations of Africa and Asia had to be freed from the shackles of white tyranny.[9]

Following his return to the NAACP in 1944, Du Bois increased his personal involvement in the pursuit of global peace. In October 1944 the black scholar participated in a national conference chaired by Undersecretary of State Edward R. Stettinius in Washington, D.C., to discuss U.S. positions on international affairs in the postwar period. Du Bois joined the U.S. delegation at the founding conference of the United Nations, held in San Francisco in 1945. As early as June 1945—two months before the dropping of the U.S. atomic bombs on Japan— Du Bois predicted, "I seem to see outlined a third World War based on the suppression of Asia and the strangling of Russia. . . . Perhaps I am wrong. God knows I hope I am."[10] With renewed vigor Du Bois lectured at both universities and public gatherings on behalf of international peace. In his widely read *Chicago Defender* newspaper column of January 11, 1947, Du Bois asserted, "The emancipation of the black man of the world is one guarantee of a firm foundation for world peace."[11]

In September 1948, after his firing as the NAACP's director of special research, Du Bois accepted an unpaid position as the vice chairman of Paul Robeson's Council on African Affairs in New York City. He used the post to publicize his opposition to the growing Cold War between the United States and the Soviet Union, as well as to promote the self-government of Caribbean and African nations. At the Cultural and Scientific Conference for World Peace, held in New York City in March 1949, Du Bois argued, "We know and the saner nations know that we are not traitors or conspirators; and far from plotting force and violence it is precisely force and violence that we bitterly oppose. This conference was not called to defend communism nor socialism nor the American way of life! It was called to promote peace!"[12]

In early 1950 a small group of American peace activists who opposed the growth of domestic anti-Communism and McCarthyism established the Peace Information Center. The primary purpose of the organization was to circulate petitions calling for the abolition of nuclear weapons. By July 1950, Secretary of State Dean Acheson attacked such "world peace appeals" as nothing less than

Soviet propaganda. Du Bois's reply to Acheson challenged the assertion that a public, educational campaign promoting international peace was tantamount to aiding the global objectives of Soviet Communism. "Is it our strategy that when the Soviet Union asks for peace, we insist on war?" Du Bois asked. "Must any proposals for averting atomic catastrophe be sanctioned by the Soviet Union?"[13]

In August 1950, Du Bois accepted a draft by the small American Labor Party to run as its candidate for the U.S. Senate for New York. The senatorial campaign was at best quixotic: the eighty-two-year-old candidate managed to deliver only ten public addresses and seven radio broadcasts that autumn. Despite being widely ridiculed as an apologist for Communism, however, Du Bois still retained a limited popular following as a public figure. Even at the height of McCarthyism, Du Bois still received nearly 210,000 votes, four percent of New York's statewide electorate, in November 1950. The senatorial campaign reinforced Du Bois's growing pessimism about the future of America's democratic institutions. The United States "never has been a democracy," Du Bois reflected. "Our industrial enterprise is dominated by vast monopolies and our freedom of thought increasingly chained by law, police spies, and refusal to let anybody earn a decent living who does not think as he is told to think."[14]

The Peace Information Center was disbanded in late 1950. However, the publicity surrounding Du Bois's unsuccessful Senate campaign may have been responsible for the Justice Department's decision to prosecute Du Bois and other peace proponents as "unregistered" Soviet agents. There was absolutely no truth in the government's assertions against Du Bois. Du Bois had possessed a long, contentious history with American Communism, and he did not actually join the Communist Party U.S.A. until late 1961, several days before embarking on permanent exile to Ghana. The U.S. government's real objectives, it appears, were to disgrace and smear the venerable Negro leader, to discredit his politics, and to intimidate his supporters.

In Battle for Peace recounts Du Bois's personal anxieties and fears during his prosecution and defense with a frankness that is often missing from his other works. Du Bois was bitterly disappointed with the NAACP's failure to rally to his defense. The association's national secretary, Walter White, had even informed associates that Justice Department officials possessed "definite evidence" that would secure Du Bois's conviction as a pro-Soviet agent. To his longtime friend Judge Hubert Delany, Du Bois wrote on December 21, 1951: "I have heretofore refrained from any attack upon the NAACP, since it is, in part, my child. But since this indictment the executive officers of the NAACP have warned and frightened their branches from helping in my defense."[15] Throughout much of the world, however, millions of people voiced support for Du Bois during his terrible public ordeal. *In Battle for Peace* recounts in great detail the impressive range of international associations and institutions that protested Du Bois's prosecution.

Du Bois's remarkable sojourn continued another twelve eventful years after the publication of *In Battle for Peace*. Throughout the 1950s Du Bois remained steadfast to his dual visions of black freedom and peace. To many Americans during these years Du Bois was, as his wife Shirley Graham later wrote, a "tower of strength. . . . He was constantly being called upon: to speak to some embattled harassed group, to appear as a witness before some committee, or even in court, to sign a petition, to visit a family bowed in grief because one of its members had been 'taken away.' "[16] On December 5, 1961, Du Bois departed from the United States for Ghana, where he died two years later. But even through his final years, as the revealing *In Battle for Peace* makes clear, Du Bois sought to be true to himself and to his ideals.

NOTES

1. W. E. B. Du Bois, *In Battle for Peace: The Story of My 83rd Birthday*, with comment by Shirley Graham (New York: Masses and Mainstream, 1952).
2. *In Battle for Peace*, pp. 11 and 51–56, and William E. Foley to W. E. B. Du Bois, February 2, 1951, in *The Correspondence of W. E. B. Du Bois*, edited by Herbert Aptheker, vol. 3 (Amherst: University of Massachusetts Press, 1978), pp. 306–309.
3. W. E. B. Du Bois, "Credo," *Independent*, October 15, 1904, p. 787.
4. W. E. B. Du Bois, "The African Roots of the War," *Atlantic Monthly*, May 1915, pp. 707–714.
5. W. E. B. Du Bois, "Close Ranks," *Crisis*, July 1918, p. 111.
6. W. E. B. Du Bois, "A Philosophy in Time of War," *Crisis*, August 1918, pp. 164–165.
7. See Byron Gunner to W. E. B. Du Bois, July 25, 1918, in *The Correspondence of W. E. B. Du Bois*, edited by Herbert Aptheker, vol. 1 (Amherst: University of Massachusetts Press, 1973), p. 228.
8. W. E. B. Du Bois, "Opinion," *Crisis*, October 1923, p. 248.
9. W. E. B. Du Bois, "Opinion," *Crisis*, March 1926, p. 215.
10. W. E. B. Du Bois, "UNCIO Dodges Colonial Issue—U.S. Becomes Colonial Power—World War III?" *Chicago Defender*, June 23, 1945.
11. W. E. B. Du Bois, "The Winds of Time," *Chicago Defender*, January 11, 1947.
12. W. E. B. Du Bois, *The Autobiography of W. E. B. Du Bois: A Soliloquy on Viewing My Life from the Last Decade of its First Century* (New York: International Publishers, 1968), p. 350.
13. *Autobiography of W. E. B. Du Bois*, pp. 358–359.
14. W. E. B. Du Bois, "The Social Significance of These Three Cases," in *Against Racism: Unpublished Essays, Papers, Addresses, 1887–1961*, edited by Herbert Aptheker (Amherst: University of Massachusetts Press, 1985), p. 283.
15. W. E. B. Du Bois to Hubert Delany, December 21, 1951, in *The Correspondence of W. E. B. Du Bois*, vol. 3, pp. 322–323.
16. Shirley Graham Du Bois, *His Day is Marching On: A Memoir of W. E. B. Du Bois* (Philadelphia: Lippincott, 1971), p. 210.

In Battle for Peace

CHAPTER I

---◆---

About Birthdays

I do not seem to remember that during my boyhood and youth any particular attention was given to birthdays as such. Certainly there were no celebrations which compared in importance with the fire crackers of the Fourth of July, the "Cattle Show" in the fall, and the presents and tree at Christmas. Indeed, I think it was not until my 25th birthday, when I was a student in Berlin, that I remember making an occasion of this anniversary. It was in the long, dark winter of northern Germany, and while I was comfortable, I felt a little lonesome and far-away from home and boyhood friends. I had candles in my room on Schoeneburger Ufer, and a dedication of my small library to the memory of my mother; and I wrote something rather sentimental about life in general:

> "I am striving to make my life all that life may be—and I am limiting that strife only in so far as that strife is incompatible with others of my brothers and sisters making their lives similar. The crucial question now is where that limit comes . . . God knows I am sorely puzzled. I am firmly convinced that my own best development is not one and the same with the best development of the world, and here I am willing to sacrifice. . . . The general proposition of working for the world's good becomes too soon sickly sentimentality. I therefore take the world that the Unknown lay in my hands and work for the rise of the Negro people, taking for granted that their best development means the best development of the world. . . ."

My first real birthday celebration was my fiftieth, when a dinner was given me at the Civic Club in New York City. This club was housed comfortably on Twelfth Street near Fifth Avenue, with members of many races. It was a successor of the defunct Liberal Club in which Walter Lippmann fought against Franklin Giddings, the sociologist, to make me a member—and from which membership presumably it soon died. The Civic Club dinner was small and intimate, and I received a silver loving cup inscribed:

> "From the branches of the National Association for the Advancement of Colored People to W. E. Burghardt Du Bois, writer, scholar, seer, on his fiftieth birthday, February 23, 1918. Given in affectionate appreciation of his great gifts, and gratitude for the consecration of these gifts to the service of his race."

The next dinner came not on a birthday but on my return from Europe and Africa in 1924. The program at the Café Savarin in New York was imposing. Ridgely Torrence read a poem by Witter Bynner—"To Du Bois and his People"; Heywood Broun spoke, and Harry Burleigh's adaptations of the spirituals were sung. James Weldon Johnson read a tribute from Zona Gale. Robert Benchley, Walter Hampton, and the Lieutenant-Governor of the State were speakers. There was a word from Eugene O'Neill:

"It seems to me that to be a Negro writer today must be a tremendously stimulating thing. They have within them an untouched world of deep reality. What greater boon than their rare opportunity can a true artist ask of fate? They are fortunate. And it is to Dr. Du Bois more than to any other man that they owe their good fortune; for by the sheer power of his own ability he has played a foremost part in convincing the world that it must await with genuine artistic respect the contribution of the Negro to modern literature."

A poem was read by Countee Cullen:

"Men raised a mountain in your path,
*   Steep, perilous with slime,*
Then smouldered in their own hot wrath
*   To see you climb and climb."*

I said in part:

"Humanity is progressing toward an ideal; but not, please God, solely by help of men who sit in cloistered ease, hesitate from action and seek sweetness and light; rather we progress today, as in the past, by the soul-torn strength of those who can never sit still and silent while the disinherited and the damned clog our gutters and gasp their lives out on our front porches. These are the men who go down in the blood and dust of battle. They say ugly things to an ugly world. They spew the luke-warm fence-straddlers out of their mouths, like God of old; they cry aloud and spare not; they shout from the housetops and they make this world so damned uncomfortable with its nasty burden of evil that it tries to get good and does get better."

This whole beautiful occasion was finely arranged for me by my long loyal friend and fellow-worker, Augustus Dill. Joel Spingarn, Chairman of the Board of the N.A.A.C.P., was not able to preside but wrote me:

"I congratulate you on your public service, and I congratulate you also on the power of language by which you have made it effective. I know that some people think that an artist is a man who has nothing to say and who writes in order to prove it. The great writers of the world have not so conceived their task, and neither have you. Though your service has been for the most part the noble one of teacher and prophet (not merely to one race or nation but to the world), I challenge the artists of America to show more beautiful passages than some of those in *Darkwater* and *The Souls of Black Folk*."

At Atlanta University I celebrated quite elaborately my 70th anniversary. There was a bronze bust by Alexander Portnoff; J. E. Spingarn and James Weldon Johnson spoke; Braithwaite read a poem written for the occasion.

All this was heartening, even if to some minds a bit exaggerated. I liked it, of course, but I came to be gradually rather fed up with this sort of celebration for two reasons: First of all it became, to my thinking, a sort of blackmail on my unfortunate friends. The cost of the dinner and presents had to be considerable, and few people had courage enough to refuse co-operation. Secondly, these celebrations put a most unpleasant emphasis on the meaning of Age in itself. It began to be customary that whenever my name or work was mentioned it seemed necessary to add a note concerning my age, indicating subtly that I was about at the end of a rather too long career, and could hardly be expected to keep sane and busy much longer. Therefore, hurry, hurry, and give the old man "a hand"!

This tendency to look upon age as abnormal and rather useless is peculiarly American. It is true in neither France nor England, nor in most parts of the Western world, and never in Asia or Africa. But with an emphasis on Youth in America, which has long lost its meaning, it is an old American custom to write off as a liability, if not total loss, the age of men in public work after they have passed fifty, and to regard them as practically dead at seventy.

I therefore made up my mind that I would stop these celebrations, so as to relieve the financial pressure on my friends, and so as to have my work still judged by its efficiency, and not by the number of its years. This good resolution was negatived by the fact that I returned to New York and the N.A.A.C.P. in 1944, and therefore my 80th birthday became a rather natural occasion for welcoming me back to an old stamping ground. It was at the Hotel Roosevelt. "Love and veneration" came from Alva and Gunnar Myrdal; and from Henry Wallace: "Warmest congratulations on your long years of service to the cause of humanity. May you go on giving courage to those who otherwise would fear to speak out." Somewhere later the giver of this urge to courage himself failed!

I protested ineffectually at the celebrations of my 81st and 82nd birthdays. Then I took a firm stand; especially when this last dinner became cause of an unpleasant argument as to who would preside. I stubbornly insisted that I alone should decide the presiding officer at my own birthday dinner. I did. Then I said: "No more birthday celebrations! Enough is too much!" But I was induced in 1951 to change this resolve, because of my long and deep interest in Africa.

COMMENT

These postscripts at the end of certain chapters are an attempt to share related confidences with the reader. God forbid that I should take upon myself the presumption of adding anything to W. E. B. Du Bois' facts or style. His is a grand simplicity that needs no clarification. The specific nature of my lines is signified by the title applied to this section and from these personal comments some enjoyment may be derived. But the title may also be looked upon as the French *"Comment"* which with the addition of the question mark is best translated into everyday English as "How come?"

It is my opinion, for instance, that frequent celebration of his birthday has not been the burden on "unfortunate friends" as imagined by W.E.B. For at least fifty years this man has played a very special part in making the history of these United States. Van Wyck Brooks writes in *The Confident Years*:

> ". . . the Negro cultural statesman . . . set out to remould the racial destinies . . . opposed conciliatory measures and fought for higher education. This unique leader, an intellectual who was also an artist and a prophet, with a mind at once passionate, critical, humorous and detached, an adviser and supporter of the interests of the young whose writings he published in *The Crisis,* had also a mental horizon as wide as the world. He was concerned with the great questions that were exercising Harlem, the cultural capital of the Pan-African cause, the possible role of the American Negroes in the future development of Africa and the larger question of all coloured peoples."

When he published his list of sixty-one Americans as "The Men Who Make Up Our Minds," Henry Steele Commager included W. E. Burghardt Du Bois along with Benjamin Franklin, Thomas Jefferson, Mark Twain and John Dewey. John Gunther in his *Inside U.S.A.* says that Du Bois "has a position almost like that of Shaw or Einstein, being the most venerable and distinguished of leaders in his field."

While in his considerations he tends to overlook such judgments, W.E.B. proudly includes a letter from Joel Spingarn, who from about 1912 until Spingarn's death was his closest friend.

Joel Spingarn was a poet and professor of American literature at Columbia University. But he became so deeply involved in protesting the arbitrary dismissal of a fellow professor that he brought down upon his own head the wrath of the administration. Nicholas Murray Butler forbade the airing of Columbia University affairs before the general public and when Professor Spingarn could not be silenced he also was dismissed. Spingarn not only considered these dismissals an affront to justice and academic freedom but because of the handling of the case he was rudely reminded that he, Spingarn, was a Jew. And this consideration turned his attention to the problems of discrimination and intolerance. He knew William English Walling, Oswald Garrison Villard and Charles Edward Russell, who had a short time before combined their efforts with others in the organization of a National Association for the Advancement of Colored People. Now, upon visiting the offices of this association, Spingarn met a small, alert brown man who was enthusiastically getting together a magazine which he called *The Crisis.* Such a literary effort alone would have deeply interested the former English professor, but the man himself with his Harvard accent and continental manners intrigued him. After several weeks of inquiry and exploration Joel Spingarn threw himself—mind, heart and hand—into the exciting work of these pioneers in human rights. He accepted for himself the credo of this incredible Dr. Du Bois:

> "We will not be satisfied to take one jot or tittle less than our full manhood rights. We claim for ourselves every single right that belongs to a free-born

American, political, civil, and social; and until we get these rights we will never cease to protest and assail the ears of America. The battle we wage is not for ourselves alone, but for all true Americans."

In 1912, Du Bois' voice was like one crying in the wilderness. Even his associates in the N.A.A.C.P. attempted to soft pedal such expression. "Advancement," yes, but "one step at a time." When the N.A.A.C.P. really went out to expose and report on lynchings, many "good" people resigned in disgust. But with Joel Spingarn as Chairman of the Board, Du Bois was free to wield *The Crisis* like a powerful sword cutting through tangles of ignorance, stupidity and indifference. The two men believed in the power of the word and that great writing was writing which serves humanity greatly. They were about the same age and being so much alike in temperament their close friendship was quite natural.

For them, however, it was exceptional. This was the period in which W. E. B. waged total war against white America. Proudly he rebuffed any offers of what he considered "special" overtures being made to him. For his own reasons there must have been something of the same exclusiveness about Spingarn. His brother, Arthur Spingarn, has told me that the two friends addressed each other in familiar terms which neither tolerated from anybody else. They had fun together. Having heard that the old City Club on 44th Street, of which he was a member, had refused service in their dining room to a Negro, Spingarn promptly set out with Du Bois for lunch there. Since at this time no downtown restaurant in New York City served Negroes, the two were simply asking for trouble. The story goes that neither really enjoyed the excellent meal because nothing happened!

Early in World War I, Joel Spingarn applied for and was given a commission. He was sent to Washington to the Department of Intelligence. Almost immediately he was confronted with the complications of a segregated army. Complaints were pouring in from all over the country. With the country actually at war, Major Spingarn's hands seemed tied. Largely through his efforts, camps for the training of Negro officers were set up. But he knew it was essential that there be some Negro in high authority who could give his attention to the treatment of Negro soldiers. He recommended the proper man: William E. B. Du Bois.

Since civilian morale—even for Negroes—was important, the suggestion was favorably received. Jubilantly W. E. B. joined his friend in Washington. At the conferences of ranking military he made a good impression. Spingarn had recommended that he be given the rank of major, which would correspond to his own. This, it was decided, was a little too much. Du Bois accepted the assignment with a captain's rating. He was told to return to New York where the proper papers would be sent him.

They never came and quite naturally, for soon the Army was aware of the dangerous Negro radical it was about to receive into its ranks. It was pointed out that this man had opposed Booker Washington and was openly advocating "social equality" of black and white. The whole plan was quietly dropped. Spingarn was sent to the front lines in Europe, while Du Bois remained to edit the *Crisis.*

In the months which followed, the circulation of *The Crisis* passed the 100,000 mark, at that time an unprecedented event in the history of Negro journalism.

I remember how my father eagerly awaited his copy of the magazine and how he read aloud to me and my brothers the stirring editorials of W. E. B. Du Bois. I remember how I held my breath as I listened.

More years passed and then one day I found the courage to send a poem to *The Crisis*. It had been published in our high school journal after it was praised by my English teacher. I doubt if any publication can ever bring me the same pride with which I read my poem from the smooth, white page of *The Crisis*—nor the joy and inspiration which came to me from the editor's letter. This was my first sight of the now world-famous signature: W. E. B. Du Bois.

And I was only one of the many hundreds. No, I do not think celebrating his birthday was merely a bothersome chore. I read of some of those dinners. While the glittering details were always interesting, it was the few, well-chosen, perfect words of Dr. Du Bois for which we all waited. He was the symbol of our hopes and aspirations; the one who from a high place described the vision. From the vision which he presented to us who were growing up in America came such a first poem as mine. I called it "Black Man's Music":

> *A fantasy of sound, scarce heard*
> *And yet insistent as a heartbeat in the night time*
> *A song, so irresistible with charm*
> *   That straight into the soul it sinks*
> *And breaking down all bars of prejudice and pride,*
> *   There it remains.*

CHAPTER II

◆

The Council on African Affairs

I am not sure just when I began to feel an interest in Africa. Some folks seem to assume that just as Irish Americans have a sentimental regard for Ireland, and German Americans and Americans of Scandinavian descent look back to their mother countries, either through their own experience or that of their parents, so in similar ways Negro Americans should regard Africa.

This was true in the 17th and early 18th centuries, when there actually were, in the United States, Negroes who either remembered Africa or inherited memories from their fathers or grandfathers. In my mother's family, the Burghardts sang an African song that came down from great-grandparents; but that was rather unusual.

Among the Negroes of my generation there was not only little direct acquaintance or consciously inherited knowledge of Africa, but much distaste and recoil because of what the white world taught them about the Dark Continent. There arose resentment that a group like ours, born and bred in the United States for centuries, should be regarded as Africans at all. They were, as they stoutly asserted, Americans. My father's father was particularly bitter about this. He would not accept an invitation to a "Negro" picnic. He would not segregate himself in any way.

Notwithstanding all this, I became interested in Africa by a sort of logical deduction. I was tired of finding in newspapers, textbooks, and history, fulsome lauding of white folk, and either no mention of dark peoples, or mention in disparaging and apologetic phrase. I made up in my mind that it must be true that Africa had a history and destiny, and that one of my jobs was to disinter this unknown past, and help make certain a splendid future. Along this line I did, over a stretch of years, a great deal of reading, writing, research, and planning, of which I have written elsewhere.

When I returned to New York from Atlanta in 1944 to become Director of Special Research for the N.A.A.C.P., it was specifically for the purpose of concentrating on study of colonial peoples and peoples of Negro descent throughout the world, and to revive the Pan-African Congresses. From this plan came the Fifth Pan-African Congress in England, 1945; and my book, *The World and Africa*, in 1947. I should have liked to join the Council on African Affairs, and expected to be invited, but the secretary, Max Yergan, did not seem to want my co-operation, although in past years I had helped in his African work.

Nothing illustrates more clearly the hysteria of our times than the career of the Council on African Affairs. It had been the dream of idealists in earlier days that the stain of American slavery would eventually be wiped out by the service which American descendants of African slaves would render Africa. Most of those American Negroes who gained their freedom in the 18th century looked forward to a return to Africa as their logical end. They often named their clubs and churches, their chief social institutions, "African." But the Cotton Kingdom and Colonial Imperialism gradually drove this dream entirely from their minds until the Negroes of the post-Civil War era regarded Africa as renewal of color caste and slavery. They regarded the colonization and "back to Africa" movements of Lincoln and Bishop Turner with lackluster eye; and when in 1918 I tried to found a social and spiritual Pan-African movement, my American Negro following was small.

The Council on African Affairs was planned in London in 1939, when Max Yergan, a colored Y.M.C.A. secretary, returning from long and trying service in South Africa, met Paul Robeson returning from a visit to West Africa. They set up an organization in New York. In 1943 they were joined by Alphaeus Hunton, son of the greatest Negro secretary the American Y.M.C.A. ever had; himself a doctor of philosophy in English, and a professor for seventeen years at Howard University.

With the co-operation of Frederick V. Field, a fine African library and collection of African art, along with offices for the new organization, were secured. A monthly fact sheet devoted to developments in new Africa was issued. Money was raised for starving people in South Africa and striking miners in West Africa. African visitors were welcomed, and lectures delivered.

Then came the witch-hunting scare, and the Council was put on the Attorney-General's list of "subversive" organizations. Immediately, without consulting his board, Yergan, as secretary, issued a newspaper release attacking "Communists," although Yergan himself had often been attacked as a sympathizer with the Left. Robeson protested. His position was that the Council was not a Communist organization, and was doing a specific and needed work; that the political or religious opinions of its members or officials were their own business, so long as the actions of the organization as such were legal.

A division arose within the ranks of the Council, and many of the members of the board resigned. At this time, on invitation of Robeson, I was asked to join the Council, which I did. I joined on account of my faith in his sincerity, and my belief in the necessary function of the Council on African Affairs. Since Yergan now was at odds with the board, he was dismissed from his office. Legal complications followed due to Yergan's claims to property which the Council and Mr. Field considered theirs. When settlement was finally made, the Council resumed work, hampered by its proscription by the Attorney-General.

When I was dismissed by the N.A.A.C.P. as Director of Special Research in 1948, I was offered the honorary position of Vice-Chairman of the Council on African Affairs, without salary but with an office rent-free, and the services of a secretary to be furnished by the Council. I accepted for two reasons: first, because of my belief in the work which the Council should do for Africa; and secondly, because of my belief that no man or organization should be denied the right to a legal career because of political or religious beliefs.

The Council was, however, on shaky foundations so far as funds were concerned. Membership fell off, and money-raising efforts were not very successful. One promising effort presented itself in May, 1950.

We had received from South Africa a moving appeal for assistance from a native musician, Michael Moerane. We turned to the brilliant, young, black orchestra leader, Dean Dixon, and asked him to arrange a concert of symphonic music by Negro composers of all lands, including Moerane. The concert was successful. We gave it at Town Hall. A thousand persons paid to listen. Critics applauded.

But alas for our dream! The concert cost $4,617, and our receipts were $3,236, leaving a loss of $1,381. This was not bad in itself; but since we had very limited funds and a dwindling income, this result made any plans for repeating the concert annually, as Dixon so ardently desired, impossible. Yet the Voice of America broadcast news of this concert as proof of the encouragement of Negro culture by the United States! It failed to add that this was done by an organization listed by the United States as "subversive."

The ability of the Council to finance even my rent and clerical help decreased, and by 1950 it seemed my duty to relieve them of this obligation. However, the officers came to me and asked me earnestly not to do this, and disclosed a plan which they had considered; and that was that I would consent to a celebration of my 83rd birthday in February, 1951, for the declared purpose of raising a publication fund; that this fund would go to maintaining the office and my connection with the Council on African Affairs, and also for re-publication of some of my works long out of print, and new publication of certain unprinted manuscripts. They were sure that such a proposition would be welcomed by a large number of people, and would mean not only forwarding of my work, but the renewed activity of the Council on African Affairs, at a time when its services were greatly needed. Somewhat to my annoyance, then, I found myself facing another birthday celebration.

It was a particularly difficult situation because the increased costs called for a high charge a plate, and other expenses meant a great outlay of money. Yet I did not feel free to refuse. I consented. A committee was organized, and the dinner planned at the Essex House. Publicity sent out by Dr. E. Franklin Frazier of Howard University, past president of the American Sociological Association and chairman of the sponsoring group, said:

"More than 200 prominent individuals from all sections of the United States, among them Dr. Albert Einstein, Mrs. Mary McLeod Bethune, Dr. Kirtley F. Mather, Langston Hughes, Lion Feuchtwanger, and Hon. J. Finley Wilson, have joined in sponsoring a testimonial dinner honoring Dr. W. E. B. Du Bois on the occasion of his eighty-third birthday this month.

"Honorary chairmen of the sponsoring group for the dinner include Dr. Mordecai W. Johnson, President of Howard University; Rabbi Abba Hillel Silver of

Cleveland; Thomas Mann, noted author; Mrs. Mary Church Terrell of Washington; Miss Mary White Ovington, a founder of the N.A.A.C.P.; Dr. Alain Locke; Dr. William H. Jernagin; Carey McWilliams; and Bishop William J. Walls."

With the dinner invitation went this appeal for a special fund:

"At the peak of his unparalleled experience, learning, and skill we have the rare opportunity of paying tribute to him in a tangible way by assuring continuing facilities for his research, writings, and publications. His priceless library must be kept intact and preserved. His unique collection of scores of thousands of letters and manuscripts must be edited and published. Most important of all, his basic works now out of print must be made available through the publishing of *The Collected Works of Dr. W. E. B. Du Bois.*"

So another birthday dinner was launched, by an organization whose objects and difficulties I have outlined. But now there arose an obstacle which cannot be made entirely clear until I have reminded my readers that because of a habit of world travel which I had fallen into since I went to Germany on a fellowship in 1892, I had gained interests which went beyond Africa and her children. It was these interests which came to dinner before we had opportunity to sit down.

CHAPTER III

---◆---

My Habit of Travel

My early interest in the color problems in the United States and Africa led to the habit of travel which followed my college years, and in time to my advocacy of Peace and the Peace Information Center.

My attitude toward current problems arose from my long habit of keeping in touch with world affairs by repeated trips to Europe and other parts of the world. I became internationally-minded during my four years at Harvard, two in college and two in the graduate school. At this time every student who wanted a modern education yearned to study in Europe, and especially in Germany. Study in England by Americans was not as common, because English universities did not recognize American degrees. This was true also in France, but in Germany Americans were welcomed, and most of the new scholars at Johns Hopkins and Chicago were German-trained. It early became my ambition, then, to study in Germany, and when finally I obtained a fellowship from the Slater Fund, I made plans through Albert Bushnell Hart, my Harvard mentor, to enroll at the University of Berlin.

Since that first trip in 1892 I have made thirteen trips to Europe, one of which circled the globe. I have been in most European countries, in Asia, Africa, and the West Indies. Travel became a habit, and knowledge of current thought in modern countries was always a part of my study, since before the first World War the best of American newspapers took but small account of what Europe was thinking. During my vacations at the University of Berlin I traveled in east, west, and south Germany, in Switzerland, Italy and Austro-Hungary, and to the borders of Russia.

In 1900, on the basis of work on an exhibit done for the United States government, I went to the Paris Exposition, and attended a Pan-African Conference in London. Eleven years later, Felix Adler and I were made secretaries of the American section of the World Races Congress in London, where I spoke twice in the Great Hall of the University of London.

In 1918, when President Wilson was planning to attend the Congress of Versailles, I wrote him a letter saying:

"The International Peace Congress that is to decide whether or not peoples shall have the right to dispose of themselves will find in its midst delegates from a nation which champions the principle of the 'consent of the governed' and 'government by representation.' That nation is our own, and includes in itself more than twelve million souls whose consent to be governed is never asked. They have no members in the legislatures of states where they are in the majority, and not a single representative in the national Congress."

In November the same year, after the Armistice, I went to Paris on the "Creel" boat, and tried to get the President and other Americans interested in a Pan-African Congress to set forth the demands of African peoples. I talked to Colonel House, and received courtesy, but no action. Then I turned to the French, and through Blaise Diagne, the Senegalese Deputy who had brought 100,000 black Africans to defend France, secured permission from Prime Minister Clemenceau to hold a Pan-African Congress in Paris, despite martial law. There were fifty-seven members from fifteen countries, and we demanded that the League of Nations bring the status of African peoples under its purview. One result was the Mandates Commission. Two years later I brought together a second and more representative Congress, meeting successively in London, Paris, and Brussels. There were 113 accredited delegates from twenty-six different groups, including Africa, the West Indies, Europe and the United States. The Congress declared:

"Surely in the 20th century of the Prince of Peace, in the millennium of Buddha and Mahmoud, and in the mightiest Age of Human Reason, there can be found in the civilized world enough of altruism, learning and benevolence to develop native institutions for the native's good, rather than continue to allow the majority of mankind to be brutalized and enslaved by ignorant and selfish agents of commercial institutions, whose one aim is profit and power for the few."

Afterward, in 1923 and later, other such congresses were held, but they were smaller and less effective because of the growing opposition of the imperial countries toward these meetings. We said in London and Lisbon in 1923:

"We ask in all the world that black folk be treated as men. We can see no other road to Peace and Progress. What more paradoxical figure today fronts the world than that of the official head of a great South African state striving blindly to build peace and good will in Europe by standing on the necks and hearts of millions of black Africans."

That same year, by a peculiar political situation, I was made Minister Plenipotentiary to Liberia. Liberia had made application too late for the funds which the United States Congress gave various countries to help their post-war economy. Since I had gone to Africa to visit Liberia after the session of the Pan-African Congress in Portugal, it occurred to certain colored politicians that it might be a fine gesture and one not too costly, to give me diplomatic status and let me represent the President at the second inauguration of President King. Thus, to my surprise, in 1923 I became Dean of the diplomatic corps in Monrovia, with the status of Special Minister Plenipotentiary and Envoy Extraordinary.

I took occasion to greet the President, and to recall the connection between the black people of America and West Africa.

Meantime, my attitude toward the problems of peace and progress had slowly become revolutionized. Formerly I had assumed with most folk that the path of human progress lay necessarily through war, and that if the colored peoples of the world and those of America ever secured their rights as human beings, it would be through organized violence against their white oppressors. But after the First World War, I began to realize that under modern conditions such means to progress were self-defeating. With modern techniques in world war, there could be no victory. The victor was, in the end, as badly off as the vanquished. Reason, education, and scientific knowledge must replace war.

I am not certain just when this change in my thinking came; but I can remember meeting in London in 1911 a colored man who explained to me his plan of leading a black army out of Africa and across the Pyrenees. I was thrilled at his earnestness! But gradually all that disappeared, and I began building a new picture of human progress.

This picture was made more real in 1928 when it became possible for me to take a trip to Russia. I saw on this trip not only Russia, but prostrate Germany, which I had not seen for thirty years. It was a terrible contrast. I visited Leningrad, Moscow, Nizhni Novgorod and Kiev, and finally came home by way of Odessa and Constantinople. It was for me a never-to-be-forgotten experience, and it strengthened my basic belief in Socialism as the one great road to progress.

Ten years later, impelled by puzzled curiosity at the changes that were taking place in Europe, I applied to the Oberlaender Trust, part of the Carl Schurz Foundation, for a fellowship. I proposed a study of the former German colonies in Africa, and an investigation in Germany as to her present attitude toward colonies. This was refused, but later I was offered a fellowship to study industrial education in Germany. As a result, I spent five months in Germany in 1936, and then, going to the Soviet Union, made the trip from Moscow to Manchuria, travelling ten days over the Trans-Siberian Railroad. Finally I spent two months in China and Japan, returning to the United States by way of Hawaii.

I thus saw Asia for the first time, and began to get a new idea of the place of the colored races in the world. I lectured in Japan, met with Chinese leaders in Shanghai, and discussed the future of the darker races, colonialism, and world peace.

Returning to the United States, I continued teaching at Atlanta University until 1944, when I returned to the N.A.A.C.P. in New York as Director of Special Research. I went as Consultant to the U.N.O. in San Francisco, which led me later to edit an "Appeal to the World," to be presented to the Commission on Human Rights of the United Nations. I said in that small volume:

"A discrimination practiced in the United States against her own citizens and to a large extent in contravention of her own laws, cannot be persisted in without infringing upon the rights of the peoples of the world and especially upon the ideals and the work of the United Nations.

"This question, then, which is without doubt primarily an internal and national question, becomes inevitably an international question, and will in the future become more and more international as the nations draw together. In this great attempt to find common ground and to maintain peace, it is, therefore, fitting and proper that the thirteen million American citizens of Negro descent should appeal to the United Nations and ask that organization in the proper way to take cognizance of a situation which deprives this group of their rights as men and citizens, and by so doing makes the functioning of the United Nations more difficult, if not in many cases impossible."

By 1945 all these contacts with foreign peoples and foreign problems and the combination of these problems with the race problem here was forced into one line of thought by the Second World War. This strengthened my growing conviction that the first step toward settling the world's problems was Peace on Earth. Being then invited and urged, I took part in 1949 and 1950 in three congresses which stressed peace. From this arose the Peace Information Center in New York, over which I presided; then to an indictment by the Government as an agent for a "foreign principal." Of this let me now tell, and of its effect on my birthday dinner.

CHAPTER IV

---◆---

Peace Congresses

The peace movement in the United States is old and respectable. I began to study it early and tried to get in close touch with it. I wrote in the *Crisis* in 1913— concerning the meeting of the peace societies at St. Louis:

> "Peace today, if it means anything, means the stopping of the slaughter of the weaker by the stronger in the name of Christianity and culture. The modern lust for land and slaves in Africa, Asia and the South Seas is the greatest and almost the only cause of war between the so-called civilized peoples. For such 'colonial' aggression and 'imperial' expansion, England, France, Germany, Russia and Austria are straining every nerve to arm themselves; against such policies Japan and China are arming desperately. And yet the American peace movement thinks it bad policy to take up this problem of machine guns, natives and rubber, and wants 'constructive' work in 'arbitration treaties and international law.' For our part we think that a little less dignity and dollars and a little more humanity would make the peace movement in America a great democratic philanthropy instead of an aristocratic refuge."

At the Congress of Versailles in 1919, I was on the outside looking in, and my contribution was the Pan-African Congresses, and appeals to the Mandates Commission and the International Labor Organization. In 1945, as Consultant to the American delegation to the U.N.O. in San Francisco, I tried to have this delegation give colonial peoples a real place in the International Bill of Rights. I wrote May 16, 1945:

> "The attempt to write an International Bill of Rights into the San Francisco Conference without any specific mention of the people living in colonies seems to me a most unfortunate procedure. If it were clearly understood that freedom of speech, freedom from want and freedom from fear, which the nations are asked to guarantee, would without question be extended to the 750 million people who live in colonial areas, this would be a great and fateful step. But the very fact that these people, forming the most depressed peoples in the world, with 90% illiteracy, extreme poverty and a prey to disease, who hitherto for the most part have been considered as sources of profit and not included in the democratic development of the world; and whose

exploitation for three centuries has been a prime cause of war, turmoil and suffer-ing;—the omission of specific reference to these peoples is almost advertisement of their tacit exclusion as not citizens of free states, and that their welfare and freedom would be considered only at the will of the countries owning them and not at the demand of enlightened world public opinion."

I discussed this with John Foster Dulles and other leaders. Nothing was done.

In 1949, I was asked to be one of many sponsors of a peace meeting in New York to bring together representatives of the nations of the world. On February 5, 1949, O. John Rogge, formerly Assistant Attorney-General of the U.S., wrote me:

> "The recent development in American-Soviet relations places a new emphasis on the need for a meeting such as our Cultural and Scientific Conference for World Peace. Certainly intellectuals today are faced with no greater challenge than to give the best of their talent, skills and special knowledge to the problem of how we achieve a real peace.
>
> "We are most eager to make this Conference a real contribution to the solutions of the problems that now block the way to peace. For that reason we are asking you and a small group of key individuals among our sponsors to meet with us to help in the preparation of the subject matter and program as well as speakers for this Conference. . . ."

The Conference took place in March, 1949, at the Waldorf-Astoria Hotel, and marked an era in the cultural history of the United States. It was sponsored by 550 of the outstanding leaders of American cultural and liberal thought. It suc-ceeded in bringing together an extraordinary representation of the leaders of modern culture, and especially cultural leaders of the Soviet Union.

The treatment of this peace meeting was extraordinary. So rabid was its reception by the American press, that a concerted and directed movement against peace and in favor of war against the Soviet Union was made clear. Distinguished cultural figures like Picasso were refused visas to attend. The meeting became a matter of bitter recriminations; the sessions were picketed, and the distortion of the whole enterprise in the press was unprecedented. Every kind of attack and misrepresentation was made. Henry A. Singer (in the *Journal of Educational Sociology*) concluded that out of 2,062 items, comprising headlines, feature sto-ries, articles, editorials, cartoons and captions, which appeared in the New York press from March 23 to 30, 1949, there were:

1,090 emotionally charged words and phrases

205 unsupported charges

139 falsehoods

468 statements in opposition to the congress

132 statements neutral in tone

28 statements in favor of the congress

Thus a conference called by persons of the highest standing in science, liter-ature and art, and conceived with the best motives, became as the New York

Times said, one of "the most controversial meetings in recent New York history"; and a signal expression of the witch-hunting and calumny in this nation which has driven free speech and the right to inquire and reason into almost total eclipse.

At the final meeting in Madison Square Garden I said in introducing the Chairman, Harlow Shapley:

> "We know and the saner nation knows that we are not traitors nor conspirators; and far from plotting force and violence it is precisely force and violence that we bitterly oppose. This conference was not called to defend communism nor socialism nor the American way of life. It was called to promote peace! It was called to say and say again that no matter how right or wrong differing systems of beliefs in religion, industry or government may be, war is not the method by which their differences can successfully be settled for the good of mankind."

The next month I was urged by O. John Rogge, Albert E. Kahn and others to attend a world peace meeting in Paris. The American committee offered to pay a part of my expense, and I paid the rest. I went to what seems to me the greatest demonstration for peace in modern times. For four days witnesses from nearly every country in the world set forth the horrors of war and the necessity of peace if civilization was to survive. On the concluding Sunday, 500,000 pilgrims from all parts of France, coming on foot, by automobiles, by train and plane, filed through the vast Buffalo Stadium crying "Peace, no more war!" At this world conference I emphasized colonialism and said:

> "Let us not be misled. The real cause of the differences which threaten world war is not the spread of socialism or even of the complete socialism which Communism envisages. Socialism is spreading all over the world and even in the United States. . . . Against this spread of socialism, one modern institution is working desperately, and that is colonialism, and colonialism has been and is and ever will be one of the chief causes of war. . . . Leading this new Colonial Imperialism comes my own native land, built by my fathers' toil and blood, the United States. The United States is a great nation: rich by grace of God and prosperous by the hard work of its humblest citizens. . . . Drunk with power we are leading the world to hell in a new colonialism with the same old human slavery which once ruined us; and to a Third World War which will ruin the world."

In July, 1949, I joined with Linus Pauling, John Clark, Uta Hagen and O. John Rogge to call an "American Continental Congress for World Peace" to be held in Mexico City in September.

Again in August, 1949, twenty-five prominent Americans were asked to attend an all-Soviet peace conference in Moscow. For reasons which arose directly from the violent reception given the peace congress in March, I was the only one who accepted the invitation. I addressed the 1,000 persons present.[1]

My trip to the Soviet Union made it impossible for me to get to the Congress in Mexico City, but I watched with interest other peace conferences: in Cuba in August; in Australia in April, 1950; the delegations to the Parliaments of the world, projected by the Defenders of Peace in Paris in February, 1950. I joined a group to welcome persons selected to come here, including the Dean of Canterbury, and the great painter, Picasso. They were refused visas. A Mid-Century Conference for Peace was called by the Committee for Peaceful Alternatives in May, 1950, in which I was to conduct a panel; but a previous engagement kept me away. I was asked to attend the meeting of the Executive Committee of the Paris Defenders of Peace in Prague in August, 1951, and accepted. This meeting was to call a Second World Congress and make a new plea for disarmament.

But before this meeting, we had succeeded in forming in the United States an organization to work for peace. This was the Peace Information Center.

COMMENT

Certainly none of the Americans who went to the Paris World Congress for Peace in April, 1949, had the wide experience in international gatherings of W. E. B. Few of us who decided to go were actually delegates from any organization, though some were sent by trade unions and loosely organized citizens' committees. I had derived such tremendous benefit from my participation in our own Scientific and Cultural Conference for Peace held in New York the month before that, as a writer, I wanted to see the larger world picture. I had just finished my book on Benjamin Banneker, but in order to undertake such a trip it was necessary for me to turn in another short book (from which I could collect an advance). For this reason I was not ready to leave with the group which flew out over the Atlantic early Easter morning. Only a quirk of fate prevented me from making the trip with our good friend and enthusiastic advocate, Mr. O. John Rogge. A legal case was holding up his departure and he had made a reservation with Air France to leave several days after the others. He offered to make a second reservation for me. However, I turned in my book sooner than I had dared hope and was fortunate enough to get a ticket on the American Line to leave April 19th. Mr. Rogge told me I had settled for a far less enjoyable trip. "They serve champagne with meals on the Air France," was his parting remark.

It so happened, therefore, that I landed at the Paris airport at the very moment Paul Robeson was making that much discussed speech in the Salle Pleyel. The Paris Committee had reserved a room for me at the Hotel Claridge where they had sent Dr. Du Bois. I was quite over-awed by the hotel's splendors and knew I'd have to move out pretty quick; but since it was already evening and I had found a note from W. E. B. inviting me to join him for dinner, I changed into something suitable and went downstairs.

Hardly had we found seats in the gold-and-mirror-paneled dining salon than we were joined by Paul Robeson at whose appearance the orchestra swung into "Old Man River" while guests all over the room stood up and applauded. I recall how Paul Robeson modestly shrugged aside Dr. Du Bois' compliments on the "remarks" Paul had made upon being introduced to the Congress that afternoon. He was leaving almost immediately for Norway. At the close of our delicious meal, we wished him bon voyage and all good fortune in his Scandinavian concert tour.

For me the Peace Congress was simply breath-taking. Whether I sat in my seat, earphones clamped to my head so that every word of the speaker up front came to me in English, or pushed through the crowded corridors, I had the realization that I was at the cross-roads of all nations, of all peoples of the world—where past, present and future, east, west, north and south did meet. That this feeling was shared was evidenced by the joyous reception of the whole Congress to speakers from the many different countries.

As I look back over the program which unfolded before us I find it difficult to pick out high points. There was the morning when Dr. Du Bois was introduced to deliver his address and the packed assembly rose to its feet while men and women, young and old, applauded and cheered. Afterwards he told me that as he stood waiting for the waves of acclamation to subside he was overwhelmed with amazement that these peoples from the far corners of the earth "seemed to know me." Indeed this fact was obvious on every shining, lifted face—black faces from Africa, brown faces from India, yellow faces from the Orient. These people did know that the slight, dignified gentleman they were seeing for the first time had been their champion for many years!

Another event which would have made interesting reading in our press was the appearance of the Metropolitan Nicolas, head of the Russian Orthodox Church. When, as a child, I attended my father's Sunday School, I was given each Sunday beautifully colored picture cards. Now when I saw the Russian prelate, I could only think of the imposing figures of Old Testament patriarchs as they were reproduced on those cards. His sweeping robes with jeweled breast-plate, his stately headdress, long white beard and flashing eyes made him a magnificent representative. Newsmen with cameras rushed forward, bulbs flashed and pencils scribbled feverishly as the ringing voice resounded through the hall in an address which closed with an invocation to "our Father God for blessings to shower down upon the head of our beloved son, Joseph Stalin!"

Yes, the Metropolitan Nicolas furnished reporters with copy for thrilling headlines, but so far as I know not one word of this appeared in our commercial press.

On Monday, April 25th, during the last session of the Congress, a Peace Manifesto was adopted. This historic document whose Preamble declared it was drawn up by representatives of the peoples of seventy-two countries, "men and women of every creed, philosophy, color, and type of civilization," solemnly proclaimed that "the defense of Peace is henceforth the concern of all peoples." In the name of the 600 million represented, the Congress sent out this message: "We are ready and resolved to win the battle for Peace, which means to win the battle for Life."

The Congress adjourned and the delegates returned to their seventy-two countries. The Manifesto traveled with them and so it reached Denmark before I did. I had accepted the invitation from a publishing house in Copenhagen to attend a national festival in honor of Scandinavia's most celebrated living writer, Martin Andersen Nexö. I was in that lovely little green country during June. On the night of June 26th, the 80th birthday of the great Danish novelist, I witnessed another spectacular demonstration for Peace.

The day had been one continuous festival beginning early in the morning at Martin Andersen Nexö's home in Holte, then in the afternoon at a big public park in Copenhagen, hung with flags and banners, with music and dancing and speeches, followed by a lavish banquet in a huge, old, paneled banquet hall. The northern sky was not even dusky until after eleven o'clock. Then we were driven to the large central square of the city, overshadowed by the copper-covered towers of castles built by ancient kings and ringed about by smart, gleaming shops. I climbed into a guests' stand built in the center of the square; and then, converging on the plaza from the corners of the city, came what seemed to be an unending four-pronged torchlight procession. As they circled into the square, singing and waving, they flung the torches onto a bonfire that mounted until it seemed to reach the heavens. Then, packed into the square and extending into the streets as far as I could see, they chanted: *This, Martin Andersen Nexö, is our birthday gift to you. Here we have lit a fire for Peace. May its light be seen high in our sky, may people everywhere see our bright sky and may it light the way to Peace!*

I lingered in Denmark and did not return home until the last week in July. By that time there was talk of a Continental Peace Congress to be held in Mexico soon. But I put that out of my mind. I knew I must get back to work. Yet, even before I had unpacked my bags I was asked to attend a Peace Conference to be held in Havana in preparation for the Congress in Mexico. After what I had seen and heard, I certainly was interested in Americans enlisting in the cause of Peace. I did not believe that Europeans were any more interested in maintaining peace than we were. After failing in my efforts to encourage others to go to Cuba, I found myself on August 5th in a plane sweeping down towards multi-colored lights gleaming in the tropical night.

This conference, which held its first session at the University of Havana, so swelled and expanded that each of the three days it was moved to larger quarters. Nobody had expected the more than 2,000 delegates who came from all parts of the country. Perhaps for the first time in Cuba's turbulent history descendants of Spanish grandees sat down with descendants of African slaves, and orthodox Catholics as represented by Dr. Emilio Ochoa with the militant socialist adherents of Garcia Gallo. Peasants joined their voices with members of Rotary Clubs, Protestant pastors, priests, black and white, educated and une-ducated, united in drawing up the final resolution.

I returned home filled with enthusiasm and eager to tell mothers in America: "Don't worry! The peoples of the world all want peace just as you do. Everybody wants peace!"

NOTE

1. See Appendix A for the text of this speech.

CHAPTER V

---◆---

The Peace Information Center

There were some sixty Americans who attended the World Congress of the Defenders of Peace in Paris in April, 1950. We were all tremendously impressed and enthused, and we discussed many times the question as to what we could do when we returned to America. As a matter of fact, we did nothing for nearly a year, because in the state of hysteria and war-mongering which we found in the United States, it was not at all clear as to what could be done legally. Evidently under the new legislation we could not form a branch of the Partisans of Peace. Indeed, when delegates of great prominence from a number of nations proposed to make a journey to the Parliaments of the world to plead for peace, they were denied permission to enter the United States.

The Continental Peace Congress in Mexico in the fall of 1949 was attended by many Americans. But almost no notice of its meeting was published in the United States. American newspaper men were called into the Embassy in Mexico City before the Congress, and given kindly advice to ignore the sessions. They obeyed almost to a man. Organized effort in the United States remained difficult.

Finally I received this telegram from O. John Rogge:

"Strongly urge your participation meeting my house 400 East 52 Street at 8 o'clock Wednesday evening March 1st. Purpose is to discuss certain vital problems relating to current activities for promotion of world peace."

I went to the meeting and found that the thirty or forty persons attending had already in previous meetings been exploring methods of organizing for peace in the United States. The first idea seemed to have been some federation of the various peace movements already in existence. That had fallen through. Then a committee to welcome the prominent advocates of peace who proposed to visit the United States proved useless when they were refused visas. We appointed a committee to explore possibilities.

A number of the participants in this initial meeting went to Europe to attend a meeting of the Bureau of the Partisans of Peace in Stockholm, and also to visit Russia under the plan of approaching Parliaments in the interests of peace. Our committee adopted a plan which seemed to us all unusually apt and legal, and that was, as we decided at a later meeting in a private home, to form a Peace Information Center, the object of which should be simply to tell the people of the United States what other nations were doing and thinking about war.

Johannes Steel proposed that we publish what he called a "Peace-gram" at intervals, and in that way we could collect information and send it over the United States. The proposal was made by the chairman of the committee, Elizabeth Moos, and we proceeded to locate offices and start organized work. I became chairman, for the rather simple reason that due to long experience I was used to getting committees and groups of persons to transact business smoothly without entangling themselves in procedural technicalities; and also I had the questionable habit of being on time, and seeing that meetings adjourned well before midnight.

I was not personally acquainted with many of the people at the meeting, although at the Peace Congress in Paris I had met Mrs. Moos. But as we organized and got to work they proved a most interesting and companionable group. Elizabeth Moos was a small, white-haired woman of typical New England culture although born in the Middle West. She had an alert mind, was educated at Smith College, and had been a teacher of youth. She had a pleasing personality, was deeply interested in social developments here and abroad, and was a good executive. She became our first executive secretary, and launched the project efficiently.

She brought in Abbott Simon to head the campaign to secure signatures to the Stockholm Appeal. Simon was a typical devotee of a great cause. He had been graduated from college at sixteen, had been a leader of youth movements, was a musician trained under Schoenberg, and was a veteran of World War II. As an officer under MacArthur, he had been wounded, had seen the results of the atom bomb at Hiroshima, and was deeply devoted to peace.

Then in July, Mrs. Moos, on account of ill-health, resigned with regret after having put the organization on its feet. She went to Europe for rest, hoping eventually to take up again her study of education of youth. After our indictment Mrs. Moos returned voluntarily to stand trial with us.

Abbott Simon was her obvious successor and became our executive secretary from July to our dissolution. Kyrle Elkin was a young business man, educated at Harvard, and engaged in small manufacturing. He had never been especially active in social work, but was attracted by our program, and in his quiet way helped us by accepting the duties of treasurer. Here his business methods were of great importance, but beyond that he willingly accepted responsibility of raising funds among his personal friends and from the public. Our young and pretty stenographer and clerk, Sylvia Soloff, ought never to have been indicted with the officials, as the judge finally decided. She helped run the office but had no part in policy-making.

This was the main group in the Peace Information Center. They were all straightforward people, unencumbered by personal ambitions or petty idiosyncrasies. They simply saw a job worth doing and they were willing to try to do it. There was an advisory committee invited to meet once or twice a month to exercise general control. It varied in composition, but the usual members who attended were: Albert E. Kahn, O. John Rogge, John T. McManus, Paul Robeson, Shirley Graham, Johannes Steel, Dr. Gene Weltfish, C. B. Baldwin, Leon Straus, and others.

We all worked together smoothly and effectively. We issued the "Peacegrams," and then reprinted and circulated the Stockholm Appeal to abolish the atom bomb. We distributed this over the nation, and collected in all 2,500,000 signatures. We printed and distributed other demands and arguments for peace, like the Red Cross Appeal, the statement of the Friends, and many others.

The greatest piece of literature which came out of the World Wars was the Stockholm Appeal. In simplicity, clarity and sincerity, the eighty words of this message swept the world as few other pronouncements ever have. The statement was French in origin and stemmed from the horror of Hiroshima and the shudder of apprehension over the world when Truman casually stated the possible renewed use of the atom bomb in Korea. At a meeting of the World Partisans of Peace in Stockholm on March 15, 1950, attended by 150 delegates from 18 of the leading nations of the world, including the United States and the Soviet Union, this statement was unanimously adopted:

> "We demand the absolute banning of the atomic weapon, an arm of terror and of mass extermination of populations.
>
> "We demand the establishment of strict international control to ensure the implementation of this ban.
>
> "We consider that the first government henceforth to use the atomic weapon against any country whatsoever will be committing a crime against humanity and should be treated as a war criminal.
>
> "We call on all people of good will throughout the world to sign this appeal."

The half billion persons who signed this Appeal and the billion who would have signed if given the chance, were moved not by the thought of defending the Soviet Union so much as by the desire to prevent modern culture from relapsing into primitive barbarism. The reputation of Dean Acheson, United States Secretary of State, will never recover from his deliberate attempt to misrepresent the origin, intent and word of this great appeal. The effort to imprison five officials of the Peace Information Center culminated his campaign.

The first direct public attack on the Peace Information Center came from a broadside from the United States Secretary of State, Dean Acheson, released July 12:[1]

> "I am sure that the American people will not be fooled by the so-called 'world peace appeal' or 'Stockholm resolution' now being circulated in this country for signatures. It should be recognized for what it is—a propaganda trick in the spurious 'peace offensive' of the Soviet Union. . . ."

I replied immediately on July 14, saying in a release to the press:

> " At a moment in history when a world fearful of war hangs on every American pronouncement, the Secretary of State, simultaneously with the Committee on Un-American Activities of the House of Representatives, join in condemning any

effort to outlaw atomic warfare. There is in your statement no intimation of a desire for peace, of a realization of the horror of another World War, or of sympathy with the crippled, impoverished and dead who pay for fighting.

"Surely throughout the world hundreds of millions of people may be pardoned for interpreting your statements as foreshadowing American use of the atom bomb in Korea. Nowhere in your statements can be found evidence of a spirit which would seek to mitigate by mediation the present dangers of war.

"The best answer to these assertions is to list a few of the great minds and figures of our times who with more than 200,000,000 ordinary men and women who want peace, have signed their names to the World Peace Appeal. George Bernard Shaw; Arnold Zweig; former President Cardenas of Mexico; former Premier Vittorio Orlando of Italy (who was one of the Big Four at Versailles); Osvaldo Aranha, Brazilian statesman and former president of the UN General Assembly; M. Mongibeaux, Chief Justice of the French Supreme Court; M. Mornet, Attorney General of France; Dr. Sholem Treistman, Chief Rabbi of Poland; Edouard Herriot, President of the French Senate and former Premier; Mme. Sun Yat Sen; Jose Bergamin, renowned Catholic philosopher; Cardinal Sapieha, Roman Catholic Primate of Poland—these are but a few of the great names in other countries.

"Nobel Peace Prize winner, Emily Greene Balch, in signing declared: 'A statement like the World Peace Appeal is essentially important at this time because it cuts across all ideological and political lines and merits the support of all those who want peace, regardless of any other difference among them.'

"Thomas Mann, one of the great figures of the world, writes: 'The atom bomb is a great threat to humanity. I have signed the Stockholm Appeal. I support any movement which has peace as its aim.'

"In our own country, among one million American men and women who are sick at the threat of war and have therefore signed the World Peace Appeal are scientists like Dr. Anton J. Carlson of the University of Chicago, cancer specialist; Dr. Philip R. White of Philadelphia; the Rt. Rev. Arthur W. Moulton, Protestant Episcopal Bishop (retired), of Utah; Bishop S. L. Greene, A.M.E. Church of Birmingham, Ala.; Justice James H. Wolfe of the Supreme Court of Utah; Dr. I. N. Kolthoff of the University of Minnesota; publisher Aubrey Williams.

"The appeal has been endorsed by the Egyptian Council of State, by the Roman Catholic Episcopate of Poland, by eight Catholic Bishops of Italy, by the Prime Minister and Cabinet of Finland, and by the Parliament of the Soviet Union. . . .

"The main burden of your opposition to this Appeal and to our efforts lies in the charge that we are part of a 'spurious peace offensive' of the Soviet Union. Is it our strategy that when the Soviet Union asks for peace, we insist on war? Must any proposals for averting atomic catastrophe be sanctified by Soviet opposition? Have we come to the tragic pass where, by declaration of our own Secretary of State, there is no possibility of mediating our differences with the Soviet Union? Does it not occur to you, Sir, that there are honest Americans who, regardless of their differences on other questions, hate and fear war and are determined to do something to avert it? . . .

"We have got to live in the world with Russia and China. If we worked together with the Soviet Union against the menace of Hitler, can we not work with them again at a time when only faith can save us from utter atomic disaster? Certainly, hundreds of millions of colonial peoples in Asia, Africa, Latin America and elsewhere, conscious of our support of Chiang Kai-shek, Bao Dai and the colonial system, and mindful of the oppressive discrimination against the Negro people in the United States, would feel that our intentions also must be accepted on faith.

"Today in this country it is becoming standard reaction to call anything 'communist' and therefore subversive and unpatriotic, which anybody for any reason dislikes. We feel strongly that this tactic has already gone too far; that it is not sufficient today to trace a proposal to a communist source in order to dismiss it with contempt.

"We are a group of Americans, who upon reading this Peace Appeal, regarded it as a true, fair statement of what we ourselves and many countless other Americans believed. Regardless of our other beliefs and affiliations, we united in this organization for the one and only purpose of informing the American people on the issues of peace."

The Peace Information Center continued its work. The evidence of the desire for peace came in from all parts of the United States, and especially from those regions where the newspapers were suppressing information. Surprising interest and support came to us especially from the West and South.

In the midst of this campaign I made the trip to Russia to attend the peace congress in August, and on my way home viewed briefly the terrible destruction in Warsaw and the brave and increasingly successful effort to rebuild the land; and again I saw Prague after an interval of fifty-six years.

Although on the program, I could not attend the peace congress in Mexico because of my inability to get back from Russia in time. In August, I had a cablegram from Paris inviting me to attend as a guest the meeting of the Bureau of the World Congress of the Defenders of Peace in Prague. They offered to pay my expenses. They were meeting for two main purposes: to broaden the Stockholm Appeal by asking for disarmament; and to arrange a Second World Peace Congress. I regarded this as important and applied for a visa on my unexpired passport.

The young man in the New York office looked over my note of application and asked whom I knew in the country. I realized that I was under suspicion for the request, and I promised him details the next day. I appeared with a long letter in which I noted all the facts: that I had attended peace congresses in New York, France and Moscow in 1949, and now wished to attend a meeting of the Bureau of the World Partisans of Peace as their guest in Prague.

He scanned the letter and said that I must add that I was aware of the risk of post-war conditions; I assented and started to write: "If war conditions prevent permission to go, I shall understand," when he interrupted me and said: "You must say that you know of the unsettled conditions in Czechoslovakia." But I objected that I had no such knowledge. He assured me that the State Department had so notified his office. I said I was quite willing to say that the State Department had so informed him. That would not do. "You know," he added, "that Russia controls Czechoslovakia?" "No," I said, "I do not; I was under the impression that the Czechs were in control." He then gave up and passed me to an older official.

This man looked annoyed and hunted at length through a file of instructions. He finally explained that the State Department had ordered them to obtain from all prospective visitors to Czechoslovakia an acknowledgement that they were aware of conditions there. Very well, I answered, and I appended to my letter this statement: "Whatever the conditions are in Czechoslovakia, I wish to make this trip." He eyed this disparagingly, but finally said, "All right."

It took ten days of deliberation in Washington and two telephone calls before my passport came. Even then it was carefully limited to sixty days in Czechoslovakia and "necessary lands" en route, and "was not to be validated for additional countries without the express authorization of the Department of State." I felt like a prisoner on parole.

When asked at Prague to speak, I said:

> "For fifty years I have been in touch with social currents in the United States. Never before has organized reaction wielded the power it does today: by owner-ship of press and radio, by curtailment of free speech, by imprisonment of liberal thinkers and writers. It has become almost impossible today in my country even to hold a public rally for peace. This has been accomplished by inducing Americans to believe that America is in imminent danger of aggression from communism, socialism and liberalism, and that the peace movement cloaks this threat. . . .
>
> "Manifestly, to meet this hysteria, it is not so much a question of the concept of war under any circumstances, as the far deeper problem of getting the truth to the masses of the citizens of the United States who still in overwhelming majority hate murder, crippling destruction and insanity, as a means of progress. By personal contact, by honest appeal, by knowing the truth ourselves, we can yet win the peace in America. But it is going to take guts and the willingness to jeopardize jobs and respectability. . . ."

After this meeting in Prague where the Bureau of the Defenders of Peace finally voted to broaden the Stockholm Appeal so as to ask disarmament and condemn aggression and armed intervention, I started home; but on the way I received two messages in Paris, which led to a political campaign and a crimi-nal indictment.

The Peace Information Center was in existence from April 3, 1951, to October 12 of that year, when it formally disbanded. After that, the closing down of our activities, answering continued correspondence, paying our bills, and ending our lease, kept our office partially in existence until the end of the year. During the seven months of active work, we took in a total of $23,000 from small donations, public and house meetings, and sale of literature for which there was a large demand. We printed and distributed 750,000 pieces, of which 485,000 were peti-tions for signatures to the Stockholm Appeal. These sold for a cent and cost us a half cent. We also issued a hundred thousand stickers, and thousands of pam-phlets for children, Negroes, Jews, Catholics, Spanish and Italian speaking minori-ties whom we tried to interest in peace. In addition came the regular "Peacegram" with its news of the world peace movement. Our largest two items of expense were about $9,000 for printing and $8,000 for rent and salaries. We had, finally, a mailing-list of 6,000 persons in all parts of the nation especially interested in peace.

This was the story of the Peace Information Center, and this was my connec-tion with it. In this way our indictment for crime came with my 83rd birthday dinner, with a defense of my honor and decency, and started a crusade which actually reached around the world.

For this fantastic legal case, which never at any time had a scintilla of proof or plausibility behind it, the Government of the United States, relying on the testimony which O. John Rogge presented to the Grand Jury in the District of Columbia, brought us finally before the bar of justice on November 8, 1951. Trusting in the further testimony of Rogge and twenty-seven other witnesses whom the Department of Justice had subpoenaed, but only seven of whom they dared call to the witness chair, the Government tried to put us in jail and thus stop any citizen or organization from daring to advocate Peace in the United States.

NOTE

1. *The New York Times*, July 13, 1950.

CHAPTER VI

◆

My Campaign for Senator

As I started home from Prague in August, 1950, I received two messages from the United States, both important. One was from John Abt of the American Labor Party, asking if I would run for United States Senator from New York. The other was from Abbott Simon, executive secretary of the Peace Information Center, informing me that the Department of Justice had demanded our registration as "agents of a foreign principal."

Arriving in Paris on August 2, I hastened to my favorite little hotel on the Rive Gauche, only a block from the beautiful flowers, sculpture and children of the Luxemburg gardens. As soon as I was settled I telephoned to Abt and he asked my decision on his proposal. I laughed.

I laughed because I remembered my grilling by the State Department when I asked for a passport to visit Czechoslovakia. I was amused to think what such a reputation could add to any campaign; then I recalled that laughter over the long distance telephone is as costly as words, and I proceeded to remind Abt of my age and political inexperience and my unwillingness to run for public office.

But Abt said a number of things, of which two sunk in: (1) That this campaign would afford a chance for me to speak for peace which could be voiced in no other way. (2) My candidacy would help the campaign of Vito Marcantonio. I thought this matter over gravely. Because of my support of the Progressive Party in 1948, my acceptance of an honorary and unpaid office with Paul Robeson in the Council on African Affairs, and my activity in Peace Congresses in New York, Paris and Moscow, I found myself increasingly proscribed in pulpit, school and platform. My opportunity to write for publication was becoming narrower and narrower, even in the Negro press. I wondered if a series of plain talks in a political campaign would not be my last and only chance to tell the truth as I saw it.

Beyond this, of all members of Congress, Vito Marcantonio has acted with courage, intelligence and steadfast integrity in the face of ridicule, mud-slinging and cheating. Liberals like Graham, Pepper and Douglas have wavered, backed and filled and deserted their principles; the colored members of the House have generally been silent or absent. If I could do anything for Marcantonio, I decided to try. On August 31, I wired, "Accept. Du Bois."

Of course, whatever contribution I could make would, I knew, be small and not very effective. I did not have the strength for a hard, active campaign; I was no orator or spell-binder, but only one who could reason with those who would listen and had brains enough to understand. I had no large group of close personal friends, and many of those whom I had, dared not speak or act because of fear for their jobs—a fear which was real and restraining; finally, I had no money to spend or moneyed friends to contribute; and anyone who thinks that money does not buy American elections is a fool.

The matter of registering the Peace Information Center as a foreign agent I did not take too seriously. It was, I was sure, either a mistake or an effort begun to intimidate us. I cabled a statement to Simon, setting forth our work and aims. I suggested sending an attorney to Washington, and promised to go there myself as soon as I could get passage home. Then I forgot it and turned to what seemed then the more serious matter of my campaign.

My experience in practical politics had been small. First of all I had been reared in the New England tradition of regarding politics as no fit career for a man of serious aims, and particularly unsuitable for a college-bred man. Respectable participation in political life as voter, thinker, writer and, on rare occasions as speaker, was my ideal. This preoccupation was strengthened by the fact that for Negroes entrance into political life was especially difficult. Spending as I did the first thirteen years of my active life in Georgia, I was disfranchised on account of my race, and confined my political work to advice to my students and to writing.

When I came to New York in 1910, my political activity was exercised through the *Crisis* magazine which I founded and edited. As it gained influence and circulation, I began to give political advice to Negro voters. In 1912, I tried to swing the Negro vote to Woodrow Wilson for President and away from Taft, in order to break our servitude to the Republican Party, and to rebuke Taft for his "lily-white" Southern policies. Many Negro voters took my advice to their regret and my own embarrassment, as Wilson surrendered in many instances to the Negro-hating South. Next I tried to influence Theodore Roosevelt and the Bull Moose movement to make the Negro problem a main plank in their platform. Roosevelt would not yield, and preferred alliance with the "progressive South," which he lived to regret. I remembered this in 1919 as I introduced him to an audience in Carnegie Hall, when he made his last public speech.

From 1921 to 1933, under Harding, Coolidge and Hoover, I pushed the political fight against lynching and for civil rights in editorials and lectures, with my only personal participation in politics the chance appointment as special minister to Liberia, and membership on the New York state commission to celebrate emancipation. When Ferdinand Morton, colored leader of Tammany and a man of extraordinary ability, suggested that I run for Congress on a Tammany ticket, I refused flatly, partly on account of my dislike of Tammany, and partly because I knew I had no personal fitness for a political career. I began to lean toward the Marxian view of politics as at bottom economics, and said so in the resolutions which for years I wrote for the annual meetings of the N.A.A.C.P. I strongly supported LaFollette in 1924.

With the depression and the reign of Roosevelt from 1933 to 1945, I embraced the "New Deal" in writing and lecturing and in socialist thinking; stressing the disabilities of the Negro and criticizing the failure adequately to deal with them, but believing firmly in state planning for social welfare. At this juncture, in 1934, I returned to the South to teach and re-enter my Ivory Tower. War came, with Hitler, and Stalingrad, the United Nations and the disaster of Truman. I returned to the N.A.A.C.P. in New York in 1944, and soon in frantic recoil from a program of war and economic reaction, I cast my political lot with Henry Wallace. This cost me dear, although I took no active part in the campaign of 1948. But I did lose my job indirectly because my political thought was deemed too radical.

During the next two years I worked with the Progressive Party in minor roles, without pay. I had some influence in forming the Progressive Party platform for 1950, and I made the personal acquaintance of Henry Wallace. He was a kindly and warmhearted man. He induced Anita McCormick Blaine, his close friend, to help me out of financial difficulties in 1949, when for a time it seemed that I would no longer be able to continue my writing and study.

But as I came to know Henry Wallace, I realized the uncertainty of his intellectual orientation, and the strong forces close to him which wanted respectability and feared too close association with unpopular causes. In a sense Wallace lacked guts and had small stomach for martyrdom; and all this despite his facing of Southern rotten eggs in 1948. I tried gingerly to strengthen his faith, when I saw him wavering in 1950. I wrote him to call his attention to the way in which, a century before, respectable folk who disliked slavery recoiled from being classed with "Abolitionists," because the word connoted so much that was not respectable at the time. I noted the same attitude today toward "Communism." I received no reply, and on July 15, 1950, Wallace deserted the Progressive movement. Thereafter, and perhaps ungenerously both to him and the slender little animal who, after all, can fight, I thought of Wallace as no longer the crusader, but as Wallace the Weasel.

I went into the campaign for Senator knowing well from the first that I did not have a ghost of a chance for election, and that my efforts would bring me ridicule at best and jail at worst. On the other hand, I did have a message which was worth attention and which in the long run could not fail to have influence. The leaders of the American Labor Party and my colleagues on the ticket were more than kind and solicitous; they reduced my participation to a minimum, themselves bore an unfair part of the work, and gave me every help to keep my efforts within my strength and ability.

I delivered, in all, ten speeches and made seven broadcasts. I began with a press conference in Harlem, to which the *Times* and *Herald Tribune* sent reporters, and the Associated Press; only one Negro paper was represented. I addressed mass meetings in Harlem, Queens, Brooklyn and the Bronx, each attended by 1,000 to 2,500 persons, who gave me careful attention and generous applause. This was encouraging because I used manuscript, no gestures, and few jokes. This method I have used before popular audiences for years, and while an audience always sighs at the sight of a roll of manuscript, I am convinced that intelligent persons prefer to have a speaker really say something, rather than entertain them with shouting and acting. My last speech in the city of New York was at that marvelous gathering of 17,000 persons at Madison Square Garden on October 24, news of which was nearly blacked out by the press.

On an upstate tour from Buffalo to Albany beginning October 15, I spoke four times to audiences of a few hundred persons in small and rather obscure halls. There was a distinct air of fear and repression. "Free" Americans slipped in almost furtively and whispered many stories of how the industries of Rochester and Syracuse threatened their workers. In Albany political pressure was tense. While the press was courteous, we evidently were permitted just to touch the edges of real publicity.

I realized from this how much money and effort in halls, advertisement and personal contacts was needed to get our message over to the mass of voters. Once reached even in small groups, they were eager and enthusiastic. They listened, leaning forward with rapt faces. But they and we were gripped by defeatism. Tom Dewey and Joe Hanley, the Republican candidates, could talk to ten thousands while we spoke to a hundred. Even if they said nothing, which they often did, their message reached every end of the state. Senator Lehman and his Democratic Party friends did not have to go hungry in order for him comfortably to cover the state. I winced at our little collections for expenses at meetings; they drew blood. My colleagues, like John McManus, Frank Scheiner and George Murphy, spent day and night in personal contacts and conversation while I slept with guilty conscience. We needed a hundred workers where we had one.

I had another handicap and paradox. Of the utter unfitness of Hanley for public office, especially after his notorious letter revealing disreputable political bargaining came to light while I was in Albany, there was not the slightest doubt. Lehman was different. He was an honest man and wealthy; he had behind him a fairly good record of public service. Yet he ought not to sit in the United States Senate because he represented finance and foreign investment, and because of this was frantically backing Truman in the Korean crime which Big Business precipitated.

All that my candidacy, however, could possibly accomplish, in the immediate present, would be to draw enough votes from warmonger Lehman to replace him with a venal politician. Many voters were indignant at this prospect, and some accused me of being deliberately a catspaw or at best of poor judgment. For a time the political leaders were worried over this; and this angle gave me more publicity than any other.

Yet, I am sure, I was right to persist, and that even the threat of Hanley was not worse than that of World War; and that overwhelming defeat today of my fight for peace and civil rights would some day prove worth while.

The ten speeches I made in this campaign were based on three themes, represented by my talk on "Peace and Civil Rights" at Madison Square Garden; my address on "The American Way of Life" at the Brooklyn and Queens rallies; and my lecture on "Harlem" at the Golden Gate Ballroom. All my other speeches were combinations and adaptations of these.

For the seven broadcasts, I adopted another method: I planned a connected series of expositions on the underlying basis of the demand for peace and civil rights, emphasizing in succession the rule of propaganda, the misconception of property, and the concept of democracy. These were interlarded between two general statements, one delivered on television, and one in our final symposium.

My main thesis was thus summed up:

> "The most sinister evil of this day is the widespread conviction that war is inevitable and that there is no time left for discussion. It is doubtful if the mass of Americans who accept this judgment realize just what its implications are. War is physical force exercised by men and machines on other men so as to compel submission to the will of the victors. Unquestionably in primitive times there were repeated occasions when such recourse to force was the only path to social progress. But as civilization has progressed and included larger and larger masses of men and portions of the earth, two things have become increasingly clear: one, that the costs of war have become too great for any nation to pay no matter what the alternative; and two, that in war as now carried on, there can be no victorious party. In modern world war all contestants lose and not only lose the immediate causes of strife, but cripple the fundamental bases of human culture."

On the whole I enjoyed this unique excursion into political activity. I encountered little open race prejudice, although of course few New Yorkers wanted to be represented in Washington by a Negro—because of their prejudice and also because they suspected I was more Negro than American. To counteract this at least in part, I made no appeal to the Negro vote as such. I wanted the people of New York to know that as Senator I would represent the interests of the state and not merely those of one minority group. At the same time I knew, and Negroes knew, that I would regard Negro emancipation as a prime prerequisite to American freedom. The Negro voter of Harlem was in a quandary; he knew that no candidate would defend Negro rights as I would; he also knew I would be defeated and that he must depend on Lehman or Hanley. His path was cloudy.

Above all, I was amazed and exasperated by the overwhelming use and influence of money in politics. Millionaires and corporations, not record and logic, defeated Marcantonio. Dewey could afford to spend $35,000 for one day on radio; when friends of mine the nation over sent $600 to further my campaign, it represented more honesty and guts than all the millions spent on Lehman and Hanley. Small wonder the result of this election throughout the land sounded like a "tale told by an idiot."

Five million persons voted in this election; of these, 4 per cent voted for me (15 per cent in Harlem), which was far more than I expected. More than a million of the voters stayed away from the polls.

After a great social effort like the election of 1950, one must feel the let-down. Even the victors gain less than they wish, while the losers wonder if it was worth all the effort, all the worry, all the breathless disappointed hope. Yet there is a sense in which no sound effort is in vain, least of all a struggle with high ideal and personal integrity. One feels that, in the end, all of this can never be lost; that somehow, somewhere, whatever was fine and noble in this campaign will triumph; and what was vicious and low will remain contemptible, no matter what the returns may say.

Of course I was disgusted at the re-election of an acknowledged demagogue and opportunist like Thomas Dewey as governor of the Empire State and the continued threat of his elevation to presidency. I was insulted to know that two million New Yorkers wanted a man like Joe Hanley to be continued in public office. I was sorry to see Herbert Lehman go back to Washington to work to keep us in war and chains. But most of all I could not understand how a sane and intelligent electorate could reward the brave, lone fight of Vito Marcantonio with defeat. It just did not make sense. But dollars did it—just plain cash to purchase the election of as reactionary and characterless a nonentity as ever sat in Congress.

As for myself, having never expected anything but defeat I would not have been surprised if no more than 10,000 persons had voted for me. I was astonished by a vote of 205,729, a vote from men and women of courage, without the prejudice against color which I always expect and usually experience. This meant that these faced poverty and jail to stand and be counted for Peace and Civil Rights. For this I was happy.

I had slapped no backs during the campaign which I had not slapped before; I had begged no man for his vote as a personal favor; I had asked no vote simply because I was black. It was a fine adventure. But it proved only a prelude to the most extraordinary experience of my life: my indictment as a criminal.

CHAPTER VII

◆

The Indictment

The first letter from the Department of Justice to the Peace Information Center was received August, 1950. It read:

> "The Peace Information Center is engaged in activities within the United States which require its registration with the Department under the terms of the Foreign Agents Registration Act of 1938, as amended. There is enclosed for your information in this respect a pamphlet which contains a reprint of the Act, together with the rules and regulations prescribed thereunder by the Attorney General. . . .
>
> "In view of the length of time that has elapsed since the Peace Information Center has been acting as an agent of a foreign principal without having filed its registration statement as required by law, it is expected that the registration statement will be submitted forthwith."

The executive secretary, Abbott Simon, replied August 18, saying that I was out of the country but was expected to return in the near future, and that I would immediately take up the matter with the Department after returning. On August 21 the Department informed us that the absence from the United States of any officer of an "agent of a foreign principal" would not relieve the agent from the obligation to file a registration statement. Mr. Simon answered two days later, saying, in part:

> "The Peace Information Center is American in its conception and formation. Its activities were intended to and do relate only to the people of the United States. It acts for and is responsible only to itself and to the people of this country. It has never agreed, either by contract or otherwise, to act as a 'publicity agent' for a 'foreign principal' as defined in the Act, nor does it purport or assume to act as one.
>
> "Since the Peace Information Center acts only for itself and has no 'foreign principal,' you can well realize our inability to understand the basis for your request that we register pursuant to the terms of the Foreign Agents Registration Act."

At the same time, Mr. Simon sent our attorney, Gloria Agrin, to Washington, and she verbally and in writing, reiterated the position of the Peace Information Center:

> "The Peace Information Center was conceived and formed by a group of American citizens, apprehensive lest the growing tensions among the governments of the

world burst into a terrible conflagration which might well snuff out civilization as we know it. They believed that the overwhelming desire of the American people was for peace. They also believed that the avoidance of the mass destruction and human misery of a Third World War was dependent, in large measure, on the expression by the American people of their desire for peace. They conceived that the Peace Information Center would serve the American people by informing them of the issues of peace; by making available to them data concerning the great struggles being carried on for the maintenance of international peace; and by providing the means and forums for expressing their desire for peace.

"The inference which you and the Department have made seems to be founded only on the fact that there are people throughout the world who may have, and be expressing, ideas and concepts similar to those expressed by the Peace Information Center. In fact, it might even be surprising to find that this were not so. The minds and desires of men have always transcended national barriers. This is so in every field of endeavor, whether it be art, music, literature, science, or politics. Respect for an Einstein, a Mann, a Picasso, a Pasteur, or a Disraeli, has never been diminished by the fact that they were not American aborigines, nor has esteem for their ideas lessened. It would seem, therefore, to be a startlingly new pattern of reasoning that any idea or activity which is not indigenous to, and confined to, the United States, will subject its holder to the inference that he acts for some person abroad. Concomitantly, such a concept would limit the thought processes of American citizens to the four corners of the United States boundaries."

On September 19, Mr. Foley of the Department of Justice wrote us that the Center's registration "should be submitted without further delay" and added, "Again let me stress the point that registration under the act is in no way intended to interfere with the operation of the Peace Information Center in its present program."

Miss Agrin told the Department, September 29, that I, as well as several other officers of the Peace Information Center, strongly desired to discuss the matter further with them, and wanted to arrange a conference; but that since I was standing for election to the United States Senate I wished the conference postponed until after election day. "If you feel that the matter cannot wait until then he has informed me that he will be available after October 26."

The Department replied that "no useful purpose would be served in any further discussion, consequently it is requested that the registration statement of the Peace Information Center be submitted without further delay."

I then took over the correspondence myself and wrote to the Attorney-General, October, 1950:

"I cannot but feel that, in a matter of such serious concern, Mr. Foley's denial to me of an opportunity to be heard must necessarily reflect adversely upon the Department of Justice. I should think that the possible consequences of an unjustified enforcement of the Act, would impel the Justice Department to bend every effort to make certain of its conclusions. The Department's arbitrary and capricious refusal to confer with me compels me to infer that either the Department is unaware of the import of the statute which it seeks to enforce, or that it is unwise enough to deal cavalierly with the rights of American citizens. . . .

"Although, as you know, I am a candidate for the U.S. Senate from the State of New York, and, therefore, am laboring under a heavy schedule, I shall seek to accommodate myself to any date you may set, if it is at all possible."

This letter brought no answer, but later we heard that a Washington Grand Jury was investigating the possible violation of the Foreign Agents Registration Act, and that our case was under consideration. While in Washington on another matter, in January, 1951, Miss Agrin met John Rogge emerging from the Grand Jury room. It was hard to say which was the more surprised. Rogge blurted out that he would dislike very much to appear as witness against us, which was our first intimation that he was the informer; a man who had been our associate and responsible for our original organization. Miss Agrin started to ask why, then, Rogge felt impelled to appear against us in any event; but she desisted and merely reported the incident. I wrote to the Department, sending copies of the letter to both McGrath and Foley:

"This is surprising to me, in the light of the fact that the Peace Information Center and your department were engaged in discussions concerning the position of your department that this organization was obliged to register pursuant to the terms of this law. . . .

"Furthermore, it seems to me that the entire matter is now moot and academic, since the governing body of the Peace Information Center, on October 12, 1950, voted to disband the organization, which since then has been in the process of winding up its affairs and has undertaken and conducted no new business. Even this last process, I believe, is all but completed.

"In any case, however, I again urge the importance of a discussion with you in which I may have the opportunity to participate. Any confusion as to the position either of the Department of Justice or the Peace Information Center may, in this way, be clarified, and both the Government and the organization save the unpleasantness and expense of unnecessary legal contests."

We were informed February 2 that dissolution of an organization did not relieve it or its officers from complying with the provisions of the Act. Finally, on February 9, we were notified that the Grand Jury in Washington had indicted the Peace Information Center and its officers for "failure to register as agent of a foreign principal."

The indictment said in part:

"Continuously during the period from April 3, 1950 to and including the date of the return of this indictment, Peace Information Center has been an agent of a foreign principal, because within the United States (1) it has acted as, and has held itself out to be a publicity agent for; (2) it has reported information to; and (3) it has acted at the request of, the Committee of the World Congress of the Defenders of Peace and its successor the World Peace Council. . . ."

The Bill of Particulars added:

"During the period mentioned in the indictment, the officers, directors and representatives of the Peace Information Center, at the request of its said foreign principal, published and disseminated in the United States the 'Stockholm Peace Appeal' and related information pertaining primarily to prohibition of the use of atomic weapons as instruments of war. . . .'"

To this indictment the Peace Information Center replied in a release to the public, setting forth the truth about the organization:

"For the information of the public, the facts concerning the indictment of the officials of the Peace Information Center should be clarified. These five persons are not accused of treason or conspiracy against the United States. The Government admits that the activities of this organization in advocating peace and circulating petitions on the atom bomb were legal exercises of citizens' rights. The Department of Justice has indicted them not for these acts but for refusing to declare that in its activities the Center was acting as an agent of a foreign person or foreign organization. This the accused vehemently deny. They declare that in their work for peace through this Center they were acting as Americans for America, and that their work was supported by funds raised solely in the United States.

"The defendants deny that Peace is a foreign idea; but they gladly admit that they gathered and publicized ideas and news of action for peace from everywhere they could obtain them. They assert that any attempts to curtail such free inter-change of thought, opinion and knowledge of fact the world over is clearly an interference with the constitutional rights of Americans citizens. The function of this Center was to give to the citizens of this country those facts concerning the worldwide efforts for peace which the American press for the most part was ignor-ing or suppressing. It did this with the same object that other Americans have spread information of medical advance, efforts for labor uplift, scientific discover-ies, plans for housing, suppression of crime and education of youth. The United States has as yet laid no embargo on the importation of ideas, or knowledge of international effort for social uplift; and surely there can be today no greater need for information than in the peace movement and the effort to remove the horrible threat of a Third World War."

Our board of advisors had voted October 12 to dissolve the Center. We had no intention of running counter to the government, but only wished to make it clear that we did not believe we should register under the law. But closing the office of such a movement takes time. Letters kept pouring in asking for petitions, asking about further peace congresses, asking what anyone could do to help. We answered the letters and used our remaining stock of stationery for this correspondence. We tried to break our lease on the office, but could not do this immediately. Above all we tried to turn all public interest in peace into other channels: into local peace organizations and especially toward a second world peace congress to be held in England. A special committee was organized for this end, and they opened a separate office. But all this closing activity was held against us eventually by the Government as evidence of our deliber-ate flouting of orders. The Department of Justice thus assumed that our real crime was peace and not foreign agency. It was reiterated that the Peace Information Center continued to exist until the indictment was handed down in February, 1951.

COMMENT

February 9th had already been chosen by us as a rather special day. We had told only our immediate families that we were going to be married. True, the papers carried an "unconfirmed rumor," but we had made no announcement. We were not planning a wedding. I intended to telephone a few intimate friends and invite them out to my home in St. Albans, Long Island, the evening of February 27th. And after a quiet ceremony we would immediately fly to the Bahamas where W. E. B.'s grandfather Du Bois was born. It was on the birthday dinner February 23rd that we wanted to focus public attention. Therefore we planned to get our marriage license and the wedding ring well ahead of time. Also we would go for the first to Queens County Court House rather than to the City Hall in New York. We had set aside Monday morning, February 9th, for these preliminaries.

It was a beautiful, cold, clear day and I was up early. He was coming out from New York and would meet me at Sutphin Boulevard at ten o'clock. Everybody knows W. E. B.'s reputation for promptness and I found myself at the last minute running for the bus. I was not late, but as always he was waiting for me. He had already walked over to the Court House and located the license bureau.

Notwithstanding this fact I don't think the clerk in charge thought us particularly bright. I giggled as I copied one of the sheets, thus acutely embarrassing my husband-to-be. The whole thing seemed pretty complicated and we both resolved never to go through that again! But when we came outside the sun was shining brighter than ever. The trip in town to Cartier's was very short. There we matched my engagement ring with a wedding band which we left for inscribing.

"Now," he said, "let's have a celebration luncheon!"

Cartier's is just around the corner from Henri's, and French restaurants are always high in W. E. B.'s favor. And he is loved by the waiters because he consults them in French, giving his undivided attention to their words and following their recommendations. On this day our dessert was *crêpes suzette*, which lends the final glow of satisfaction to any meal. It must have been three-thirty when we left Henri's and walked slowly back to Fifth Avenue. There he took the bus downtown to his office and I went uptown to look at an advertised apartment and for a visit to the tailor for a suit fitting.

About seven-thirty I was back at home. The house was dark and as I switched on the lights I thought happily of how before so very long he would always be home waiting for me. It was a silly thought but I remember how it flitted through my mind. I wanted no dinner so I turned immediately to other things. In the course of the evening I called a friend and asked for the exact address of a mutual friend at that time in Paris. I found the friend strangely unresponsive and impertinently inquisitive. "Well, what's the matter with her?" I asked myself impatiently. After she had made two or three utterly meaningless remarks, I hung up.

When the phone rang around nine-thirty I knew it was W. E. B. I answered and started talking gayly. No, the apartment wouldn't do . . . the suit was coming along fine, etc., etc. Now, W. E. B. is not the world's most eloquent phone conversationalist, but after a moment I was struck by the unusual silence on his part. When I paused he said something I didn't understand at all. What came later has completely wiped whatever it was from my memory, but I remember asking, "What? What did you say?" He answered with a question, "Haven't you heard?"

"Haven't I heard what?"

"We've been indicted—the Peace Information Center—arraigned in Washington next Friday."

For once his clipped, precise words failed to convey meaning! I heard, yet I stood shaking my head. I must have mumbled something. He named the four indicted with him. Then I had hung up and was sitting on the edge of my bed staring at the wall. Indicted! That really meant arrested—summoned to Washington—a trial! Jail! Maybe they wouldn't allow bail! Waves of thought struck me now with full force. By the time I dialed his number my vision had cleared and my voice was steady.

"Dear," I said, "this changes our plans. We must be married right away."

Now it was his turn to exclaim, "What did you say?"

This, I knew, was no time for maidenly coyness. I did not want to let him know the terror which had engulfed me—him in jail where only a wife would be permitted entrance. With him in jail, only a wife could carry the case to the people. *I must be in a position to stand at his side*—this I felt was essential. Without being emotional I managed to sound convincing enough now for him to say we'd discuss it further in the morning. Then he told me soothingly to go to bed and "not worry."

By morning I had a program worked out.

The next few days were crammed full of action. Outwardly my attention was focused on the Birthday Dinner. News of the indictment electrified Harlem. Now invitations began to move at an accelerated pace. Space for the Dinner Committee had been donated by the African Art Shop on 125th Street and now the phone rang continuously with requests for dinner reservations. From all over New York the little white cards began coming in. We sent out an S.O.S. for assistance to get out the mailing.

Wednesday evening, February 14th, at the home of Reverend Edward McGowan, we were married. The witnesses were my son, David, and a close mutual friend. Neither knew until that moment why we asked them to accompany us to the Bronx. They assumed that the call had something to do with the indictment and needed no urging. After the short ceremony I returned to St. Albans and W. E. B. to his apartment on Edgecombe Avenue.

Thursday at twelve-thirty, three defendants, Kyrle Elkin, Abbott Simon and Sylvia Soloff, with the lawyers, took the train to Washington. David went along to be of assistance if needed. Mrs. Elizabeth Moos was still in Europe and W. E. B. had a speaking engagement that night. He was to fly down.

The meeting was at a large union hall in East New York. Vito Marcantonio presided. He knew we had to catch a plane and so placed W. E. B. in the first half of the program, but the usual forthright, precise voice of the ex-Congressman faltered as he introduced the chief speaker, and the audience rose to its feet without the usual scraping and bustle. Almost in silence those assembled paid sincere tribute to that man who the next morning must defend their rights in a Federal Court. He employed no histrionics that night, asked for no personal consideration. He talked simply and directly of the struggle for peace which we, the people, must wage. I saw tears in the eyes of those who shook his hand afterwards.

We caught the eleven-twenty plane for Washington and were warmly welcomed at the airport by the others. I use the adjective "warmly" though it is inadequate to describe the close, sensitive relation which typified this group from the very beginning. It was after one o'clock and they had all had a long and trying day, but they were cheerfully alert and solicitous only about us.

We had made reservations at the Dunbar Hotel. This is a Negro hotel in segregated Washington, operating under extreme difficulties with all the odds against it. Police had raided the place a few nights before. As I remember, no infringement of the law was found but the management had been accused and guests were routed out of bed. We were caught in a quandary. Five defendants and a battery of lawyers would be involved in our case; four of the defendants and the New York lawyers were white; one of the defendants and the Washington law firm were Negro. The matter of where we would lodge in Washington during what would probably be a long trial was a question. Everybody agreed that it would be most convenient to put up at the same place. None of the defendants were familiar with criminal proceedings; they were ignorant as to courtroom etiquette, had little idea what to expect. Since they were charged with a blanket indictment there was the natural tendency to "stick together."

And so for this first night which would usher in our day of uncertainty we took the course offering the least resistance. Six white and three Negro Americans summarily called to their capital city to answer criminal charges asked the small, crowded Negro hotel to take them in. The Dunbar courteously obliged and gave the best their facilities afforded.

Two taxis set us down in front of the hotel in short order. Immediately the attorneys, Miss Gloria Agrin, Bernard Jaffe and Stanley Faulkner gave W. E. B. a quick summary of how things stood at the moment. Then everybody insisted that he go to bed. We were to be in court at nine-thirty. David grinned at me sympathetically while Abbott accompanied my husband to his room. After a few minutes Abbott joined us in Kyrle's room where we settled down for a long and detailed discussion.

The room was small and soon "smoke-filled"; the one radiator was cold. Yet the sky outside was gray before we separated. As a matter of fact, neither Abbott nor David went to bed at all. They secured a typewriter from the hotel clerk and worked right through the dawn.

Yet we were simply a casual, pleasant group of guests which gathered in the hotel lobby at eight o'clock that morning. The hotel "lunch room" was not yet opened and so we traveled to the Pennsylvania Station where we found places at the lunch counter and had coffee. We had managed to stick together—the hard way.

A half hour later we mounted the stone steps to the Federal District Court. It is an imposing building with high columns. As we reached the statue of Abraham Lincoln, located midway up the broad staircase, I saw cameras pointing in our direction. I looked up at the rugged, sorrowing face of Lincoln and proudly slipped my hand through the arm of W. E. B. Du Bois.

CHAPTER VIII

◆

The Birthday Dinner

February is to me an unusual month, as indeed it is to many others. It is the month of St. Valentine's day as well as that of the birth of Abraham Lincoln and George Washington. Neither Frederick Douglass nor Booker T. Washington knew the exact dates of their births, but by long consent the birthdays of both of these great Negro leaders have been celebrated in February. Carter Woodson, the Negro historian, on this account placed the celebration of Negro History Week in this month. In this month I was born, and gradually its advent took on increasingly solemn and fateful significance in my life. I was not only getting older, but now passing the limits which folklore custom had long allotted to human existence.

In 1950 the month had for me added meaning. I was a widower. The wife of fifty-three years lay buried in the New England hills beside her first-born boy. I was lonesome because so many boyhood friends had died, and because a certain illogical reticence on my part had never brought me many intimate friends. But there was a young woman, a minister's daughter, to whom I had been a sort of father confessor in literary affairs and difficulties of life for many years, especially after her father's death fifteen years ago. I knew her hardships and I had rejoiced in her successes. Shirley Graham, with her beautiful martyr complex, finally persuaded herself that I needed her help and companionship, as I certainly did; so we decided to get married a few days after my next birthday, which gave it added significance.

Preparations for the dinner to be held at the Essex House were going unusually well. E. Franklin Frazier of Howard University, a sociologist and colleague, was Chairman of the Dinner Committee; Walter Beekman, my friend and dentist for thirty-five years, was treasurer, and my cousin, Alice Burghardt Crawford, was the active secretary. The list of sponsors was imposing and growing daily. Before the indictment about three hundred people had made reservations and paid in over $2,000.

Then came a strange series of events: on February 9th I was indicted for an alleged crime; on February 14th, I was married secretly to Shirley, lest if I were found guilty she might have no right to visit me in jail; February 16th I was arraigned in Washington and on February 19th, four days before the dinner, the hotel at which the dinner was planned cancelled our contract by telegram saying:

"Pursuant to our rules and regulations and for other sufficient reasons we hereby advise you that reservation of our facilities for Friday evening, February 23rd for the W. E. B. Du Bois testimonial dinner is cancelled. Deposit is being returned. Vincent J. Coyle, Vice President and Managing Director, Essex House Hotel, Inc."

The Essex House, on Central Park South, is a successful corporation, directed by the president of the Arnold Constable store, which is rated as worth seven and a half million dollars. Several bank directors are also on the board, especially directors of the Sterling National Bank and Trust Company, besides commercial corporations, railroads and oil wells. The hotel is mortgaged for five million dollars to one of the great railroad chains of America. It is affiliated with the New York City Hotel Association, which lays down a common policy for its members, not mandatory but enforced by strong pressure. It covers such matters as rates, food, labor policies, rents, etc.

Its organ is the *Hotel World Review*. The policy of this review is close cooperation with the Department of Justice and the F.B.I. On December 10, 1949, it printed the Attorney-General's "subversive list," and warned against serving any organizations on this list, referring to peace meetings at two hotels as giving the hotels "unfavorable publicity." It went on to say that any hotel serving these organizations might incur "a definite cloud of suspicion" and get into "serious trouble" with the government.

We had five days before the dinner to find a place to entertain our 300 guests. In addition to this, our three speakers, Charlotte Hawkins Brown, Mordecai Johnson, and Rabbi Hillel Silver, hastily declined to appear. Some of the sponsors withdrew, but I do not know how many of the original list remained.

I can stand a good deal, and have done so during my life; but this experience was rather more than I felt like bearing, especially as the blows continued to fall: my colored graduate fraternity, which I had helped found forty years ago, voted down a birthday greeting to me, and accompanied the action by bitter criticism in its private debate on the matter. In Washington I had been fingerprinted, handcuffed, bailed and remanded for trial. I was more than ready to drop all thought of the birthday dinner.

But my remaining friends said No! I could do no less than stand beside them, although without Shirley's faith and strength I probably would not have allowed the dinner to take place. Franklin Frazier, the chairman, stood firm. He said the dinner must and would go on.

There ensued a period of wild search for a place of meeting; of securing other speakers and of notifying participants. Subtly the whole picture changed; instead of a polite, friendly social gesture, this dinner became a fight for civil rights, and into the seats of timid and withdrawing guests slipped a new set of firmer men and women who were willing to face even the United States government in my defense and for the preservation of American freedom. They carried on the battle while I sat uneasily in the background.

The program was hastily rearranged. No white downtown hotel would harbor us, and turning to Harlem we found Small's Paradise, well-known to the cabaret world, much too small but with a proprietor willing and eager even to lose money by the venture. Belford Lawson, head of the Alpha Phi Alpha fraternity, volunteered and made a fighting speech; Paul Robeson spoke courageously and feelingly. A strong letter from Judge Hubert Delany was read. Franklin Frazier presided and spoke. The room was crowded to suffocation, and many could not get to their seats. But the spirit was what the Germans call "feierlich!" Finally, amid cheers, birthday cakes and flowers, I made my speech. There were about 700 persons present who paid $6,557 in dinner fees and donations.

All the speeches were brave and clear. The audience of familiar and unknown faces was inspiring. There were so many birthday cakes that hundreds marched around while Shirley cut them pieces. Letters and cablegrams from the ends of the civilized world were read,[1] and although afterward I crept to bed with influenza, I was glad that we had stood to our guns and faced an accusing world.

Then, after repeating our marriage in public ceremony, Shirley and I flew to Nassau. We did not know if the government would allow this trip, but no opposition was offered, and the sunshine and emerald sea healed us both at least of our more superficial wounds.

Our reception by the inhabitants was deeply cordial, as if to returning natives. We traced the wanderings of the white revolutionary loyalist Du Boises. We found the landgrants to them by Governor Dunmore of Virginia, and we imagined the first journey of the little mulattoes Alexander and John Du Bois to the United States in 1818. We came home in their tracks and spent the spring campaigning for freedom.

COMMENT

We did have a big wedding after all. On the morning of the hearing in Washington, standing on the steps of the Federal District Court, I gave the details to a sympathetic *Afro-American* reporter. And so, along with the story of the arraignment, the newspapers announced that we were to be married February 27th in "the bride's Long Island home." When arranging for bail, our Washington attorneys, Cobb, Hayes and Howard, put in the special request that Dr. Du Bois be allowed to travel to the Bahamas on a wedding trip for which reservations had already been made. To insure this permission, Mr. Perry Howard, Jr., son of the Mississippi Republican National Committeeman, presented himself as personal bondsman for my husband.

We returned to New York, to the dismay and confusion caused by the Essex House cancellation of the Birthday Dinner, to the frantic search for another place, to the awakening of Harlem's pride which swamped the Dinner Committee with more paid dinner reservation than could possibly be accommodated. Reporters came out to St. Albans, News Reel called for permission to take pictures of the marriage, friends offered to decorate my house; wedding presents began to arrive. From Baltimore, Mrs. Yolande Du Bois Williams, W. E. B.'s only daughter, wrote that she would be up to the dinner and would stay over for the wedding;

similar notes came from friends all up and down the eastern seaboard. I found myself trying to make up a list of guests for a caterer and choosing decorations for the cake.

Meanwhile New Yorkers were enjoying typical February weather. On Wednesday night, February 21st, W. E. B. went out in a blizzard of rain and snow for a big A.L.P. rally in Harlem. He expected to address empty benches surrounding a small knot of faithful standbys. Not only was the Golden Gate auditorium filled with an enthusiastic crowd but at the close of the meeting he was presented with two dozen long-stemmed red roses and a huge three-tier birthday cake. It took two men to carry the cake up to his apartment. My poor darling was so overwhelmed that his voice on the phone sounded plaintive: "What shall I do with it?" I suggested that he call up Harlem Hospital the first thing in the morning and he went to bed somewhat relieved.

The Eighty-Third Birthday Dinner was an event none of us will ever forget. So much valor, good will and happy wishes were packed into Small's Paradise that night that the walls expanded. We solved the problem of the many birthday cakes necessary to hold eighty-three candles by cutting them right there so that everybody shared in their creamy richness. It was after midnight before the last well-wisher left the platform. W. E. B. had been beaming all evening but now I saw lines of exhaustion in his face. His voice was hoarse but he was still jubilant:

"You and Yolande must come and have breakfast with me Sunday morning!"

Every woman will understand my dilemma. The "big wedding" was Tuesday night; I was going away on my honeymoon; I had a thousand things to do that week-end.

Yet, Sunday morning, there we were sipping the famous Du Bois coffee. Everything went famously until, without warning, W. E. B. dropped his after-breakfast cigarette and said his head was aching. We insisted on his lying down while we cleaned up the dishes. He stretched out on the couch and continued sharing in the conversation. When we had finished he told me to "run along." I elicited the promise from him that he would telephone Dr. Carey. He might drop by during the afternoon. Yolande had to get back to her high school teaching job. We left the apartment about two o'clock.

Before night Dr. Carey ordered W. E. B. to bed. Mental strain, exposure to bad weather, extreme fatigue had brought him down with what threatened to be pneumonia. Of course he didn't tell me all this when I phoned but what he did say and the way he sounded so alarmed me that Monday morning I was back at the apartment. Until the arrival of the doctor the prospect for our Tuesday wedding looked dim. Dr. Carey was optimistic.

"It's sunshine and rest you need more than anything else. We'll keep you in bed until tomorrow evening. I can bolster you up so you'll be able to get to St. Albans. Then off you go to the land of sunshine. As soon as you reach Nassau put yourself in the hands of a physician. I'll guarantee that in a week's time you'll be fully recovered."

One hour before the wedding guests arrived I was certain the whole thing was a mistake. Everything was wrong. Yet, miraculously things did fall into place. W. E. B. was, as usual, well ahead of time. He was faultlessly attired in gleaming black and white and looked like his usual self. However, he went immediately to my spare room to lay down. Flowers filled the house, candles flickered, soft music and the low murmur of voices. Yolande had pulled my dress over my head and then stood back saying nice things. Eight-thirty—time for the ceremony—and no preacher! As the moments dragged I began getting frantic, but word reached me that W. E. B. was quite calm and unperturbed. For once he was not upset by tardiness!

"We don't have to be married twice. Tonight we leave on our honeymoon! That's enough for me!" David reported his words to me and added, "Relax, mamma. Reverend McGowan will be here."

Somebody suggested a minister who lived across the street, but since the license had already been signed and witnessed I knew we couldn't call him in.

Eventually, Rev. McGowan got there. The friend driving him out to Long Island thought he knew the way. They wound up somewhere in the vicinity of the United Nations!

And so, preceded by Yolande as my matron-of-honor, accompanied by my son, in a bower of flowers, surrounded by friends and with music in the air, for the second time we promised to "love and cherish." Then everybody kissed us, there was the cake cutting, the change into traveling suits and the dash for La Guardia Field.

Not until the plane was lifting itself from the ground did we remember something:

"My God, we forgot the sandwiches!"

The gleaming bridal table with its huge white cake, bowl of sparkling punch, platters of toasted sandwiches and plates of dainty canapés floated in front of us. We saw our friends back there in St. Albans still spooning velvety ice cream! I groaned. Neither of us had eaten that day—W. E. B. because the doctor had ordered a fast and I because there had been no time for anything except a hasty cup of coffee that morning. Our caterer friend had prepared a special box filled with delicacies which we were to take with us. Who, I wondered dismally, would enjoy the contents of that box? (Which reminds me, who did?)

"Do you suppose the stewardess could bring us anything?" I asked hopefully.

She brought two cups of lukewarm coffee. I took one sip and shuddered. It was *not* Du Bois coffee.

Then he took my hand. And my fingers closed about his wrist—the wrist encircled a few days before by iron manacles. Down there on the earth now rapidly falling away from us THEY were waiting! We were flying away now only because in Washington another man stood pledged to forfeit his freedom as a bond for our return. This moment only was ours—our honeymoon. We had our honeymoon! We would breakfast in Nassau!

NOTE

1. See Appendix B.

CHAPTER IX

◆

An Indicted Criminal

Up to this time my experience with courts of law had been limited. In my home in western Massachusetts we had deep respect for law and legal processes. To be arrested was in itself a serious matter which involved social condemnation. We assumed that no one was ever arrested without sufficient cause. Among my playmates were the daughters of Justin Dewey, a prominent lawyer who afterward became a judge of the Supreme Court of Massachusetts. I remember him as a portentous figure to whom no one ever spoke lightly. I often wondered how Mary, Sarah and little Margaret dared sit down in his company. I saw the courthouse from afar, and only felt near to it later when my high school classmate, Walter Sanford, was made the local judge.

So far as I knew, no member of my family or of my class of acquaintances was ever arrested, much less jailed. Undoubtedly some such incident must have occurred, but in that case the family carefully refrained from ever referring to it in my presence.

As I grew up and went South, naturally my attitude changed. I saw police and courts in Tennessee and Georgia as instruments of cruel oppression of Negroes and poor whites; yet my personal contacts were but slight. I avoided the police, never asking information or help, and was never arrested while in the South. Once in Atlanta I was unfairly threatened with arrest for "trespass" by a policeman. He desisted when I suggested paying a "fine" to him; he accepted ten dollars.

In the North I soon learned what police and courts meant to the poor, and shared their distrust of both. It was not until 1918 when I was 50 years old that I ever personally came in contact with the courts. I had bought my first automobile and was driving quite happily back from Coney Island to Manhattan, when I was ordered to the side of the road by a bicycle policeman; I was told that I was exceeding the speed limit of New York State, which at that time was 20 miles an hour. I was given a summons and eventually fined $25, after having been strongly advised by the arresting policeman to make no defense. He assured me that this would make the matter much easier, and take less time. He was right. I paid my fine philosophically, and drove more carefully thereafter.

My attitude toward the courts in general was to avoid them; I was sure that in them, as a Negro I could not expect justice, and that no ordinary, certainly no poor citizen, would be much better off than I. I did, however, assume that with competent lawyers one had a good chance if wrongly accused. I did not think it usual for a decent citizen of good repute to be treated as guilty before he had stood trial. This was, of course, usual with Negroes in the South, and was not uncommon in the North with persons who were not properly defended or who had a criminal record.

In this indictment of the Peace Information Center I received a severe jolt, because in fact I found myself being punished before I was tried. In the first place, the Department of Justice allowed to spread, or certainly made no effort to correct, the impression that my colleagues and I had in some way betrayed our country. Although the charge was not treason, it was widely understood and said that the Peace Information Center had been discovered to be an agent of Russia.

When we were arraigned in Washington February 16th, the proceedings were brusque and unsympathetic. We were not treated as innocent people whose guilt was to be inquired into, but distinctly as criminals whose innocence was to be proven, which was assumed to be doubtful.

Before we were summoned to the bar, several accused felons appeared before the presiding Judge Letz to have dates set for their trials. They were respectively charged with "Manslaughter—assault to commit robbery—housebreaking and larceny—violation of lottery laws—theft—forgery." Such was the category within which the case of the Peace Information Center was placed.

Judge Holtzoff, later assigned to this case, was arrogant; he enjoyed talking about himself and his wide experience. Especially was he disdainful of all lawyers from New York, and tried pointedly to ignore our chief counsel, Gloria Agrin, who had the misfortune not only of being from New York, but in addition was a young, pretty, and well-dressed woman.

After some motions, the time of trial was set much earlier than we possibly could arrange to be ready. Miss Agrin argued for more time, and for relief in a number of ways, and the judge began to brush aside her objections and motions; later he realized that here was a well-versed lawyer, even though she was from New York. He had to take some of her motions under consideration, or chance reversal in a higher court, an occurrence with which he was familiar. Eventually we got a postponement.

After the arraignment I was told to follow the marshal, and walk down some narrow stairs at the back of the courtroom into a small basement room, perhaps ten feet square. There I was fingerprinted and asked details as to my life and work; told to remove my coat and empty my pockets, and then examined carefully by an orderly for concealed weapons! As I turned around to go upstairs where the matter of bail was to be arranged, the marshal put handcuffs on me and Mr. Elkin, so that for ten minutes we were manacled together. Then a stir and murmur rose sharply from beyond the grated partition where the public could look through and see what was happening. I heard one of our attorneys protesting sharply. The marshal grumbled, looked disconcerted, but finally unlocked our handcuffs, and we walked out into the corridor. The matter of arranging bail took but a short time, and we were soon free, with the bail set at $1,000 each.

From then until the trial actually took place six months later, I went through a gruesome experience. Despite my knowledge that I was not accused of any action whatsoever involving moral turpitude, but only indicted because I had refused to admit that I was "agent of a foreign principal"—notwithstanding this, I was walking through the world as an indicted criminal with a possible sentence of five years in prison and a fine of $10,000; and being pointed out by word of mouth and publication as guilty of some heinous offense against my country.

It was increasingly difficult to explain my position. Up until the time of acquittal, whenever I made a plain statement of the case to a person or an audience, I could see upon their faces a reaction of the utmost astonishment. Usually they said, "This is preposterous; the government cannot hold you on any such charge, and you have nothing to fear." And then, afterward, I could always see the reaction: "You have nothing to fear—unless as a matter of fact you are really guilty of treason, and are acting in the United States as the agent of the Soviet Union." To such an accusation or such suspicions there was absolutely no answer, and curious instances strengthened the paradox.

By invitation, for instance, I went once to meet a group of writers in Greenwich Village. We met in an author's home, and in the presence of a dozen persons who represented a liberal group of writers and correspondents. I stated briefly and clearly just what the situation was. They were filled with indignation and disbelief, and also, I am afraid, with some latent suspicion: "The case was all too clear." Out of that meeting, although we expected and had been promised articles in the liberal press making our status clear, not a single article appeared in the periodicals represented that night.

Another of our projects was to secure the names of a dozen nationally prominent Negroes to this statement:

> ". . . We are not here concerned with the political or social beliefs of Dr. Du Bois. Many of us do not agree with him on these and other matters. But we are concerned with the right of a man to say within the law what he thinks without being subject to threat and intimidation. Especially are we concerned with Dr. Du Bois as a leader of the Negro American for 50 years. In that time until now his integrity and absolute sincerity has never been questioned. . . ."

We did not, however, succeed in getting enough such signatures to this statement to warrant its circulation. Possibly this effort was not pushed as long and hard as it might have been. Probably I expected too much too soon; but I was deeply disappointed. I recognized the fear in the Negro group, especially among the educated and well-to-do. One said to me sadly, "I have a son in government employ; he has a well-paid position and is in line for promotion. He has worked long for this start and has had many and humiliating disappointments. I am sorry, but I dare not sign this!" Others, of course, had less excuse.

The white commercial press treated our case either with silence or violent condemnation. The New York *Herald Tribune* had this editorial, February 11:

> "The Du Bois outfit was set up to promote a tricky appeal of Soviet origin, poisonous in its surface innocence, which made it appear that a signature against the

use of atomic weapons would forthwith insure world peace. It was, in short, an attempt to disarm America and yet ignore every form of Communist aggression. A lot of 'men and women of good will through the world,' to quote the petition's bland phrasing, were snared into signing without quite realizing that this thing came straight out of the Cominform."

Other dailies like the *World-Telegram* had similar diatribes. The New York *Times*, August 29, 1951, published a letter of protest by William Mandel concerning the treatment of one of his books; but before printing the letter the editor "tried to get me to delete the reference to Dr. Du Bois and Dr. Struik."

Outside of the Negro press I got support from radical periodicals alone, like the *Daily Worker*, the *People's World, Masses and Mainstream*, the *Daily Compass*, and the *National Guardian*. Jennings Perry of the *Compass* said:

> "We ought to withdraw the prosecution. . . . Dr. Du Bois is genuinely and, I hope, incorrigibly a peace-seeker. Wars disturb and disappoint him. In better than four-score years, he has observed that wars beget wars and that peace is not, as our President habitually puts it, 'won.'"

So far as the general public of the nation was concerned, Alice Barrows secured 220 leaders of the arts, sciences, clergy and other professions in thirty-three states, including thirty-five universities, to sign "A Statement to the American People," released June 27, calling for the withdrawal of the prosecution. The statement, initiated by the National Council of the Arts, Sciences and Professions, described the indictment as "but one of numerous recent actions against individuals and organizations that advocate peaceful solutions to the world's crisis. In this time of hysteria, the attempted labeling of 'foreign agent' on a distinguished scholar and leader of a peace movement can fairly be interpreted as an effort to intimidate and silence all advocates of peace."

The Methodist Federation for Social Action defended the Peace Information Center. The National Executive Board of the National Lawyers Guild called on the Attorney General to withdraw the indictment.

The response of Negroes in general was at first slow and not united, but it gradually gained momentum. At first many Negroes were puzzled. They did not understand the indictment and assumed that I had let myself be drawn into some treasonable acts or movements in retaliation for continued discrimination in this land, which I had long fought. They understood this and forgave it, but thought my action ill-advised. The Norfolk *Journal and Guide* expressed this clearly. The Chicago *Defender* said:

> "Dr. Du Bois has earned many honors and it is a supreme tragedy that he should have become embroiled in activities that have been exposed as subversive in the twilight of his years."

These papers, however, were exceptions. Most of the Negro press from the first showed unusual leadership. They reacted against the court hearing in particular and in singular contrast to the attitude of other sections of the Negro bourgeoisie. Editors evidently sensed the reaction of the Negro masses who buy the papers as against that of the Negro professional classes who so often criticize and repudiate even the idea of a separate Negro press. But beyond this, editors like Percival Prattis of the Pittsburgh *Courier*, Carl Murphy of the *Afro-American*, and columnists like Marjorie McKenzie, J. A. Rogers, and others, showed a courage and real intellectual leadership which was lacking elsewhere. The *Courier*, which has the largest circulation among Negro papers, started out with its columnist, Marjorie McKenzie, February 23rd:

> "We have to take a stand here and now with Dr. Du Bois . . . else it will be dangerous for a Negro to belong to anything but a church."

Prattis, the executive editor, said:

> "Dr. Du Bois represents Negro leadership at its best and strongest. . . . Now a government which has found itself unable to protect the rights of an entire people against criminal intrusion of a prejudiced majority finds the means to handcuff the man who has fought most insistently for those rights.
> "I cannot forget, or ignore, what he (Dr. W. E. B. Du Bois) has done for me, fighting for my rights and serving as an example of my possibilities in a world which spurned me as an inferior. They could not look at him and call me inferior."

The *Afro-American* said:

> "It was a calculated humiliation based on race when 83-year-old Dr. Du Bois was herded into an iron-cage chute with human derelicts. . . . Outside the barred room, hard-boiled newsmen looked grim. . . . Seasoned attorneys swore audibly while Shirley Graham . . . wept bitterly. . . ."

The Philadelphia *Tribune* said:

> "Whenever it becomes a crime to spread information advocating peace, the doors of civilization might as well close up."

The Boston *Guardian* added:

> "In this third period of his life, Dr. Du Bois has emerged into world citizenship, and has taken on his heart the burdens of colonial peoples and the problem of securing peace by outlawing war and bringing to the backward peoples the blessings of modern civilization. He has developed into a world statesman."

The reaction of Negroes to this case revealed a distinct cleavage not hitherto clear in American Negro opinion. The intelligentsia, the "Talented Tenth," the successful business and professional men, were not, for the most part, outspoken in our defense. There were many and notable exceptions, but as a group this class was either silent or actually antagonistic. The reasons were clear; many believed that the government had actual proof of subversive activities on our part; until the very end they awaited their disclosure.

Other Negroes of intelligence and prosperity had become American in their acceptance of exploitation as defensible, and in their imitation of American "conspicuous expenditure." They proposed to make money and spend it as pleased them. They had beautiful homes, large cars and expensive fur coats. They hated "Communism" and "Socialism" as much as any white American. Their reaction toward Paul Robeson was typical: they simply could not understand his surrendering a thousand dollars a night for a moral conviction.

This dichotomy in the Negro group, this development of class structure, was to be expected, and will be more manifest in the future, as discrimination against Negroes as such decreases. There will gradually arise among American Negroes a separation according to their attitudes toward labor, wealth and work. It is still my hope that the Negro's experience in the past will, in the end, lead the majority of his intelligentsia into the ranks of those advocating social control of wealth, abolition of exploitation of labor, and equality of opportunity for all.

I have belonged to a Negro graduate fraternity for forty years—indeed, was consulted at the time of its first formation. Today it contains in its membership a large number of the leading business and professional Negroes in the United States. Yet of its thirty or more chapters covering the nation, only one expressed any sympathy with me, and none offered aid. It is probable that individual members of the fraternity gave my cause support, but no official action was taken save in one case.

While, then, most of my educated and well-to-do Negro friends—although by no means all—were scared by the war propaganda and went quickly to cover, an increasing mass of the Negro working class, especially the members of the so-called left-wing unions, rallied to my side with faith and money. This gave me a new outlook on social stratification within this group, which I once hoped would never develop. My faith hitherto had been in what I once denominated the "Talented Tenth." I now realize that the ability within a people does not automatically work for its highest salvation. On the contrary, in an era like this, and in the United States, many of the educated and gifted young black folk will be as selfish and immoral as the whites who surround them and to whom Negroes have been taught to look as ideals. Naturally, out of the mass of the working classes, who know life and its bitter struggle, will continually rise the real, unselfish and clear-sighted leadership. This will not be automatic or continuous, but the hope of the future of the Negro race in America and the world lies far more among its workers than among its college graduates, until the time that our higher training is rescued from its sycophantic and cowardly leadership of today, almost wholly dependent as it is on Big Business either in politics or philanthropy.

Our appeal to the officials of the Defenders of Peace resulted in wide publicity for our case all over the world. Messages began to come to us from Europe, Asia, and Africa; from the West Indies and from South America. We received letters from England, Scotland, and France; from Belgium, Holland, Luxemburg, and Scandinavia; from Germany, the Union of Soviet Socialist Republics, Austria, Czechoslovakia, Poland, Rumania, Albania, Hungary, Trieste and Switzerland; from Canada, Cuba, Martinique, Jamaica, British Guiana and Brazil; from West

Africa, South Africa, Southeast Asia, China, Viet Nam, Indonesia, India and Australia. International bodies sent their support, including the International Union of Students, the World Federation of Teachers Unions, the International Federation of Women, the World Federation of Scientific Workers, and others.

Most Europeans do not understand the American custom of burying Negroes under a pall of studied silence and ignoring them; so that the average American himself knows little of persons or problems within the Veil of Color. When Europeans realized that a man whom they knew as the author of certain books which they had read, and whom some had heard speak, was threatened with jail, they reacted quickly and widely; so much so that it is no exaggeration to say that their interest and indignation kept me out of prison. Most Americans will be astonished and skeptical at this assertion, but there is wide proof, some of which may be noted.

On the 18th of July, seventeen Frenchmen of national prominence sent a joint letter to Mrs. Elizabeth Moos and myself, which said:

"We have heard with deep feeling the attitude of the government of the United States because of your unremitting and generous activities for Peace. We cannot miss this opportunity offered us today to express to you the complete unity with you of the French movement for Peace, which embraces citizens of every opinion and belief and realizes national union in the service of this noblest of causes. . . ."

These distinguished Frenchmen assumed that this manifesto would reach the American people, not realizing that since it was sent to a woman and a Negro it would not be regarded as "news" in the United States, and would be ignored.

This statement was followed later by the formation of an "International Committee in Defense of Dr. W. E. B. Du Bois and his Colleagues." The original signers included a university professor from Holland; two professors from Switzerland; a judge of the Court of Appeals and a federal judge in Brazil; two magistrates from Colombia and Iran; an Italian senator; and the president of the French Court of Cassation; together with ten Americans, eight white and two Negro. Eventually this committee grew to 200 with 33 Frenchmen, 30 Poles, 12 Belgians, 11 Germans, seven Englishmen, six Italians, five Brazilians, four each from Switzerland, the Soviet Union, Hungary and China; from one to three each from Romania, Bulgaria, Iran, Lebanon, Martinique, Holland, Austria; and 59 from the United States of whom six were colored.

This committee sent out a circular, saying, after giving the facts of the case:

"We would be startled to learn that in the United States of America, a nation with such generous and liberal traditions, every public manifestation of a desire for peace is considered a crime, especially if inspired by a foreigner."

What the foreign signers of this appeal did not realize was that in the United States a Negro is not regarded as an American; as a Negro who works for Negroes, he has certain nuisance value, which is often recognized as natural; but his contribution to the nation, much less to humanity at large, is practically never considered. And appeals such as this are not so much disregarded as unheard because no American periodicals having national circulation would think of printing them.

From London came messages—from the distinguished scientist, J. D. Bernal, from the President of the International Association of Democratic Lawyers, D. N. Pritt, and from Ivor Montagu, leader of the British Peace Movement. Montagu told of his first meeting with Dr. Du Bois in Moscow, 1949:

> "Dr. Du Bois for forty minutes led his rapt hearers through an analysis of the history of the United States. He picked out the threads that go to make its tangled present, the forthright pioneers as well as the luxurious shareholders, the tradition of freedom as well as the ruthless monopoly. As the sole American guest he conceived it his duty to seize an opportunity, perhaps unique, to contribute fundamentally toward the understanding of the two peoples. He was already over eighty and the task he set himself must have constituted a physical ordeal. But he did not falter. Nor will he falter today. . . ."

Vigorous protests came from groups in Luxemburg and Finland, and the Very Reverend Dr. James Endicott, leader of the Canadian Peace Congress, wrote:

> "If the cause of peace, as advocated by Dr. Du Bois, should become a crime under American law, then all mankind will know that the policy and purposes of the Government of the United States of America are a serious threat to international peace. . . ."

The British Columbia Peace Council and branches of the Canadian League for Democratic Rights joined in protest. Latin Americans were further informed and alerted to the dangers of this attack of the United States upon "defenders of the peace" by a long and moving statement written by Pablo Neruda and Jorge Amado and addressed to the National Assemblies and various intellectual and labor organizations in Brazil, Mexico, Chile, Paraguay and Argentina.

Of the reaction in the Soviet Union, the British journalist Ralph Parker wrote:

> "The Soviet public learned of the trial of Dr. W. E. B. Du Bois with a sense of profound indignation. The fact that this great American who has devoted his life to the service of peace should be prosecuted in his advanced age is considered here as an act of inhumanity which makes mockery of America's present leaders' pretensions to be protectors of human rights.
>
> "Dr. Du Bois is remembered here as a dignified noble-looking figure who two years ago took the tribune in the House of Trade Unions during the first all-union conference for the defense of peace.
>
> "For nearly an hour Du Bois held their attention as he analyzed the history of his country. He was the only American guest present and his contribution to the understanding between the American and Soviet peoples was one of which all good Americans past or present would have approved.
>
> "When he, at the close of his address, returned to his place, the standing ovation he was accorded was the public's recognition of him as a patriotic American."

From Poland, Czechoslovakia, Romania and Albania organizations representing many million persons sent protests to the United States Government. Orthodox priests in Bulgaria protested, "since our Lord Jesus Christ himself preached world peace for all men of good will." Students from the Free Territory of Trieste, scientists and artists of Hungary, and forty-three signers of the Stockholm Appeal in Switzerland joined in appeals and protests.

Articles were published in Austria, India, the Soviet Union, the *Shanghai China News* and the *Edinburgh Review* in Scotland. The story was told in at least a dozen different languages. From the West Indies came letters, from the Professors of the University of Havana and outstanding Cubans like Dr. Fernando Ortiz, Latin America's most famous sociologist; Dr. Domingo Villamil, eminent Catholic jurist; and Juan Marinello, Senator and poet.

Other protests came from the French West Indies, British Guiana and British West Indies. The All China Students Federation wrote, and the students of Viet-Nam. Indonesian students living in Holland said: "This is not only an attack on the democratic principles of the United States but also an intimidation of the Negro population." The Southeast Asia Committee held a meeting in London, and five Indian writers joined in declaring: "Your name belongs to us too, and will live in our annals as a bright inspiration to those who seek to build."

George Padmore, a colored West Indian, long resident in London, spread information among a large number of Negro periodicals in Africa and the West Indies. He said:

"Colored colonial organizations in this country are watching with keen interest the outcome of the indictment. . . . The League of Colored Peoples and organizations of Negroes throughout the world have sent resolutions and telegrams of protest to President Truman, expressing indignation. . . .

"Dr. Du Bois was the father of 'Pan-Africanism,' which proclaims the right of the Africans to govern themselves.

"He presided over the fifth Pan-African Congress in Manchester in 1945, under the joint secretaryship of Dr. Kwame Nkrumah, Leader of Government Business in the Gold Coast, and George Padmore.

"That was Dr. Du Bois' last visit to Great Britain, where he had many friends among whom were . . . H. G. Wells and Professor Harold Laski of the London School of Economics and Political Science, where Dr. Du Bois was guest lecturer."

Communications came from many parts of Africa, from the Gold Coast, Nigeria and the Union of South Africa. Sam Kahn, Communist member of the House of Assembly, Cape Town, South Africa, wrote:

"Dr. Du Bois does not belong to America alone, he is a citizen of the world, and those who revere and cherish liberty, peace and freedom will have no hesitation in responding to requests to protest against the vindictive action of the United States Department of Justice."

The World Federation of Scientific Workers, through its Secretary General, J. G. Crowther; National Peace Committees in seventy-eight countries; The

International Democratic Federation of Women and the International Union of Students sent communications and protests. The students wrote to the Department of Justice:

"On behalf of over 5,000,000 students in 71 countries, the International Union of Students expresses indignation at the prosecution of Dr. Du Bois and associates. Du Bois [is an] internationally known scholar and spokesman for peace. [His] work for peace is in best traditions of the American people. Prosecution is an attack upon peace supporters, upon Negro people and upon right of professors and students to act for peace. We join with peace-loving people throughout the world in demanding that you dismiss Du Bois' indictment and end persecution of United States peace supporters."

From Africa came many communications. J. A. Wachuku, barrister and founder of the New Africa Party, on his arrival at Accra, Gold Coast, British West Africa, to attend the West African Court of Appeal, said:

". . . the philosophy of Pan-Africanism enunciated by Dr. Du Bois is the dominating influence of my life. On behalf of New Africa and the youths of West Africa, of whom I am one, we protest against the high-handed action of the American government in this act of inhumanity against one of the greatest sons of the black race."

A letter from Lagos, Nigeria, exclaimed:

"Indeed! you have been degraded, but the ignominy is that of the American nation globally, and rather than deter us, the struggle for a place under the sun for the colored races will rise in its tempo until a man is accepted as a man. . . ."

An editorial in the *West African Pilot*, Gold Coast, B.W.A., said:

"We must state categorically that we are alarmed at the insane and savage way world personalities like Paul Robeson and Dr. W. E. B. Du Bois are persecuted, simply because of their opinions. Whither America? Do the descendants of the Pilgrim Fathers realize why the Huguenots fled from religious persecution and made the Mayflower Compact?
"Can we expect anything constructive from American leadership, globally? As black peoples, we cannot but resent in unequivocal terms the victimization of our fellow black folk in America."

Just as the newspapers suppressed foreign statements and petitions about me and about this case because of my connection with it, so consciously and according to specific orders from the High Command they suppressed, or their editors cut out, all news about the white defendants and the general aspects of the case. Instead they continuously built up the case against the Soviet Union and implied or hinted that there was more than ample proof that we were part of the "Russian pro-war front." This was calculated to range behind the case for the prosecution all the anti-Communist hysteria. Nevertheless, I persisted in facing this propaganda openly. With jail in sight I hammered at the proposition that the Soviet Union did not want war, while our masters did; that we in demanding peace were opposing Big Business which wanted war, and that we did this as free Americans and not as tools of any foreign or domestic power.

You see, one knows personalities in reality not by newspaper notoriety—that but flashes highlights on vaguely familiar features. Acquaintanceship comes from walking, eating together, meeting in clubs and homes; it is a matter of intimate, continuous association and unhampered exchange of experience and thinking, of friendship. How many white Americans have Negro friends? What social clubs have a single black member? What would a white American say if his friend brought home a colored man to lunch? A few such friendships and real knowledge of souls exist—a very few. For the most part, black and white in America live in separate worlds, and often complete foreigners have to introduce each to the other.

This was largely the case in this prosecution. What did the ordinary employee of the Department of Justice or even an under secretary in the Department of State know of me save that I was colored? That labeled me completely until "interfering" foreigners referred to me as an author and student of science. Then they looked me up. A white employee of the Department of Justice, who also is a part-time teacher in the colored Howard Law School, was ordered by his Department to prepare a "dossier" on me and my career. His colored colleagues in the law school protested, but he had his orders and carried them out. During the trial, agents of the Department of State queried persons in the audience about me. This is the result of a caste system.

What irked me most in this proceeding was the "cat and mouse" technique of the judicial process. I do not suppose that it was worse in our case than in others, but to me it was nerve-wracking to have a sudden indictment thrust on me February 9, with arraignment set for the 16th. Where in "Jim Crow" Washington was I to stay? Could white and colored defendants and counsel stay together or within consulting distance? Where would we eat? These were, of course, the peculiar difficulties of citizens in what the Beau Brummel of the State Department calls the "Free democracies of the West."

Trial date was set for April 2. This was much too soon; we had yet to secure our panel of lawyers; to study this case under a new and seldom evoked statute; and above all to raise money. We secured an extension only after insistent struggle to secure the time we actually needed to prepare our motions adequately. Motions could be argued April 27 and May 1, touching place of trial, settling matters of jurisdiction, and bringing up the case of our clerk, Miss Soloff, who, as a clerical worker, ought never to have been indicted, as was eventually decided.

The date of the trial was at last fixed for May 14; again much too soon. We knew that we would need evidence from the officers of the World Peace Council to help our defense. On May 11, 1951, before Judge Holtzoff had even decided our motions to dismiss the indictment, which, if granted, would have ended the proceedings, we were constrained to make our motions to take the foreign testimony. These motions were so well founded that they had to be immediately granted, and the trial postponed to October 3rd to give our lawyers time to go to Paris to take the testimony. In the time thus afforded us, Shirley and I made pilgrimages across the nation twice, to make known a situation which the press was completely blacking out. We got an office set up, and with difficulty secured a bank account. (Many may not know that the brave fight against "subversion" uses the techniques of inducing banks to refuse to hold the funds of unpopular causes.)

Despite the difficulty of securing meeting places in New York where we could defend our cause, we succeeded late in September in organizing a meeting in Town Hall. The National Council of the Arts, Sciences and Professions put on an interesting program, with Professor Henry Pratt Fairchild presiding. Here Bishop Wright, Corliss Lamont, and Lawrence D. Reddick, former curator of the Schomberg Collection and now Librarian of Atlanta University, spoke. Dr. Reddick said in part:

> "I have just come from a part of our country where the flag of the Confederacy is more popular than the flag of the United States of America; where Robert E. Lee is not only more of a hero than Ulysses S. Grant but also more than George Washington; and where the Governor threatens to close down the State's entire system of education if the courts should compel the public, tax-supported institutions that are presently maintained for whites only to admit a single Negro.
>
> "In such a land, the struggle for life and liberty is real and the issues raised by the case of Dr. W. E. B. Du Bois are clear. . . ."

When the head of the Criminal Division of the Department of Justice returned with our lawyers from Paris, he may have learned something. He was to call our attorney in an hour. He remained in conference with the High Command for four hours. He could consent only to a postponement until November. The High Command was apparently adamant; McInerney was withdrawn from active participation. The trial, first called for November 2, finally took place November 8. Personally, I was glad of no more delay, unless it meant entire quashing of the indictment, of which there was no longer hope.

Moreover, we were now ready for trial, as we certainly were not in May. Our lawyers had become acquainted with each other and assumed their respective roles. Six or more times all the defendants met with the attorneys and went over the case point by point. Our "cause was just," but "thrice-armed" was not enough.

Just before the trial I spoke to an Inter-Faith Committee for Peace which held public meetings at three centers in New York City. I said:

> "Peace is not an object in itself; it is a method, a path to an ideal. We who ask for peace and peace now in Korea and elsewhere in the world, do not for a moment believe or pretend to believe that peace will settle all or any of the deep and serious differences between men and nations. What we say and insist upon is that by no other method save by peace can we be in a position to begin the settlement of world problems. We affirm that the clear lesson of the awful history of the last half century is that the military force as now used cannot compel men to alter their beliefs and ideas, nor can it ultimately change their actions against their will."

I also wrote this statement for the defendants:

"This case is a blow at civilization: by instituting thought control; by seeking to stop the circulation of ideas; by seeking to shut off the free flow of culture around the world and reducing all American culture to the level of Mississippi and Nevada; by making it a crime to think as others think, if your thought is against the prejudices or graft or barbarism of some backwoods partisan; by making it treason to brand the hoary lie that War is the path to Peace; by crucifying fathers and mothers who do not want their sons raised to murder men, women and children. . . .

"The Government can put into absolute control of our thinking, feeling and culture any set of half-educated fanatics from Southern rotten boroughs or western mining camps or Missouri gang politics in order to: curtail and misdirect education in America; limit thought and twist ambition; send school children hiding under desks instead of learning to read and write; to make saints of spies, informers and professional liars; make a prisoned nation call Freedom that which is slavery and to change a Democracy into a police state!

"Wake up, America. Your liberties are being stolen before your very eyes. What Washington, Jefferson and Lincoln fought for, Truman, Acheson, and McGrath are striving desperately to nullify. Wake up, Americans and dare to think and say and do. Dare to cry: No More War!"

CHAPTER X

The Pilgrimages for Defense

We knew well that we were in serious danger. We were not lulled to sleep by the flimsiness of the case against us or by fatuous reliance on "justice." The situation was clear. The nation was ruled by the National Association of Manufacturers, the United States Chamber of Commerce, and like affiliated organizations. That is, concentrated control of the whole industrial process coupled with direction of public opinion through nationally organized propaganda. This new concentration of economic power guided the rapidly accumulating profits of national enterprises, and planned to increase them by buying labor and using land in Asia, Africa, the Caribbean area, and South America at lower prices than they would have to pay in Europe or North America. Even in these latter lands their rate of profit was threatened by rising socialism among the organized labor vote which had now actually taken from possible exploitation the whole of Eastern Europe. It was necessary to fight or threaten to fight to stem this socialistic tide.

The nation prepared for war by intervention in China, by war scares and "police action" in Korea. Labor was frightened by shouting "Communism" and defining Communism as violence, disorder, atheism and slavery. Under the excuse of helping the poverty and distress of Europe, America was taxed to restore the control of capital over wages in Europe just when European labor was least able to assert its rights and wishes. Simultaneously America repaid itself by letting corporations buy part interest in European enterprises or start new enterprises, and paid for this partly with our tax money. We secured thought control in the United States by concentrating ownership of the press and news-gathering agencies in the hands of powerful, integrated agencies, while the periodical and book publishing business was also kept subservient.

The public fright and hysteria consequent on this policy began to get out of control, and the nation was faced with "war or bust"; with continued concentration of capital in unproductive enterprises or danger of a financial crisis brought on by inflation and unemployment. Warning or discussion of this was stopped by refusing publicity to criticism in education, art, or literature; by making it difficult for critics to earn a living, and by persecuting dissenters. The leaders of the Communist Party were thus sent to jail. A witch hunt into opinions ensued and was upheld by the courts. Screen writers and helpers of Spanish refugees, persons of reputation and integrity, were imprisoned. Negroes who complained too much of race discrimination; or read radical papers; or attended meetings where criticism of present politics was voiced; or joined organizations like the Council on African Affairs, were threatened or actually lost their jobs.

When a small peace propaganda began in America, it was ignored by giving it no publicity. The recurring peace congresses were called "Communist" propaganda, and given only unfavorable publicity. But when over two million persons signed the Stockholm Peace Appeal, it was time to act. A barrage of abuse swept over the land. Papers like the Los Angeles *Times* became hysterical:

"This is a warning.
"If anyone comes to your door, or accosts you on the sidewalk, with a petition sponsored by an association calling itself the Partisans of Peace—don't sign it! . . .
"If you really want peace, that is.
"This petition is straight from Moscow, despite the fact that it's sometimes called the 'Stockholm Peace Appeal.'
"What should you do? Don't punch him in the nose, or slam the door in his face. Reds are used to that. The thing to do is ask him for his credentials of identification; get his name and address if you can, take a good look at him, and then telephone the FBI."

Soon the Department of Justice joined the Department of State, and the leaders of the Peace Information Center were arrested. The indictment served two purposes: to stop peace propaganda which would interfere with the war scare; and to warn Negro leaders to go slow. In arresting me for peace propaganda, the traditional policy of frightening Negro leaders into conformity was re-implemented. But, at the same time, the government was not prepared to press this too far, for fear of its effect on the elections of 1952. However, all purposes would have been served if, having been indicted and thus thoroughly scared, the case against me was dropped, with my consent and connivance.

This offer was made to one of my attorneys in an office of the Department of Justice; in the comfortable atmosphere of a smoke-filled room, with feet on the table. It was all naturally "unofficial," but if Du Bois would enter a plea of "Nolo Contendere," the procedure against him would undoubtedly be dropped. In other words, I had only to lie and keep still and the case against me would not be pressed. I immediately wrote my attorney and said flatly that before I would enter such a plea I would rot in jail. I was not guilty of being an agent for anybody and would go to court and prove it, if allowed a fair trial.

This was easier said than done. Our trial would not be simply a legal procedure. We would be victims of a misled public, and would be convicted by public opinion of sympathy with plans of force and violence if not as open traitors to the nation. Already this smear was spreading. Most persons, white and Negro, were given to understand that the officers of the Peace Information Center were proven by incontestable evidence in the possession of the F.B.I. of being in the pay of the Soviet Union.

The attitude of the N.A.A.C.P. shows the reaction of a powerful national Negro organization. The white man who first advanced the idea of such a movement, William English Walling, once said:

> "We had secured, from the start, the favorable attention of the emancipated and advanced elements among the whites. But we all agreed that the organization itself had to give an example of successful cooperation of the races and that it must be founded upon the American principles of self-government and self-development.
> "So I always date the real launching of the organization from the day we secured Dr. Du Bois."

I served the N.A.A.C.P. for twenty-eight years in all. When this case came up, although I was no longer officially connected with the organization, branches and members all over the nation wanted to help me and urged the main office to join in. The president of the Board of Directors said frankly to Shirley Graham that undoubtedly the Peace Information Center was supported by funds from the Soviet Union. He admitted that it was possible that I did not know this. At a meeting, March 12, of the Board of Directors, it was urged that the Board take a position on the indictment, and as one branch said, "give active, tangible aid to Dr. Du Bois in his present plight." However, the Secretary, Walter White, reported that he had talked with Peyton Ford, Assistant to the Attorney-General in Washington, and was told that there was definite evidence of guilt in the hands of the Department of Justice, and that the four associates of Dr. Du Bois could not be prosecuted without prosecuting Dr. Du Bois.

A white member of the board had offered to take up the matter of asking the legal department of the N.A.A.C.P. to join in our defense. After this member heard our "certain guilt" stated he made no further effort.

The Board finally passed this resolution:

> "Without passing on the merits of the recent indictment of Dr. W. E. B. Du Bois, the board of directors of the N.A.A.C.P. expresses the opinion that this action against one of the great champions of civil rights lends color to the charge that efforts are being made to silence spokesmen for full equality of Negroes. The board also reaffirms its determination to continue its aggressive fight for full citizenship rights for all Americans."

Even this resolution was not given much publicity, and the main office advised the branches strongly "not to touch" this case. Some branches vigorously complained, and despite the attitude of the New York office, many branches of the N.A.A.C.P. supported our campaign.

Finally, at the Atlanta annual conference of the N.A.A.C.P., held in July, some sixty-five branches brought in resolutions in defense of Dr. Du Bois and a strong resolution was adopted:

> "Whereas, Dr. W. E. B. Du Bois is one of the illustrious founders of the N.A.A.C.P. and has devoted his entire life in uplifting minority groups in the South, in this nation and in the world as an educator, teacher, scholar, international organizer and editor for more than fifty years, and

"Whereas, the Government of the United States has caused the return of an indictment against him alleging that he is an agent of a foreign power and failed to register as such, and

"Whereas, the N.A.A.C.P. National Board of Directors has expressed the opinion that this action against one of the great champions of Civil Rights lends color to the charge that efforts are being made to silence spokesmen for full equality of Negroes, and

"Whereas, Dr. Du Bois is and for more than fifty years has been one of the leaders in the fight for democracy at home, abroad and among colored peoples (of Africa, West Indies and elsewhere);

"Therefore be it resolved that this Convention go on record as being unalterably opposed to such methods by any Government instrumentality to silence spokesmen for full equality for Negroes and reaffirms its determination to continue to fight for such citizenship rights for all Americans."

Nevertheless, on the day before our acquittal, Walter White spoke in Milwaukee at the Municipal Auditorium. He did not mention this case and no questions were allowed. After the meeting, Sidney Berger, son of the late Victor Berger, once mayor of the city, accosted White on the way out. White said confidentially to Berger that he had been to Washington and to the Department of Justice. He had talked with a top official; he had urged the dropping of the case against Du Bois lest the Communists make a martyr of him. The Department said it was too late; that they had "irrefutable proof" that the funds of the Peace Information Center "came from Moscow." White suggested that perhaps Du Bois did not know this; but the answer was that they could not separate his case from the others; all must sink together. One can see under what a mist of misapprehension we started to fight this case.

What does one do when accused of crime? This being my first experience, frankly, I did not know. There first came the question as to who was to take legal charge of the case.

In this respect we were fortunate—how fortunate we did not realize until after the acquittal; that was in the initial securing by the P.I.C. of the services of Gloria Agrin. She was a good lawyer, careful, meticulous, and untiring, who absolutely mastered the law, the facts, and the decision in this case. But that was not all. Miss Agrin was modest, self-sacrificing, perfectly willing to step aside if that assured co-operation; just as willing to step forward and take full responsibility when necessary. It was Miss Agrin who chose as her closest co-worker, the Constitutional expert Bernard Jaffe. They worked together as a team, and laid a splendid legal foundation for our defense. With them also came Mr. Elkin's personal attorney, Stanley Faulkner. It was, however, important for many reasons to have a firm of colored lawyers. I had long known Judge Cobb of Washington, who had once been a magistrate in the District of Columbia. We retained his firm, Cobb, Howard, and Hayes, because of their long and intimate knowledge of procedure in the District of Columbia, and their technical acquaintance with the peculiar ramifications of the color line. With them we associated Mr. George Parker, dean of a colored law school in Washington.

There was still another matter. A court case, especially one of this kind, was not merely a matter of legal knowledge. It was a matter of publicity. The name of some lawyer or law firm of national reputation was important. We had not realized how important it was. We began to explore and immediately encountered the ramifications of the current witch-hunt. There was no eagerness on the part of lawyers to enter this case; first, because we had little money, secondly, because we were known to be radicals in thought. We were talking about Peace when apparently the nation, and certainly the government, wanted war.

I wrote personally to perhaps half a dozen leading lawyers, asking at least advice if not actual participation. All declined. I wrote to Zechariah Chafee of the Harvard Law School and asked for the privilege of talking about the case with him, and getting his advice. He did not answer my letter. I spoke with an old acquaintance, Arthur Garfield Hays. His final answer was:

> "Having talked to some of the key men among the directors, and those who would be most favorable toward our going into the matter, and not having met support, I feel there is no possibility of the American Civil Liberties Union taking up this matter until after the trial. I am sorry because personally I should like to have helped in this case."

I made some other futile gestures, and finally we all united in choosing Mr. Vito Marcantonio, who offered his services without fee. Marcantonio is a remarkable man; he was long the most intelligent and consistent of progressive congressmen and missed re-election only because of a shameless gerrymander. He was a staunch defender of civil rights, and in addition a courageous and resourceful trial lawyer, genuinely interested in this case. We accepted his offer gladly, and made him Chief Counsel, even though some of our friends shook their heads and said that the choice of such a lawyer stamped us as allied with "subversive" elements. But we stuck to our choice.

Later some friend urged us to add to our panel a nationally known lawyer who would undoubtedly bring publicity to our case. When, however, he demanded the fee of $25,000, we dropped the matter. In the end, I am sure, this was fortunate.

But this brought forward the whole question of costs. It had not occurred to us how costly justice in the United States is. It is not enough to be innocent in order to escape punishment. You must have money and a lot of it. In the end it cost us $35,150 to prosecute this case to a successful end, not counting the fee refused by the Chief Counsel. If, as we had confidently expected, the case had gone to higher courts to determine the constitutionality of this foreign agents Act, it might have cost us $100,000. Before this prospect of sheer cost, we stood for many weeks appalled and discouraged. We realized more than ever that this trial was not going to be simply a legal process, but a political persecution, the outcome of which would depend on public opinion; and that to raise the funds necessary for our defense, we would need the contributions of large numbers of poor people and need have no hope for gifts from the rich nor from well-endowed foundations.

Our plan of appealing to public opinion in order to secure a fair trial divided itself into two parts: an appeal to the nation and an appeal to the world. The appeal to the world logically should have followed an appeal to the United States, especially to the Negro people. But because of the prior knowledge which the peace forces of the world received of our indictment, the world was alerted before we explained our case to our own nation. I have shown in the last chapter how wide and sincere this foreign movement became; and that this was accomplished before the domestic campaign got afoot, so that China knew of our plight before California. This was due not only to our appeal to the World Defenders of Peace, but to the work of the defense committee in New York.

There followed an appeal to the people of the United States, and especially to Negroes, by a lecture trip to be undertaken by myself and my wife, Shirley Graham. We wished to meet the blackout in the press by explaining our case; and besides this to collect funds for our legal expenses.

But before we started West, a central committee was formed in New York. Former Minnesota Governor Elmer Benson and artist Paul Robeson were elected as co-chairmen. Other members of the committee included Vito Marcantonio, Prof. Henry Pratt Fairchild, Doxey A. Wilkerson and Leon Straus of the Fur Workers. First came all the difficulties of setting up an office, enhanced by the nature of our particular case and the usual problems of race. After two or three volunteer workers, we secured Alice Citron as secretary. She was one of the public school teachers of New York City who had been a victim of the witch-hunt.

Alice Citron taught colored children eighteen years in Harlem. She was regarded widely as "the best of the best teachers in our system." On May 3, 1950, Superintendent Jansen of the New York City schools suspended her without pay "because she had not answered the question: 'Are you or were you ever a member of the Communist Party?'" He said that he knew nothing of her record in the classroom or in the community. He might have added that he cared less. Miss Citron was dismissed. She took charge of our defense office. I salute her!

She became our executive secretary and threw herself into the work with unfaltering sacrifice and at a nominal salary. The Hotel Breslin where our offices were first established tried to get rid of us from time to time, but she hung on even when shunted to the cold and inaccessible attic. Here she literally corresponded with the whole United States and the wide world. Press releases and personal letters were sent out in increasing numbers.

Outstanding, too, was the characteristically self-effacing and efficient work of Doxey Wilkerson. He voluntarily shouldered many tasks for the committee and his contributions were of great value.

Then, as the initial publicity and money raising venture, came the first trip to the West by Shirley and myself. Engagements were secured by peace centers, members of the Progressive Party, and Negroes. We realized that we would meet heterogeneous groups with varying points of view. This developed differently according to place and circumstance; often the Progressives formed the nucleus with few Negroes or workers; then trade unionists were to the fore with supporting Negroes and few drawn by the peace appeal. And again to our surprise, we found ourselves talking to persons who literally knew almost nothing of our case or the world peace movement, because of the almost complete blackout of the press.

We started out in the Spring, in June. Our plan was for Shirley to speak first and explain the case. Shirley spoke easily and interestingly, without notes and with an intense vigor which set the audiences on the edges of their seats. Then came the collection directed by some local person of standing. Then I spoke. What I should say was a matter of anxious conference. Over the years I had developed the habit of using a manuscript. It went rather well because I was familiar with my manuscript, could talk clear English, and my arguments got somewhere. Yet popular audiences were repelled by manuscripts, and we hesitated. Finally I tried this line of written talk, prepared to vary it from place to place or abandon it. It proved, however, popular, and left audiences something to get their teeth in. I therefore used it on practically all occasions. It was an argument for peace, and in the main went like this:

"The world is astonished at recent developments in the United States. Our actions and attitudes are discussed with puzzled wonder on the streets of every city in the world. Reluctantly the world is coming to believe that we actually want War; that we must have War; that in no other way can we keep our workers employed and maintain huge profits save by spending 70 thousand million dollars a year for war preparations and adding to the vast debt of 218 thousand millions which we already owe chiefly for war in the past. . . .

"If tomorrow Russia disappeared from the face of the earth, the basic problem facing the modern world would remain; and that is: Why is it, with the earth's abundance and our mastery of natural forces, and miraculous technique; with our commerce belting the earth; and goods and services pouring from our stores, factories, ships and warehouses; why is it that nevertheless, most human beings are starving to death, dying of preventable disease, and too ignorant to know what is the matter, while a small minority are so rich that they cannot spend their income?

"That is the problem which faces the world, and Russia was not the first to pose it, nor will she be the last to ask and demand answer. . . .

"It does not answer this world-wide demand to say that we of America have these things in greater abundance than the rest of the world, if our prosperity is based on or seeks to base itself on, the exploitation and degradation of the rest of mankind. Remember, it is American money that owns more and more of South African mines worked by slave labor; it is American enterprise that fattens off Central African copper; it is American investors that seek to dominate China, India, Korea and Burma, and who are throttling the starved workers of the Near East, the Caribbean and South America. . . .

"I have never thought I would live to see the day that free speech and freedom of opinion would be so throttled in the United States as it is today, when students in our colleges may not hear or discuss the Truth. Today, in this free country, no man can be sure of earning a living, of escaping slander and personal violence, or even of keeping out of jail!—unless publicly and repeatedly he proclaims that:

He hates Russia.

He opposes Socialism and Communism.

He supports wholeheartedly the war in Korea.

He is ready to spend any amount for further war, anywhere or at anytime.

He is ready to fight the Soviet Union, China and any other country, or all countries together.

He believes in the use of the atom bomb or any other weapon of mass
destruction, and regards anyone opposed as a traitor.

He not only believes in and consents to all these things, but is willing to spy
on his neighbors and denounce them, if they do not believe as he does.

"The mere statement of this creed shows its absolute insanity.

"What can be done to bring this nation to its senses? Most people answer:
Nothing, just sit still, bend to the storm, if necessary lie and join the witch-hunt,
swear to God that never, never, did you ever sympathize with Russian peasants'
fight to be free, that you never in your life belonged to a liberal organization or had
a friend who did, and if so, you were deceived, deluded and a damned fool.

"But there are others who say: We can do something. That America needs no
more cowards and liars. It needs honest men, and that honest citizens who are mistaken, are infinitely more patriotic than scoundrels who follow the herd. . . .

"Today the vast majority of the American people who are not crazy, do not
want war. Most Americans hate the current witch-hunt. The only way to oppose
war and the death of Civil Liberty is to elect officials who agree with you. We cannot export a Democracy which we do not possess. We cannot give Freedom to others when we are losing our own. . . .

"Therefore, for the whole world I want Progress; I want Education; I want
Social Medicine; I want a living wage and old age security; I want employment
for all and relief for the unemployed and sick. I want Public Works, public services
and public improvements. I want Freedom for my people. And because I
know and you know that we cannot have these things and at the same time fight,
destroy and kill all around the world in order to make huge profits for Big
Business; for that reason, I take my stand beside the millions in every nation and
continent and cry Peace—No more War!

"A new era of power, held and exercised by the working classes the world over,
is dawning, and while its eventual form is not yet clear, its progress cannot be held
back by any power of man."

This trip started at Chicago and went on to St. Paul, Seattle, Tacoma and
Portland. Then to San Francisco, Oakland, and Los Angeles, Cleveland, and back
to New York.

We left New York June 1 by air, and stopped in Chicago. There we attended
a dinner and rally in honor of Robert Morss Lovett, Professor Philip Morrison
of Cornell, and myself. Each of us spoke for ten minutes to a responsive audience of 700, white and colored. Then we found ourselves addressing colored
folk. On Sunday night, we had a meeting in Gary, the steel center. The Municipal
Hall had been hired, but at the last moment it was taken away, and the single
white daily paper announced on Saturday that the meeting had been called off.
But a meeting was hastily arranged at a former skating rink.

The local colored paper protested:

"The recent attempt to 'hush' Dr. W. E. B. Du Bois from speaking in Gary proves
to us the smallness of a certain element downtown, who have chosen themselves
to run the lives of the people in Gary. These self-appointed dictators put some sort
of pressure on certain leaders in the Midtown area in an effort to see that Dr. Du
Bois was not permitted to use any hall for his engagement in Gary. However, these
efforts were in vain, for Dr. Du Bois DID speak and before a largely attended and

appreciative audience, which was unafraid of the criticism which might be lev-
elled against them from the 'rulers.'"

But another aspect of the effect of our case among Negroes came in a social
gathering in Chicago.

A reception was tendered us at the residence of a well known Negro lawyer,
Oscar Brown. Many of the well-to-do social leaders of the Chicago Negro group
were present. Unexpectedly to me and perhaps to others in the group, Earl
Dickerson, now president of the National Lawyers Guild, brought up my case
during the evening and asked me to explain it. After I and my wife had spoken
and much sympathy was manifested, Dickerson with deep feeling asked for
pledges toward a defense fund. To my surprise, in a short time $1,100 was pledged
and a defense committee organized. But later a reaction took place. Of the money
subscribed only $445 was actually paid in, despite many reminders from the com-
mittee. The majority of the group, through fear of reprisal or unwillingness on
reflection to champion peace, or from actual lack of funds, refused to pay up.

In Minnesota there was a strong Progressive group in Minneapolis, while in
St. Paul my wife's family, the Bells, were a dominant force among Negroes, having resided there generations, with several graduates from the state university,
and some holding positions in the civil service. Consequently we were interviewed and photographed by the *Dispatch*. The largest Negro church in St. Paul
was thrown open to us and a numerous white delegation from Minneapolis
poured into our night meeting, making this probably the largest inter-racial
meeting ever held in this area. It served to introduce this case and the World
Peace movement to a new public. Near the close of the meeting, a man rose in
the balcony and said that he had a message. He then read this resolution from a
recent meeting of the alumni of Fisk University, which proved the first and only
national pronouncement on our case from a Negro college. It said:

> "Whereas, William Edward Burghardt Du Bois, distinguished graduate of Fisk
> University, has made an outstanding contribution to scholarship, literature, and
> social action;
> "And whereas, he has gained the respect, admiration and gratitude of his fel-
> low alumni, and has received the highest award from his Alma Mater;
> "And whereas, the Government of the United States had indicted him and is
> now about to bring him to trial;
> "And whereas, the General Alumni Association of Fisk University in its annual
> meeting are desirous of expressing at this time their continued respect, gratitude,
> and admiration of him, therefore be it resolved, that we reaffirm our faith and con-
> fidence in him and in his integrity and loyalty to the principles and ideals of his
> Alma Mater, and again express our sincere appreciation for his courageous lead-
> ership in the struggle for full emancipation of his people and the realization of
> total democracy for all men."

Of many resolutions passed in my defense by Negroes, including the
N.A.A.C.P., this was the first which expressed "faith and confidence" in my
"integrity and loyalty."

We then set out for the Northwest, that region of unusual climate, grand scenery, and independent thought. The Negro population of Seattle is small, so that our appeal was mainly to the white progressive group. There was no publicity from the press, but we stopped at a good hotel, and Progressives and trade unions gave an excellent audience of 500 persons. The Pension Union of the state, part of the once powerful Townsend movement, supported us and asked Shirley to address their convention.

At Portland the picture changed notably. There was not only a strong reactionary movement there, headed by the chief of police, but a virulent anti-Negro spirit. The pressure on the colored group was intense: a Negro home where we had been invited to stay, since we would not be welcome at a white hotel, telephoned the very morning of our arrival: "We can't take them; do not ask us why." Four Negro ministers, whose names were among our sponsors, precipitantly withdrew. The local committee was not able to get in touch with either the local N.A.A.C.P. or the Urban League. The chief of police and the American Legion were busy in the Negro section on the day of our meeting and the press was silent. I expected trouble.

But the local Progressive group was intelligent and courageous. Immediate preparations were made to entertain us in two or three white private homes, but we stayed with a singer who had taken part in the Wallace campaign and helped out the mother of the family who was expecting another baby. We were entertained in several private homes and addressed groups and answered questions. Then on Sunday night we talked to 700 enthusiastic persons, with the American Legion loafing conspicuously outside. A colored trade union official presided, a Reed College professor introduced me and the young man who took up the collection told us that this was his last public appearance as a professor of the University of Washington as he had just been dismissed as too radical.

Then the scene changed. We went down into the sun and flowers of California, to San Francisco, Oakland and Los Angeles. The trade unions sponsored us in the first two cities and the Progressive Party in the southern part of the state. The welcome in California was warm, with large delegations and gifts of flowers. Whites and Negroes were equally represented in promotion of the meetings. We stopped in the home of an eager young white woman, and talked in the hiring hall of the Marine Cooks and Stewards. Our press conference was attended by the chief city papers, colored and white, although in the white press not a word appeared. A reporter of the liberal *Chronicle* wrote a long article and I reminded him that during the U.N.O. meeting I was a columnist on his sheet. No word was printed.

We held mass meetings in both Oakland and San Francisco, in the Civic Auditorium and a large hall. Vincent Hallinan, attorney for Harry Bridges, spoke at both. In all we reached 2,000 persons. This whole area has a large Negro population, but they came chiefly because of war employment and were integrated largely into the unions. There is on that account no great race problem.

We had little or no contact with the professional and business class of Negroes in San Francisco. Most of the Negro ability and energy has been drawn into the union movement. On the contrary, in Los Angeles, the segregated Negro group had the usual Southern patterns of leadership and the wealthy and the well-to-do are bursting out of a ghetto into some of the most beautiful residential districts in the city. They are increasingly less segregated. Added to this is the colored Hollywood group of actors and entertainers who occupy a precarious position and are, for the most part, as intimidated as the whites in thought and action. I sensed from what I knew of this situation that my visit would have unpleasant repercussions.

Since my first visit to Los Angeles in 1915, I had always been the guest of a young colored professional couple who, after struggles, have achieved comfort and independence. They were kind and sympathetic with my work, and pressed me always to regard their home as mine when I came West. On this occasion I hesitated, and ventured in writing them of my coming visit, to suggest that under the circumstances it might be better for them if on this occasion I found another stopping place. I confess that it disappointed me to have them reply, politely, that it would be better; and to find later that neither of them joined any committee of welcome or courtesy, or attended our meetings. My private letter was even shown the newspapers to prove that these friends of mine were not implicated in my defense.

A good part of the Negro professional and business group joined with white progressives and the trade unions to give me the greatest hearing I had on this trip, with 2,200 persons in the main hall, another hall full and listening in and several hundred turned away. It was said Los Angeles had seen nothing like it since the Dean of Canterbury.

So the trip ended except for a small hastily arranged meeting in Cleveland with trade unions and Progressives. This was under the leadership of Hugh De Lacy, the man who left Congress to become a carpenter and grew in stature by the change.

Shirley went back to New York, with a little money but with promises of more, and with publicity for our case and the cause of peace which in the end proved decisive. I went back to Chicago for the Congress of the Peace Crusade which under Abbott Simon had succeeded the Peace Information Center for peace propaganda in this nation. It took place in July and was the result of hur-ried but wide and continuous effort all over the nation. It was helped by our western trip. It needed internal organization, and when the thousands poured in by all kinds of conveyance from north, south, east, and west, with a mass of enthusiastic young people, the program itself was hardly set.

I had, however, long before been asked to make the key speech, and, after thought, decided that I would talk plainly about the underlying causes of the war spirit today in this nation, instead of merely pointing out future organi-zation and specific work to be done. I was sure that others could do that better than I; but what I thought it best to say to that great audience of 15,000 people in the Coliseum of Chicago had a clear thesis. I wanted to dispel in the minds of the government and of the public any lingering doubt as to my deter-mination to think and speak freely on the economic foundation of the wars and frustration of the twentieth century. I think even the sponsors of this con-gress shrank at my outspoken analysis. I am sure the government gave up all hope that I would succumb to fear and sink to acquiescence and silence. I said in part:

> "Big Business in the United States is forcing this nation into war, transforming our administration into a military dictatorship, paralyzing all democratic controls and depriving us of knowledge we need.
>
> "The United States is ruled today by great industrial corporations controlling vast aggregations of capital and wealth. The acts and aims of this unprecedented integration of power, employing some of the best brain and ability of the land, are not and never have been under democratic control. Its dictatorship has varied from absolute monarchy to oligarchy, limited by organized labor and by often ineffective public opinion, trying repeatedly and desperately to express itself through free elections. . . .
>
> "If sincere dislike of this state of affairs is Communism, then by the living God, no force of arms, nor power of weath, nor smartness of intellect will ever stop it. Denial of this right to think will manufacture Communists faster than you can jail or kill them. Nothing will stop such Communism but something better than Communism. If our present policies are examples of free enterprise and individual initiative, they free crime and initiate suffering, as well as make wealth; if this is the American way of life, God save America.
>
> "There is no way in the world for us to preserve the ideals of a democratic America, save by drastically curbing the present power of concentrated wealth; by assuming ownership of some natural resources, by administering many of our key industries, and by socializing our services for public welfare. This need not mean the adoption of the communism of the Soviet Union, nor the socialism of Britain, nor even of the near-socialism of France, Italy, or Scandinavia; but either in some way or to some degree we socialize our economy, restore the New Deal, and inaugurate the welfare state, or we descend into military fascism which will kill all dreams of Democracy; of the abolition of poverty, disease and ignorance; or of peace instead of war.
>
> "There must come vast social change in the United States; a change not violent, but by the will of the people certain and inexorable, carried out 'with malice toward none but charity for all'; with meticulous justice to the rich and thrifty, and complete sympathy for the poor, the sick, and the ignorant; with Freedom and Democracy for America, and on earth Peace, Good-will toward men."

That summer, Shirley and I moved to a home in Brooklyn Heights. We had planned to buy this large house jointly with a friend and his family. But at the last moment, he had to withdraw because of his obligation to his fellows in a worthwhile fight. Shirley and I, with trepidation, alone shouldered this burden of a large mortgage, despite our otherwise precarious economic plight. Suitable homes for Negroes in this nation are rare to come by, and we dared not miss this opportunity. So in July came the nightmare of a double moving, from Shirley's home on Long Island, and my apartment in Harlem. We were by no means settled when calls came from the field, and immediate need of funds made a second western trip advisable. Time and strength made a short trip advisable, and after correspondence with a dozen places, we decided to visit Milwaukee, Detroit, Denver and Chicago.

Our second trip differed considerably from the first, and showed its effect. We received a great deal more publicity from the newspapers. The audiences were fairly large, and the money response was generous. We started out in September, flying to Milwaukee. Our host there was a prominent white business man, a member of the Mayor's Commission on Human Rights, who had long been interested in Shirley's books. He took us into his Lake Shore home, and through him we were able from the first to meet a number of prominent people: a state senator, members of the City Council, and members of the city Human Rights Commission. The two daily papers sent reporters to interview us. The Milwaukee *Journal*, which had printed a rather critical account of the meeting of the Methodist Social Action Committee in Chicago, sent the same reporter to interview us, and he wrote a very sympathetic column interview. We learned later that this had been accepted by the paper only after long argument. After that the *Journal*, in order to justify itself, was very much upset because I listed the Korean war as part of the effort of white Europe to maintain colonialism in yellow Asia. This, the *Journal* said, was a "disservice."

The mass meeting was called by our host, and the pastor of the leading colored church, who seemed a little alarmed at having this packed audience in his church, and warned against "demonstrations." None took place. Some 700 people were present, and the call to the meeting brought out the fact that in Madison, the capital of Wisconsin, a few days before, investigators found that only one out of 112 persons were willing to sign the Bill of Rights!

In Detroit, we again felt the shadow of the Terror. For the first time on these trips, our hosts insisted on a continuous body-guard day and night, which was not pleasant, but I submitted to their wish. The promoters of the Detroit meeting were not able to list the local N.A.A.C.P. among its sponsors. Without answering the invitation to co-operate, this local wrote to New York and invited Judge Hubert Delany to speak in Detroit on the same date and at the same hour in another church. However, Judge Delany "criticized those leaders of the N.A.A.C.P. who hesitated to take a forthright position on issues affecting the well-being of the Negro people, for fear of being attacked as Communists." He said that it was not the place of individuals or associations such as the N.A.A.C.P. to hunt for Communists or label their friends as such. He attacked the government's charge of "foreign agent" against Dr. Du Bois, reminding his listeners of the fifty years' struggle by Dr. Du Bois, and said that the indictment of such a man was almost unheard of.

We spoke at Bethel Church before 500 people, with Rev. Charles Hill as one of the speakers. Hill is a brave man. The Air Force once tried to take away his son's commission as an officer on account of his outspoken father; but this raised such a protest that the Air Force let the young officer stay. Hill was candidate for city council and led our effort for a hearing. Trade unions gave us strong support.

From Detroit we went to Denver. Denver gave us a new experience. For the first time a large branch of the N.A.A.C.P. dared sponsor an opportunity for us to place our cause before the public. Then, too, both in physical and mental climate, Denver seems exceptional. Not only did we have a full-fledged snowfall in September, but in other ways, this great city seemed out of the current of war hysteria. The *Rocky Mountain News* gave us all possible publicity with photographs and interviews. I had an opportunity to sit down for a long conference with some of the leading social workers, professionals and preachers of the city, white and black. In Detroit, where I have addressed the Negro Y.M.C.A. for a decade, not a single representative of that organization evinced the slightest interest; but in Denver a city branch gave us a crowded reception. The mass meeting was fine.

A young white Unitarian minister, who was having trouble keeping his views and his church, introduced me by saying, "In this monstrous year of McCarran we speak of a man who makes us still proud to be American."

That night 2,000 people crowded the colored church where we spoke under the sponsorship of the Denver branch of the N.A.A.C.P. They passed a resolution unanimously opposing my persecution by the government.

From Denver we went to Chicago, where there was a crowded meeting of trade unionists sponsored by the American Peace Crusade. It was a workers' rally, with none of the bourgeoisie, white or black. Then we returned to New York, to try to organize our house and prepare for trial in October.

Gradually during October results of our efforts, on the trips and in the New York office, began to appear. One of the most spontaneous reactions to the indictment and our publicity campaign was the formation of defense committees among students throughout the country, north and south, in white and Negro colleges. On the campuses of the University of Chicago, of Wilberforce University in Ohio, of the University of Texas, of Fisk University and others, appeared "Defense Committees for Dr. Du Bois," which published pamphlets and sent letters and telegrams to the Department of Justice and to President Truman. Most of these organizations, however, were quickly suppressed by the college authorities.

We were particularly impressed by the role of the trade unions in the new fight for preserving democracy. I began to grow sure that in the United States it is the independent trade union on which we must depend for far-sighted leadership and courageous thought and democratic control. Business is taking over philanthropy. This means not only that the ulterior motive of philanthropy must be profit and such thought and action as favors current business methods, but also it means that democracy in giving must yield to oligarchy, if not absolute monarchy. Today great corporations set down as part of their profit-making expense, contributions to the local Community Chest, to educational and religious projects, and to "social uplift." There is, therefore, small chance that free criticism of our economic system can be expected from our churches and colleges or even from democratic political elections.

In our case, appeal was made to the democracy of the trade union, the mass meeting, and the church, and not to the Rich Man or the Foundation endowed and set up by the rich. I doubt if any individual donation to our case on this trip exceeded $100. It was mainly a mass giving by poor folk, who gave a dollar or five dollars either themselves or through their unions or other organizations.

Gradually the trade unions throughout the land were aroused. Truman heard from the Fur and Leather Workers; Marine Cooks and Stewards; thirty locals of the United Electrical Workers, and others. The celebrated Ford Local 600 of the C.I.O. United Auto Workers, the largest local in the world, said:

> "Concern with Peace is the property and obligation of citizens of every land, to be informed about Peace is the right of all Americans, to speak for Peace is an inalienable and historic privilege, and the indictment of the Peace Information Center is a challenge to those rights."

Ben Gold of the Fur and Leather Workers proposed a dinner to us for raising funds. This was held Friday, December 16th. Thirteen national and international unions were represented, and $2,300 contributed to the defense. These unions communicated with unions abroad, bringing quick and wide response, from the General Federation of Trade Unions of Martinique, the Trade Unions of Madagascar, and eighty million workers represented in the World Federation of Trade Unions.

There came letters from the Progressive Syndicalists in Djibouti and French Somaliland in Africa, from the Student Labor Federation of England, the Czechoslovakian Employees in Art and Culture Services, and the Hotel, Club and Restaurant Union of Sydney, Australia.

The Negroes in the United States began to be more aware of what was taking place. An appeal to Truman was made by thirty-two Negro leaders, and many others like Bishop Wright of the A.M.E. Church, Langston Hughes wrote:

> "If W. E. B. Du Bois goes to jail a wave of wonder will sweep around the world. Europe will wonder and Africa will wonder and Asia will wonder, and no judge or jury will be able to answer the questions behind their wonder. The banner of American democracy will be lowered another notch, particularly in the eyes of the darker peoples of the earth. The hearts of millions will be angered and perturbed, steeled and strengthened."

There is no question but that our two trips aroused wide attention, not only in the West but throughout the country. Add to this the campaign of letter writing carried on by Alice Citron at our offices in New York; and the ceaseless activities of the other defendants and our lawyers and many other friends, and at last we got our case before the world. The newspaper censorship was not sufficient to keep the world, the nation, and especially the Negroes in the United States and Africa, from grasping the essential facts concerning this indictment, and as a result, a stream of contributions to meet our expenses came from all over the country, in small sums, but an aggregate which amounted to over $35,000.

Justice is not free in the United States.

CHAPTER XI

◆

Oh! John Rogge

What induced the United States Government to attempt to intimidate or jail five American citizens? We were not prominent nor especially influential. We had no wealth nor power. Of the five, I was best known; but I was known as a "Negro" and not as an American. Every reference to me was always accompanied by reference to my race. This labelled me, and excluded me from further consideration except in discussion of the Negro problem.

But what upset the State Department was that the activity of a small group of no influence was bringing out an extraordinary evidence of peace sentiment in this country which seemed to be growing. The powerful influences ruling the nation wanted this stopped and stopped quickly. Pontifical pronouncements by the State Department could get wide publicity in the monopolized press, but these ukases could be answered and were. The debate on Peace thus begun could be effectively silenced only by legal force, and legal force was most quickly available if in some way the smear of "Communism" could be applied. The best method of securing testimony on this matter seemed to be John Rogge, a co-worker with the accused, a personal friend of them and their friends, in whose home the Peace Information Center was conceived.

Of such an eventuality, we of the Center had no inkling, until, on sending our attorney to Washington, she unexpectedly met Rogge emerging from the Grand Jury room. From that day on we recognized his role, and while astonished, we were not as surprised as some might have imagined. For his friends had begun to know John Rogge.

Oetje John Rogge was born in west central Illinois in 1904, of a German immigrant father and a mother whose father was born in Germany. He writes frankly: "I went to school to equip myself to make money." He was graduated at the University of Illinois and the Harvard Law School. He began to practice corporation law in Chicago in 1925, and his firm made much money. But the crash came in 1929 and one of his partners was ruined. After a year of post-graduate study, with a view to possible teaching, Rogge returned to law practice. In 1937 he entered government service where he remained until 1946, when he was dismissed for attacking German cartels and their American representatives, who were "Big

Business"; or, if not actually dismissed, his relations with the Department of Justice thereafter remained secret.

This made Rogge a national figure. He received invitations to speak and concluded that the way to success was in alliance with progressive movements, with personal popularity, and a possible political career ahead. But it was the success that Rogge wanted; of that he had no doubt and few moral scruples. He turned away from an offer to return to corporation practice, "with the best little law shop there was, catering to blue chip clients" and labor matters "for employers." He took civil right cases, joined the Progressive Party and attended peace congresses. He let it be known that in this career he was surrendering the opportunity to practice profitable law in "as plush an office as any in Manhattan."

But in the election of 1948 the bubble of a political career burst. Wallace was badly beaten, and Rogge received only a small part of the vote he expected as candidate for surrogate in New York City. Immediately, Rogge began cautiously seeking a way back from his exposed position as a liberal as expressed in his book written in the election year.

He began neglecting his labor clients. One whom he represented was Harold Christoffel, whom he called in 1947, "as able a young labor leader as I have ever met." He neglected this client so outrageously that the Federal Court of Appeals said:

> ". . . disciplinary action on account of such neglect ought to be considered. Therefore this case . . . will be referred to the Committee on Admissions and Grievances for its consideration and such recommendation or petition to the court in respect of the conduct of appellant's [Christoffel] counsel as the Committee may see fit to present."

His speeches thereafter showed that he was seeking some middle way between the Soviet Union and the United States, to be represented by a well-to-do American liberalism, which he would lead. I met him first at the Waldorf-Astoria Peace Congress of which I was sponsor. Afterward I attended a peace meeting at his home. He was not an attractive figure to me because he was pompous and self-conscious. But his ideas were liberal, and his stinging attack on American business methods proved, as I then thought, his clear insight into the economic basis of modern political reform.

Later I wavered in my estimate of his intellectual integrity. In his speeches at the peace congresses in Mexico and Paris, and finally in Prague, I saw in him an opportunism which was disturbing. He first exhibited what might be regarded as judicial attitudes of weighing both sides of public questions, or less charitably as seeking the opportunist balance between irreconcilable positions. Especially was this shown in his public attitude toward peace. When I met Rogge in 1949, he was a prominent advocate of peace, chairman of the executive committee of the Waldorf-Astoria Peace Conference, and he invited me to participate in making out its program. He himself said at that conference:

> "The power of incorporated wealth is behind the attacks made against this meeting today. It is the same power which would plunge the world into war to preserve its profitable status quo. . . .

"The smokescreen of communism, used so effectively in the past to cloak real motives, is being used effectively again. The newspapers, which should be among the first to sound the alarm at any encroachment of our basic liberties, co-operate with, and are themselves among the most vocal of the smearers.

"This kind of program for war can succeed only if all opposition is proscribed. This is why the government itself gave official sanction to heresy hunting by its own loyalty investigation. This is why teachers, preachers, artists, writers, housewives and workers in all fields who speak out against these moves feel the whip-lash of vilification and hatred, as well as the ordeal of trial and conviction for opposing the authority of Un-American Committees. . . . This is why the police spy, the informer, and the wire-tapper are afforded positions of honor by our government today."

Sensing the growing power of war propaganda and monopoly capitalism in America, Rogge a year later was trimming his liberal sails to meet it. He said in Paris that he was opposed to the Truman Doctrine, the Marshall Plan and the Atlantic Pact, and that when he returned he would continue to oppose these policies; that he believed Communist nations could live peaceably beside Capitalist, and Capitalist beside Communist; each had its weaknesses and its truths, and in time we would distinguish between the two. At the Mexican Peace Congress, Rogge, being in the process of becoming foreign agent of Yugoslavia, denounced the United States for suppression of civil liberties, but also said:

"The Soviet Union is not free from colonialism and exploitation. It participated with the United States in the arbitrary and deliberate division of Korea and Viet Nam. I could not justify what the Russians did in Manchuria; nor can I justify what they are currently doing in Yugoslavia.

". . . we tell Western Europe to stop trading with the East. The Cominform . . . tells its countries to stop trading with the Yugoslavs."

This statement was not well received, for this Peace Congress did not believe that the Soviet Union was a colonial power, but that on the contrary, war was being brought nearer by the colonial imperialism of Britain and America.

At any rate, in 1949 Rogge strongly advocated peace, and peace with Russia; in 1950 he went to Europe as representative of the Paris Defenders of Peace. Although he had probably already become an agent of the Yugoslav mission to the United Nations, he accompanied a delegation of the Defenders of Peace to the Soviet Union to urge a world peace appeal. He then went to Stockholm to consider and sign the Stockholm Appeal, and from there to Yugoslavia to become its foreign agent in the United States. Later he returned to London for another meeting of the Bureau of the Paris Defenders of Peace, of which he was still a member, and there demanded that Yugoslavia be admitted to membership in the Paris organization. Immediately, Paul Robeson denounced him bitterly as a traitor to the Peace movement, because of Yugoslavia's attitude toward the Defenders of Peace. Rogge's demand was rejected.

After the Stockholm Appeal had been launched and the Peace Information Center formed in New York with Rogge as charter member, he joined the Acheson line of attack and before attending the Prague meeting of the Executive

Committee of the Partisans of Peace he told reporters that he was going to ask this organization to call for outlawing of aggression instead of outlawing the atom bomb. He was not optimistic about their adopting his proposal. "They may even throw me out," he said, and added that he challenged "the dogma that capitalism causes wars."

The Korean War had broken out in June, 1950. There was all the greater need of work for peace. His actions in Prague thoroughly alienated my regard for Rogge. The meeting of the Executive Committee of the Defenders of Peace was called in Prague in August 1951, about a year after the Paris Peace Congress. Rogge was a member of this committee, by virtue of his vice-presidency of the Paris Congress. Elizabeth Moos, who had not been connected with the Peace Information Center since her resignation in July, had been in Paris and was invited to the Prague meeting. I was invited to attend because, while not a member of the executive committee, I was a member of the general committee, and prominent in American peace work as chairman of the Peace Information Center.

Rogge had been a prime mover in the organization of the Peace Information Center. The only point he had then raised against the Stockholm Appeal was that it did not go far enough and include general disarmament; and that it should be reworded, not to change its meaning but to make it less vulnerable to attack as springing from foreign rather than American sources. Never to my hearing or knowledge did he intimate that its distribution in the United States would incur a penalty of foreign agency under the new legislation.

Moreover, the Prague meeting was called especially to meet the very criticism that the Defenders of Peace wanted nothing more than the abolition of the atom bomb. It was called to broaden the peace appeal by including a demand for general disarmament, and that was exactly what it did.

> "The aim of the Prague proposals is to provide such common ground on which all who want peace can come together to work out means of achieving the following:
> "1. The outlawing of all atomic weapons.
> "2. Reduction and control of all armaments.
> "3. Condemnation of aggression and of foreign armed intervention in the internal affairs of any nation.
> "4. A return to the accepted procedure of the United Nations as a preliminary to a peaceful solution to the Korean conflict.
> "5. The outlawing of propaganda making for war in any country whatsoever."

Rogge arrived in Prague late, as was his habit, and sat with the American group and directly by my side. Despite the fact that he had released to the press his speech of criticism, he did not utter a word at the meetings at any time. He complained to Oatis, the notorious American newspaper correspondent, but when French, Soviet and Czech delegates took him to task for his silence and newspaper criticism, Rogge voluntarily wrote the following statement:

> "I have not resigned from the Partisans of Peace and do not intend to do so. I shall continue to serve as one of the vice-presidents of this organization, and plan

to attend its second World Congress to be held this year in Great Britain from November 13–19. I shall continue to work with all those whose stated aim is to work for peace, for without peace we may end up without a world."

The Moscow *Literary Gazette* said, November 13:

"By the time of the Warsaw Congress the participants greeted Rogge so coldly that he could not but understand they had seen through him. After his speech, the text of which he importunately forced on all the journalists, all the participants in the Congress turned away from him indignantly, including all the members of the American delegation.

"Charles Howard expressed their attitude toward Rogge: 'I can assure the Congress that Mr. Rogge has not spoken on behalf of the Progressive Party. Nor does Mr. Rogge represent the point of view of the American delegation. Mr. Rogge is a paid agent of the Yugoslav government and I think the Congress ought to assess his speech in the light of his occupation.'"

Rogge then returned to the United States and almost immediately became the chief witness against the Peace Information Center as "agent of a foreign principal" and named, as that principal, not simply the Defenders of Peace but the Soviet Union.

What was back of this extraordinary action? Rogge was an ambitious man, not too stable in his intellectual outlook, and overborne by his sudden rise to notoriety due to his championship of liberal causes. Moreover he, like so many Americans, wanted money and a great deal of it. It is said that he had been willing to accept as clients the Soviet Union, the People's Republic of China, and Poland, before he was accepted by Yugoslavia.

Rogge returned home and found not reward but threat. He was admittedly one of the founders of the Peace Information Center; he was also a member of the policy-making body of the Defenders of Peace, with offices in Paris. Was not then the Peace Information Center, of Rogge's own knowledge, the agent of the Defenders of Peace and liable to the requirement to register? And would he not so testify?

Rogge was in a quandary. Because of the denunciation and repudiation in London, he was no longer friendly to the Peace Information Center; but he certainly knew that none of us were agents of any government or organization, but were honest advocates of world peace. When he registered as agent of Yugoslavia he declared that no movement with which he was connected was an agent of a foreign principal. He was at the time a member of the Peace Information Center.

But Rogge was confronted with difficulties. If he refused to testify, the Department of Justice, with whom it is possible that he had never severed all connection, certainly had a case against him much stronger than against any other member of the Peace Information Center. I was a member of the Defenders of Peace general committee, but not of their policy-making executive committee. Elizabeth Moos did some work for the Defenders of Peace, but not while she was connected with the Peace Information Center. Rogge belonged to the policy-making bodies of both organizations. But if he should maintain that they were not connected as agent and principal, the Department may have threatened to indict Rogge, bring in his admitted tie-up with Yugoslavia, and his visit to the Soviet Union. If Rogge would appear as chief witness against the Peace Information Center and connect it with the Soviet Union, was he offered personal immunity? At any rate, Rogge testified against us in January, 1951, before the Grand Jury which indicted the Peace Information Center. Later, during the trial, Marcantonio charged that this immunity had been given, and Rogge's attorneys did not deny it. Mr. Marcantonio said:

"If there is any foreign agent, as far as this case is concerned, it is this witness.
"The Court: But he isn't indicted.
"Mr. Marcantonio: Exactly. We say because he has been given immunity, that is why he is testifying.
"Mr. Maddrix (of the prosecution): You should let us say this, Your Honor. . . .
"Mr. Marcantonio: If there is any foreign agent here in connection with this alleged foreign principal, this Congress of the Defenders of Peace, it is this witness."

When he did testify, Rogge said of the Defenders of Peace:

". . . its objective, as it was stated, was to work for peace in the world; but I don't think that was its actual objective. . . . Actually, it identified itself and became an agency for the foreign policy of the Soviet Union."

He said of my speech at Prague:

"The substance of Dr. Du Bois' speech was that all the difficulties in the world stem from what he described as the capitalistic war-mongers in the United States."

This was true. I was saying in Prague in 1951 almost exactly what Rogge said in New York in 1949 (see page 76).

The life of John Rogge is America in microcosm. He is the logical result of our dominant thought and education. At the dawn of the century, this tall, young warrior marches out of the flat West, where there is neither hill nor width of water, but life is simple and straight. His object is the American object of "making money," for at what else should Life and Education aim? He rushed through his education, doing in eleven years what usually takes twenty, or certainly sixteen, if the college years are not skimped so as to enter a profession. At any rate, he began the practice of law at twenty-one. World war and world revolution broke out when he was in the grades, and ended while he was in high school. It is doubtful if he grasped its meaning. But in the nation's rush to get rich off the world's calamity, Rogge found his natural element: "In 1928, the firm for which I worked made so much money that toward the end of the year it stopped billing."

Then, in 1929, to the world came disaster, to his firm bankruptcy, and to Rogge sudden astonishment. In this pause, he toyed with the idea of teaching; but teaching offered no such income as law practice. So for five years of depression Rogge pursued the hard path to wealth, but with only moderate success, until he saw a rainbow that led to a Pot of Gold; until the nation under a man but twenty-two years older than Rogge began a "New Deal" for the wealth and happiness of the nation. Into this New Deal, Rogge was dropped at the age of thirty-three. He liked it, and for ten years stuck near it, for it gave him a vaster vision than that straight, simple path to wealth. This rainbow glowed with overtones of philanthropy and crusade, justice and loyalty, and apparently led just as surely to the Pot of Gold, but coupled with popularity and power.

War again swept the world from 1939 to 1945, and Roosevelt died of its wounds; but Rogge gave little heed to these matters. Corporations, pursuit of spies and cartels took his time, and gave him good income. Then again came disaster, when he was dismissed or suppressed. But he pushed ahead, believing that his Pot of Gold was still at the end of his rainbow, through popularity and political preferment. But it wasn't. Despite his crusade for peace and the promise of the progressive Wallace, Rogge realized that if he wanted to make money—and of course he did, for what else was there for a man to do?—he must make a right-about face.

Tentatively, he looked to several nations abroad for lucrative law practice. None responded except Yugoslavia. Of this deal Paul Robeson learned and scored Rogge in London. After that, Rogge hated Negroes, and was finally convinced that no Pot of Gold lay at the end of this rainbow, but only sacrifice and hard work. Rogge seized his chance to ingratiate himself with the money-grubbers by trying to send his colleagues in the Peace crusade to jail, and also by switching his type of law case: he so neglected his client, the young labor leader Christoffel, that the court rebuked him severely. In the defense of the Trenton Six, Negro youths framed for murder, he was rebuked by the court for publicity on which he had embarked against the advice of his fellow-counsel. When he was afterward permitted to take part, and had received a considerable fee, he nevertheless withdrew.

Rogge entered the celebrated Rosenberg case as counsel for Greenglass, the witness summoned by the government against the couple. Greenglass at first maintained his innocence; but Rogge entered into negotiations with the government and the F.B.I. Finally Greenglass and his wife signed statements implicating the Rosenbergs. Five other prosecution witnesses whom Rogge represented, including his own secretary, all buttressed each other and there emerged an apparent deal by which Greenglass got a light sentence, his wife went free, and the Rosenbergs were sentenced to death.

And so, in my mind—I trust not unjustly—to Wallace the Weasel I now add, Rogge the Rat.

CHAPTER XII

◆

The Trial

I have faced during my life many unpleasant experiences: the growl of a mob; the personal threat of murder; the scowling distaste of an audience. But nothing has so cowed me as that day, November 8, 1951, when I took my seat in a Washington courtroom as an indicted criminal. I was not a criminal. I had broken no law, consciously or unwittingly. Yet I sat with four other American citizens of unblemished character, never before accused even of misdemeanor, in the seats often occupied by murderers, forgers and thieves; accused of a felony and liable to be sentenced before leaving this court to five years of imprisonment, a fine of $10,000 and loss of my civil and political rights as a citizen, representing five generations of Americans.

It was a well-furnished room, not large, and poorly ventilated. Within the rail were tables for the lawyers, and back of these, seats for the defendants, with their backs to the audience behind. In front, on a low platform, sat the clerks and court stenographer; and behind, to a dais, came the black-gowned judge, announced by the marshal—"God save the United States of America!"

On either side were seats for the jurors, from whom twelve would soon be chosen to declare our guilt, or innocence, or a mistrial. All these seats were now filled with the jury panel, and an unusually large panel overflowed into the seats usually occupied by the public. There must have been 200 persons present; white and colored, from which juries for several cases would be drawn. Our first worry was this matter of the jury.

The jury system in the United States has fallen on evil days. The old English concept of a man's guilt being decided by presentation of the facts before twelve of his fellow citizens too often fails. Juries are selected in devious ways and by secret manipulation. Most Negroes are sent to jail by persons who hate or despise them. Many ordinary workers are found guilty by well-to-do "blue-ribbon" people who have no conception of the problems that face the poor. Juries are too often filled with professional jurors selected and chosen by the prosecution and expected to convict.

Our first hurdle was a long examination of the panel anent their affiliations, opinions and prejudices. The prosecution asked, among other things, if they had any prejudice against convicting a person of advanced years. The defendants asked a long series of more searching questions as to the prospective juror's attitude toward color, discrimination, and membership in certain organizations. One woman admitted that she was formerly a member of the K.K.K. and was excused.

No one on the panel admitted that he had at any time advocated segregation of the races, or racial discrimination in housing, transportation, employment, recreation, education; or in the use of places of public accommodation in the District of Columbia. Looking at the persons, this seemed to me hardly believable. Probably most of the whites had belonged to some such organizations but would not now admit it. They were asked about their attitude toward the House Committee on Un-American Activities, but none admitted prejudice. A number said that they had relatives in the armed forces, but declared that if they were convinced of the defendants' innocence they would be willing to say so even if a majority of the jury disagreed with them.

In our case there came another angle—the colored juror. In many parts of the nation, Negroes seldom or never serve on juries. But in the District of Columbia, lately, continually there are many Negro jurors drawn, so much so that there has been a distinct movement to curb their choice. Something of this was heard by the lawyers in our case, and they were prepared to fight it. But on the other hand, we sensed another and more hurtful method of opposition. There is a considerable proportion of Negroes in government employ: in the post office, as teachers in the public schools, as civil servants in dozens of branches. All such employees in Washington, white as well as black, are in fear of attack by witch hunts and loyalty tests, where often the accused have no chance to know or answer their accusers. Also, they are faced with severe competition and political influence. Negroes suffer especially, because their chance for employment outside government is narrow, and because their political influence is curtailed; and finally because of race discrimination which makes even civil service rules bow to prejudice. Suppose, now, a Negro government employee is given jury service in a case where he knows that the government is out for conviction and where the case appeals to current popular hysteria. In our case the government had allowed the distinct impression to prevail that it had unanswerable evidence in hand to prove our direct connection with Communist movements abroad against the United States. Suppose, then, a Negro with a government job and a home and family is drawn for this jury: no matter what the facts show, how will he vote? How will he dare to vote?

These facts faced us and one solution was to try to exclude government employees from the panel. This the judge offered to do, and he had the panel polled. The poll showed that if government employees were excluded, practically no Negroes would be left, since employment for educated Negroes in the District of Columbia is practically confined to government service. We faced a perfect dilemma: if we excluded government employees, we indirectly helped draw the color line; if we accepted government employees, more Negroes would face a greater risk of dismissal on trumped up charges than the whites. The white non-government worker would usually be in a job which did not employ Negroes, which would mean that he had had no contact with them and would be prejudiced. The lawyers consulted, and then Marcantonio came over and put this dilemma squarely before me. "Accept government employees!" I answered.

We did, and to my amazement got a jury of eight Negroes and four whites! I did not know whether to be glad or scared. The prosecution usually knows the jury panel fairly well, and it is thought that the panel may often be sprinkled with stooges. Was it possible that these eight Negroes might be owned? As I looked at their intelligent faces, veiled and non-committal as some were, I did not think so. My impulse was to follow the conclusion of Earl Dickerson, who said: "No eight American Negroes will ever agree to convict you!" Then he added reflectively, "If they do, I'll never defend another!" I was afraid his practice might be curtailed. Yet I could not believe that many American Negroes believed that I was a paid spy.

Next in importance came the problem of the judge who would preside. Judge Holtzoff, who had charge over our preliminary hearing in May, made a bad impression: pompous and opinionated; fond of talking about himself. He plainly disliked New York lawyers, and had a low opinion of women. On one occasion he summoned me to the bar, threatened to cancel my bond and send me to jail because of printed publicity found in the courtroom. Abbott Simon immediately stepped forward and took the blame for what was at worst an unintentional mistake, and more probably an attempt to frame us by some smart newspaper men. The judge finally dismissed us with a sharp warning against such "tirades" in his courtroom.

When, therefore, I heard that Judge McGuire had finally been assigned to our case, I was elated, until I heard that he was rumored to be the most reactionary judge on the District bench, and worse than Holtzoff! His appearance, however, was reassuring. He was from first to last, courteous and intelligent. He did not put on judicial airs; he never lost his temper; he was firm but kindly. Had it not been for the nature of our indictment and the impossibility of reconciling the attitude of Judge McGuire with that of the Department of Justice, through whose employment he had risen to the bench, I would call Judge James McGuire a great jurist, who in this case held the scales of justice absolutely level.

But my considered opinion is that what happened was that this judge at the last moment freed himself from the political pressures of the day to which so many had succumbed and that both he and the Department of State realized that the eyes of the world were fixed on this case.

In strictly legal aspect, remember what this trial was: it was not a question of our opinions and beliefs; it involved no question as to whether we were Communists, Socialists, Jehovah's Witnesses or Nudists; it involved no imputation of moral turpitude except in so far as it is a statutory crime to say what foreigners are saying at the command of those foreigners. The judge said:

> "The point in this case is whether or not this organization acted as an agent or in a capacity similar to that for a foreign organization or foreign political power, whether advocating peace, advocating this, or advocating that. They can advocate the distribution of wealth; they can advocate that all red-headed men be shot. It doesn't make any difference what they advocate."

It was not even fully admitted until the third week of the trial that the government did not allege that the Soviet Union was connected with the "foreign principal" accused in the indictment. It was never alleged that we had no right to advocate peace. It was only the question: were we "agents" of a foreign principal? Yet and despite all this, the public was deliberately given to understand by spokesmen of government and by the press that we were accused of lying, spying, and treason in the pay of the Soviet Union. As one of the attendants said in the ante-room of the court, scowling at us: "If the damned Communists don't like this country, why don't they go back to Russia?"

Jurisdictional questions were first raised, based on the fact that the organization was defunct, and on the question of the jurisdiction of the court over individual defendants. These motions were denied, although the court admitted that there was still some question as to the liability of the officers of the Peace Information Center, if it were proven that the Peace Information Center no longer existed. Marcantonio said:

> "The plea of not guilty did not in any manner, shape or form revive the dead. In other words, if John Jones were indicted and he died, and died before the indictment, certainly, he could not be found guilty and considered in being simply because counsel pleaded not guilty. And pleading not guilty they pleaded not guilty for all purposes, including the establishment of the non-existence of the individual."
>
> "The Court: You have just said what I have said, much better. So, we will leave it that way."

One of the basic reasons for the repeated miscarriages of justice in this country, is the lack of attention on the part of the respectable public to the procedures of court trials. Most persons assume that trials have to do with criminals, tricky lawyers, peremptory judges, and hard court officials. Such folk keep as far from courts as possible and let flagrant and cruel injustice escape without remark or attention. We knew this, and from the first appealed to our friends and the friends of justice everywhere to attend this trial and see what went on. As a result the sessions were crowded by a quiet, intelligent audience, who came from New York, New England, Chicago, the South and West, with usually a waiting line to be admitted. It was in every sense a public trial, and the Department of Justice knew it.

The jury having been selected, the trial began Thursday, November 8, and lasted five days, during three weeks, because of adjournments for weekends and holidays. A fussy little fat man, Maddrix, chief of the prosecution, and former Attorney-General of Maryland, stated the case for the prosecution:

> "The first count states that the Peace Information Center was an unincorporated organization, having its headquarters in New York City. It further alleges that the Peace Information Center was an agent of a foreign principal, in that it acted as and held itself out as a publicity agent for the Committee of the World Congress of the Defenders of Peace, and the World Peace Council . . . and because of it being an agent of a foreign principal, it was under a liability to file a registration statement with the Attorney General of the United States. . . .

"The material disseminated within the United States by Peace Information Center as publicity agent for its said foreign principal consisted of information about peace, war, instruments of war, and the consequences of peace and of war. . . .

"The agency relationship of the Peace Information Center with the Committee of the World Congress of the Defenders of Peace and the World Peace Council is not claimed to have existed pursuant to contractual relationship."

Maddrix added that the government intended to call twenty-seven witnesses.

Our lawyers postponed rejoinder, since the jury seemed more bewildered than impressed by the bill of particulars. We elected to await the development of the government case before stating ours. We were puzzled by the fairness of the judge, and were awaiting the nature of the evidence which the prosecution could produce. The prosecution reminded us that we had not named our prospective witnesses, as was the practice in the District of Columbia. We had determined to confine ourselves to as few witnesses as possible and to rely on the strength of our case rather than corroborative repetition. I had been chosen as the main witness, with two other witnesses to substantiate certain occurrences which took place during my absence in Europe. These were named; and then Marcantonio added that we might subpoena the Secretary of State and the Attorney-General. Later, when it seemed that I might need character witnesses, Albert Einstein offered to do "Whatever he could."

We may never know just what reactions took place in government circles concerning this indictment. At first, certainly, the government meant to scare us by the "Communist" bogey. Then by threatening indictment they aimed to cut off contributions to the Peace Information Center, or make us try to escape persecution. When we began to fight back and the volume of protest from white and black arose, and from Europe and Asia as well as Africa, the government began frantically to collect evidence which they had never possessed. They sent out agents. They interviewed and tried to intimidate every person connected in any way with the founding of the Peace Information Center. They subpoenaed a host of witnesses, including some of the defendants, which was illegal. They kept giving out intimations of the unanswerable evidence which they possessed. They scared off lawyers: one widely known attorney listened to our offer, and then told us he was dining with the Attorney-General. He finally refused his services. When the head of the Criminal Division of the Department of Justice went to Paris and interviewed the Secretary of the Defenders of Peace, he returned quite willing to postpone the case, and as we hoped, never to press it. When, by insistence of his superiors, long postponement was refused, he did not enter the case, and the three lawyers who took charge of the prosecution were distinctly not experienced or first class men.

Whatever design there was to confront us with manufactured testimony from professional spies, liars and agents-provocateurs, it was abandoned. But the very fairness of the trial raised the query as to why the government ever was induced to bring this case on so flimsy a basis? They had no case and they knew it. Their only hope of success was to raise national hysteria against us to the flaming point. This our campaign rendered impossible. No ex-spy could get away with testimony about seeing me emerge from the Kremlin with a bag of gold; no stooge could make black America believe that I was an undercover conspirator, when for fifty years I had always blurted out the truth on all occasions.

The judge continued to be fair and courteous. The prosecution was inept if not stupid. The defense was prepared to the last comma; it knew law and procedure; it was on its toes every minute with its eyes on the possible appeal to higher courts. The government spent precious time and money on proving the obvious: that the Peace Information Center existed; that it had a bank account; that it rented offices; that it distributed literature. Cautious F.B.I. men and newspaper reporters introduced literature which anyone could have gotten at any time, and which we freely admitted we had written and distributed.

The chief dependence of the prosecution was on John Rogge. Rogge the witness was a caricature of Rogge the crusader for Peace and Reform. In place of the erect, self-confident if not arrogant leader, came a worn man, whose clothes hung loosely on him, and who in a courtroom where he had conducted many cases, had difficulty locating me in the defendants' chairs. I voluntarily stood up to help him out.

He admitted his membership in the Peace Information Center. He admitted his attendance at the World Peace Congress; and declared that its actual objective was not peace, but that it was an agency for the foreign policy of the Soviet Union.

Mr. Maddrix in his opening said that the government did not intend to show and would not show that there was any contract of agency between the World Congress of the Defenders of Peace and the Peace Information Center. The Court said:

> "The responsibility of the government is to prove beyond a reasonable doubt, first of all, the nexus; and in doing that, you will have to establish, of course, that there was a foreign group, whether that group takes the aspect of a foreign political party, a foreign government or a foreign association within the purview of the statute."

The government introduced twenty copies of the magazine *In Defense of Peace*, issued by the Defenders of Peace, which led to argument as to whether their contents should be admitted. The judge said that he did not think that the prosecution ought to go into the nature and character of the activities of the principal, but to establish first the fact of agency. The prosecution insisted that it should have the right to show that the propaganda of the Defenders of Peace was political, but the judge insisted that first the prosecution should prove or indicate to the jury that the foreign group was a government, or party, or some organization within the purview of the statute, and that then it should establish a nexus between the Defenders of Peace and the Peace Information Center.

The prosecution then tried to say that the Defenders of Peace had said there was a terrible plot against humanity, and that the United States was the center of this plot, and for that reason the Defenders of Peace were attacking the United States. The defendants' lawyers objected to this. The judge reminded the prosecution that they had established the existence of a foreign group with headquarters in Paris. They should now indicate to the jury the evidence seeking to show the connection between that foreign group and the Peace Information Center.

This led to a long argument in which Marcantonio stressed the fact that it was absurd to argue that parallelism in thought or expression established the relationship of agency. "Two people may have parallel views, one at the north pole and one at the south pole. That does not establish agency." The Court agreed that two parallel lines never meet, but said that he assumed that the connection between the two lines of thought was going to be indicated. The Court said that unless this nexus was shown, "I think that at the proper time you would be entitled to a directed verdict." This was the first intimation that our case might never reach the jury; but this seemed at the time too good ever to become true. Mr. Jaffe, our Constitutional lawyer, insisted that if the government was first going into a characterization of the Defenders of Peace, that that would be damaging in the minds of the jury, and prejudice them. The judge responded:

> "I indicated that to Mr. Maddrix; but he says that he cannot (omit this), by virtue of the way his case is set up. Then Mr. Marcantonio very well says that if he expects to show the so-called connection by virtue of the similarity of activity in the nature of propaganda, then that would be, as he very aptly described it, parallelism; and the two could never meet, either in time or eternity. So there has to be a nexus shown; and I am assuming that will be shown. If it isn't shown, the Government doesn't make out a case and that is all."

Mr. Maddrix stressed the fact that the propaganda of the Defenders of Peace was that Anglo-American imperialism was the foremost champion of a new war, and the Soviet Union a great peace-loving power, the champion of peace; and that the evidence of this propaganda was admissable. Marcantonio replied:

> "After he makes that statement, all we need is a band to play 'Stars and Stripes Forever'—the United States is warlike; the Soviet Union is peaceful—you have a speech in Congress."

The defendants' lawyers had not read the twenty copies of the magazine *In Defense of Peace* which the prosecution had introduced, and had little time now to do so. I therefore undertook to read them over the weekend, and said in a memorandum to our lawyers:

> "My opinion is that we have nothing to fear from this magazine. Its references to the United States are on the whole temperate, even when critical; it does not mention this country often: during 1950, out of 156 articles only 6 were on the United States. In general, the United States is treated generously and hopefully. After the outbreak of the war in Korea, criticism is more frequent and specific but seldom or never nasty.
> "There is clear evidence of the character of the Defenders of Peace, and no assumption of any nexus of agent and principal. I have noted instances where this might be inferred by the reader but they are not important. On the other hand, the statements on peace are strong and well put. I do not believe that the prosecution can get any support for its contentions from these magazines."

On the other hand, the prosecution might easily quote single sentences or references inimical to the United States; and we had to insist that whatever this magazine said was not material until it had been proven that we were agents of the Defenders of Peace, and shared responsibility for its propaganda. The judge took the matter under advisement while he examined the magazines. He must have found much that he would be unwilling to place before the jury, for reasons which the prosecution might have shared, had they read the copies themselves carefully. The judge finally excluded all except four copies, and admitted them only to identify the Stockholm Appeal and the fact that it was sponsored by the publishers of this magazine, and that the magazine was published in a foreign country. When the prosecution wished to have all the contents of the magazine admitted, the judge said that he was not going to put mere propaganda before the jury.

It was at this juncture that Judge McGuire called the lawyers to his chambers and went straight to the kernel of Rogge's testimony. Rogge had said that the object of the Defenders of Peace was ostensibly peace, but really to carry out the policies of the Soviet Union. This was, as we suspected from the beginning, the whole intention of the Rogge testimony, and the method by which the government hoped to put us in jail. If, by this testimony, Russian and Communist controversy could be smeared across the case, current popular hysteria could be aroused against us. Witnesses like J. B. Matthews, long the propagandist of the Dies Committee, could be brought on the stand with his lurid stories about Communists, corroborated by the F.B.I. and its Budenzes and Bentleys.

The judge, therefore, came straight to the point: referring to Rogge he said:

> "This witness was permitted to state that while the stated purpose was peace, the real purpose was to promote the foreign policy of the Soviet Union.
> "Do you expect to show that the World Council for Peace was in fact an agent of another principal, namely the Soviet Union?"

Mr. Maddrix did not answer this directly, but the judge continued, saying that he let in reference to the Soviet Union because he thought the prosecution was going to show that the Soviet Union actually was the foreign principal, and that the World Council for Peace was merely the conduit to use the activity of the Peace Information Center. If this was not their case, he was going to tell the jury to disregard any reference to the Soviet Union. Mr. Maddrix objected to being restricted, but the Court insisted:

> "You cannot blow hot and cold. I have got to be advised now as to what you expect to show. . . . You are not, I take it, predicating your case or the theory of your case on the ground that the World Council for Peace was, in effect, the agent of the Soviet Union?"
> Mr. Maddrix. "We are not making that statement, no."
> The Court: "What you do not intend to prove, and I am so advised now, is that you are not going to attempt to prove formally that the activities of the World Council for Peace were the activities of the Soviet Union?"
> Mr. Maddrix: "I could not state it any better. . . . We do not intend to show that the Committee of the Congress of the World Defenders of Peace was an agent of the Soviet Union."

As a result of this admission the Court said:

> "I thought I ought to be advised at this juncture just exactly what the Government expected to show with reference to the Soviet Union being the principal or the so-called principal of the Peace Information Center. I understand the Government expects not to show, under any circumstances, the existence of another principal behind the principal we are concerned with, namely, the Soviet Union. If that is not my understanding here of what transpired at the bench, I would like to be so advised."

The prosecution then again admitted:

> "We do not charge in our indictment that the foreign principal in any way involves an element of agency as I understand this case, between the foreign principal, the Committee of the World Congress, and the Soviet Union."
>
> The Court: "You have answered my question. You are contending that the only foreign principal involved in this case is the World Congress for Peace?"
>
> Mr. Cunningham: "Absolutely."
>
> The Court: "I am not going to try the Soviet Union or make any comparison between the Soviet Union with respect to peace and America. I am going to stick to the issue."

With the jury out of the room, there was a conference of the judge and lawyers concerning other points in Rogge's testimony. Rogge had said that the purpose of the Stockholm Appeal was to concentrate the eyes of the world on the atom bomb in the possession of the United States, and to take the eyes of the world off any aggression that might and which did come from the East. The Court asked Mr. Maddrix if he considered Mr. Rogge an expert. He said no, but that no one was in a better position than Mr. Rogge to know what was going on and to answer this particular question. He was a member of the policy-making group, and had attended its meetings. The Court then said:

> "I am not trying any propaganda lines. I am not trying any foreign policy questions involving any country, including our own. You have a very simple case here. You charged this Peace Information Center and these individuals, as officers and directors, as being agent of a foreign principal, and disseminating propaganda in the United States. You have got to show a tie-up between the principal so-called and the so-called agent. If you don't do that, you are out of court."

The prosecution insisted that the agency of the Peace Information Center was going to be proved by circumstantial evidence. The judge said:

> "You have to show the connection. . . . I may be in Timbuctoo and you may be in some place in South America. I may be shaving and using Gillette brushless shaving cream and you may be doing the same thing, but there is no connection except we are both using Gillette."

Thereupon, when the jury had returned, the judge addressed them, saying that when Rogge was on the stand he was asked what the purpose of the World Council for Peace was, and he answered. The judge went on:

"You are now instructed by the Court, as emphatically as I can make words that lend emphasis to what I say, that you are to disregard Mr. Rogge's opinion of what he thought the purpose of the Stockholm Peace Appeal was. It is a very simple rule of evidence that excludes that type of opinion, because opinion is excluded, and the only opinion that is permitted to be introduced in a court of law, in certain circumstances, is the opinion of an expert. So, therefore, you will disregard entirely the characterization of the witness Rogge with reference to what he thought World Council for Peace had in view."

Although we did not at the time realize it, and still watched narrowly for trumped up testimony, it was right here that we won our case. The prosecution had rested its whole case on Rogge's testimony that we were representing the Soviet Union through the Defenders of Peace organization in Paris. They had naturally not an iota of real proof of this, but they planned to depend on public opinion. But Rogge's own testimony convicted him. He was a member of the Peace Information Center; he was a member of the policy-making bureau of the Defenders of Peace. He had visited the Soviet Union and spoken as a representative of the Defenders of Peace and the Peace Information Center. He had sworn on oath when he himself became an agent of Yugoslavia that he was not a member of any other foreign agency.

Mr. Rogge continued his testimony, mentioning the meeting of the Bureau of the Defenders of Peace in Prague. When asked as to the substance of my speech he said: "The substance of Dr. Du Bois' speech was that all the difficulties of the world stem from what he described as the capitalistic war-mongers in the United States."

Mr. Marcantonio asked that that be stricken out, and the Court said that he was not going to get off on any ideological discussion with reference to capitalism or any other form of enterprise; that the essential question was whether or not Dr. Du Bois was present. "What was said and who else was there is immaterial." The judge told the jury to disregard what Mr. Rogge had said. Later he excluded testimony about mention at Stockholm of setting up a peace movement in the United States.

Rogge was asked if he had a meeting in his home in February, 1949, with regard to the establishment of a peace organization in the United States. He answered that he had permitted such a meeting to be held. He admitted allowing telegrams to be sent out over his name inviting people to the meeting; and that it did result in appointing a committee on organization.

Then Mr. Marcantonio turned to the Congress of the Defenders of Peace in Paris, and brought out the fact that Mr. Rogge had sent a letter to Dr. Du Bois asking him to attend that Congress, showing him the letter.

Rogge admitted that when he attended the meeting in Prague in August, 1951, he was agent of a foreign country, and Marcantonio tried to get the letter which he had written in Prague, agreeing with the purposes of the World Defenders of Peace, admitted as evidence, but it was excluded.

Later in chambers Mr. Marcantonio interjected, angrily: "You have no case and why don't you admit it? I think this is one of the most deliberate diabolical plots ever pulled which is being pulled on these defendants."

He apologized for losing his temper, but added that the "prosecution wants to convict these defendants on their political views."

"You are trying to frighten us," said Mr. Maddrix.

Marcantonio replied, "I am not trying to frighten you at all. I am exposing you."

The Court finally said: "Mr. Marcantonio, you have indicated your surprise and your righteous indignation. They say of nuns they never get angry; it is always righteous indignation."

Mr. Cunningham of the prosecution intervened and tried to say that the Peace Information Center acted and held itself out to be a publicity agent, "that the proof of that does not require the showing of any nexus or any direct connection between the Peace Information Center and the foreign principal."

The Court: "Let's stop right there. Why doesn't the statute require that?"

Mr. Cunningham tried to refer to the legislative history of the bill, but this the Court refused to allow, and said: "You have got to show nexus and you have got to show nexus either by direct or circumstantial evidence. If you do not do that, the case fails."

The next witness, Victor Lasky, a screen writer formerly on the New York *World-Telegram and Sun*, testified that he had visited the offices of the Peace Information Center and received copies of the Stockholm Petition, and that "I made it quite clear that I abhorred the Petition." The Court excluded that because, as he said, the jury is not concerned with the witness' views on the petition.

Mr. Maddrix tried to get in the record the fact that Lasky had written a book against Communism, but that was excluded.

An F.B.I. agent, John J. Kearney, came next, and told about attending a meeting of the Peace Information Center at the Hotel Capitol. He tried to refer to Peace Information Center propaganda among Catholics, but the judge excluded all matters about race and religion:

> "Now, as I said before, no matter what form of political propaganda it takes, if it is propaganda upon the part of the foreign principal, then, the American people, under the statute, are entitled to know who is paying the bill or who is behind the gun. That is all there is to it. For that reason I excluded everything else, foreign policy of Russia, foreign policy of the United States, the appeals to Catholics, appeals to Jews, appeals to all sorts of groups, minority or otherwise; that is out of the picture."

He also excluded hearsay evidence and pictures of certain persons produced in the magazine, *In Defense of Peace*, which Mr. Maddrix introduced. Mr. Marcantonio asked, "Is Dick Tracy coming in next?" When the judge was asked to admit the picture of Dr. Du Bois, the Court rejoined that he was in the courtroom, and that the picture was not material.

The prosecution asked if reference to the withdrawal of soldiers from Korea by the Committee of the World Congress and the Peace Information Center should be offered. The Court rejoined that it had not been offered. All that had been offered was the Stockholm Appeal and the statement made in the "Peacegrams" that the Peace Information Center was not affiliated with the World Congress of Peace.

Then came a nervous medical student, William B. Reed, who testified that he had visited the offices of the Peace Information Center four times, and once had listened in on a telephone conversation. He finally admitted that he had been in the employ of the F.B.I. He identified certain material which he had been given in the office of the Peace Information Center, and said that he had entrusted it to "somebody," which somebody finally proved to be J. B. Matthews, formerly Chief Investigator of the House Committee on Un-American Activities, who expected to testify but was never called by the government.

A letter to the public on the Peace Information Center letterhead was admitted in evidence to show our criminal activities:

"Dear Friend,

"You will be interested to learn that a Peace Information Center has been set up in New York City. It will, we believe, be of help to the millions of people in our country who ardently seek peace and an end to the cold war.

"The purpose of the office is to bring news of peace activities here and throughout the world. We plan to do this by issuing Fact Sheets and Bulletins from time to time; by co-operating in arranging for delegations from the United States to attend Peace Conferences; and co-operating in the tours of persons who come to this country to speak for peace.

"The interests of peace transcend all boundaries and all present and past differences. All people must unite who agree with the proposition that war must and can be averted, that the horrors of a Third World War are unthinkable, and with its corollaries that universal disarmament should start immediately and atomic weapons be outlawed. . . .

"Peace sentiment is growing throughout the United States, petitions are being circulated and meetings held. We would appreciate any information about peace activities in your area. Copies of material being used or news items would be most helpful to us.

"We hope you will indicate your interest and desire to continue to receive our material by sending us the enclosed card.

> Sincerely yours,
> (signed) W. E. B. Du Bois
> Chairman"

The prosecution, out of hearing of the jury, called attention to the fact that the Department of Justice had made repeated demands on the defendants to register as foreign agents; intimating that our failure was wilful. The judge reminded them that the statute did not require the government to make any demands on anybody to register. The statute merely said that if the person representing a foreign principal did not register and did not maintain that it came within the exemptions, then that person was liable to the penalty imposed. The Court also pointed out that wilful failure to register must be proven, and said that he assumed that the defense was going to allege that the failure to register was not wilful.

The question of Miss Soloff's connection with the case was then discussed, and she was, the following day, acquitted by the Court on the ground that she was evidently a salaried employee and not a policy-making official. This ruling, which was based on a perfectly clear fact, we had tried to get at our first arraignment in May. Judge Holtzoff refused, and for eight months Miss Soloff was an indicted criminal, with absolutely no grounds for the charge.

The government then, to our surprise, rested its case, having called but seven of its twenty-seven witnesses. We immediately began to prepare for our presentation of our case. I was to be the main witness, and the only one of the defendants to take the stand. There was, however, a period when I was absent in Prague, and corroborative witnesses would be needed for certain actions.

We would call two members of our advisory board, the business manager of the *National Guardian,* and a professor of anthropology at Columbia, for this purpose.

Then, too, we had the sworn testimony of the executive secretary of the World Defenders of Peace, accused of being our "foreign principal." At considerable cost we had sent three of our lawyers to Paris in July. The government also sent three of their representatives, including the head of the Criminal Division of the Department of Justice, to take depositions from Jean Laffitte, the Secretary of the World Defenders of Peace. At this interesting inquiry, held at the offices of the United States Embassy, sworn testimony was taken, which we were ready to introduce but never got the opportunity. Mr. Laffitte, a man of training and manners, member of the Legion of Honor, declared that the Committee of which he was Secretary General was

> ". . . instituted by the First World Congress of the Defenders of Peace. Its definite task was to circulate and make known the information given and the decisions taken by the Congress. It was also in charge of circulating the various information concerning activities on behalf of Peace throughout the world. Its task was also to denounce all propaganda which predisposed public opinion in favor of war and to support all initiatives tending towards peace. It had the duty of encouraging all cultural activities in favor of peace. And it was in charge of preparing a further World Congress of Peace."

He was asked if he had ever heard of the Peace Information Center and if the Center had authority to act as publicity agent. He answered that he had heard of the Peace Information Center, but that it had never had such authority; that the Committee had not appointed the Peace Information Center as its agent for the circulation of the Stockholm Appeal, nor had the Peace Information Center asked to act as publicity agent; that it expended no funds belonging to the Committee, and had no authority to make contracts; that it made no reports orally or in writing to this Committee.

He was then asked about national committees which were in co-operation with the World Committee. He said there were such committees in about eighty countries, but that there was none in the United States. He said that his committee had co-operated with the Peace Information Center in a very simple way:

> "We had heard of the formation of an Information Center in the United States which had assumed the task of circulating information relating to the furtherance of peace. This naturally resulted in our sending the Center information concerning peace movements, and allowed us to hope that in this way such information would become more widely known than other matter which we sent to the United States."

Then came an interesting colloquy. Mr. Laffitte was asked, "Do you regard Soviet Russia as the strongest advocate for peace among governments?" Mr. Laffitte's attorney immediately objected to his client's answering. Mr. McInerney, head of the Criminal Division of the Department of Justice of the United States, demurred and said that he was unable to understand Laffitte's "reluctance to express a viewpoint which he has proclaimed to the world." Mr. Laffitte's attorney replied that his client had made a point of answering all questions which were closely or remotely related to this matter, but that there was no obligation on his part to answer as to his personal opinions and beliefs:

> "If he were called to testify before a French court, and if inconceivably he were asked to what political party he belonged or what was his belief concerning a given problem (a thing which could never happen), I would urge him not to answer such a question, since he is a French citizen entirely free as to his opinions; a freedom guaranteed by the Constitution of his country."

Mr. McInerney, taken aback, and probably remembering the Constitution of his own country, replied, "I wish to apologize if I have intruded upon his constitutional rights under French law."

When Mr. Laffitte was further asked if he had been in direct communication at any time with the Peace Information Center, he said that he had not. He was asked if the Peace Information Center was organized at the time that Dr. Du Bois was present in Paris at the Peace Congress. He replied that it was not, and that the Paris Committee did not hear of its organization until a year later. He was then asked if he had had personal correspondence with Dr. Du Bois, and he replied:

> "I told you that I had not had any personal correspondence, properly so-called, with Dr. Du Bois. We confined ourselves to sending Professor Dr. Du Bois, who is a member of the World Committee, the information which we transmit without distinction to all members of the World Committee; that is to say, the Secretariat regularly sends all members of the World Committee information concerning the different meetings of the Bureau or the decisions taken at such meetings, and also any publications which may arise therefrom,—always with a covering letter which we send as a matter of courtesy and a mark of respect for these personalities."

He denied that he had ever requested the Peace Information Center to disseminate the Stockholm Appeal as an agent of the Committee. This interesting testimony we were given no chance to introduce.

The prosecution had rested before the morning session was finished. We prepared during the remainder of the morning to present certain motions, and then if they were denied, to go into our defense, introducing the Paris depositions, then character witnesses for me, after which I would take the stand. I was ready.

CHAPTER XIII

◆

The Acquittal

Armistice Day, November 11, had interrupted the trial and given a three day recess. I took the occasion to fill a conditional promise to speak at the Community Church in Boston, where for some years I have made annual addresses. Mr. Lathrop, the minister, in introducing me, reminded the congregation that a spiritual founder of this church, Theodore Parker, had also once been an indicted criminal. I said in part:

> "The real causes of World War will persist and threaten so long as peoples of Europe and America are determined to control the wealth of most of the world by means of cheap labor and monopolies. Against this a resurgence of the revolt of the poor will raise a new Russia from the dead if we kill this one, and birth a new theory of communism so long as Africa, Asia and South America see the impossibility of otherwise escaping poverty, ignorance and disease. . . .
>
> "We who have known a better America find the present scene almost unbelievable. A great silence has fallen on the real soul of the nation. We are smearing loyal citizens on the paid testimony of self-confessed liars, traitors and spies. We are making the voice of America the babble of cowards paid to travel. . . .
>
> "My words are not a counsel of despair. Rather they are a call to new courage and determination to know the Truth. Four times this nation has faced disaster and recovered: Once at the end of the 18th century when we hesitated between separate independent colonies and a disciplined federal state; again when in the age of Jackson the uncouth, democratic west overbore the oligarchical well-mannered east; once more in the 19th century when human slavery cut the heart of the nation in two and we had to cement it with blood; finally, when in 1929 our boasted industries fell in vast ruin and begged on their knees for government aid, until Roosevelt rescued them with socialist planning, and gave his life to rebuilding our economy.
>
> "What we have done, we can do again. But not by silence—not by refusing to face the ugly facts."

On Tuesday afternoon, November 20, the defense began its argument for a judgment of acquittal. It first based a plea for dismissal on the ground of "lack of jurisdiction." The Peace Information Center in order to be under the jurisdiction of the court must be in existence, and the government must prove its existence. The judge remarked: "You say that the Peace Information Center is dead.

I say to you, there is a general presumption that a condition of affairs once existing is presumed to continue to exist until the contrary is shown."

Marcantonio replied: "There is only one presumption in criminal law, the presumption of innocence."

Here Marcantonio gave the prosecution an opportunity to give up the case on a technicality which would have saved their faces. He tried to get Maddrix to admit that the Peace Information Center had ceased to exist before its indictment. Had Maddrix admitted this, the case would undoubtedly have been thrown out of court then and there. But Maddrix stubbornly and indignantly refused to make the admission. On the other hand, while this fact was true, it would have been difficult for us to prove. When does an organization close? We voted in October to close and did no new work after that; but all vestiges of the old work could not suddenly stop. Letters concerning peace and peace movements continued to pour into the office and we answered them; we could not easily cancel our lease. So that while we transacted no new business we were closing out odds and ends in January and February.

Marcantonio then turned to the argument for a directed acquittal:

"The organization did not register because it is not an 'agent.' If it is not an agent as defined in the statute, therefore, the defendants could not have failed to cause it to register; and, hence, the judgment of acquittal should, by right, be directed to the individuals as well as the organization."

Attacking the Government's brief, he continued:

"The Government is seeking to spell out here a theory of the law which is something out of this world. And I read that language:

'While it is believed that evidence of a connection between Peace Information Center and the Committee has material probative value, the statute does not include "connection" as a necessary element in the proof of this phase of the charge.'

"Now, I submit, and I think that your Honor has indicated quite clearly, that connection must be established. Here, again, the Government reveals itself in its very last sentence.

"Now what is the Government saying here? It is saying that a statute states that the relationship does not have to be one pursuant to a contractual relationship; therefore no connection has to be established; no connection has to be established because no contractual relationship is required to be shown.

"I contend, and I believe Your Honor has indicated time and time again, that unless connection has been shown, there is no relationship of agency and principal. . . ."

Marcantonio insisted that the basic definition of "agency" in the law of 1938 was not changed by the law of 1942, and that 1) the Government must establish that the Peace Information Center was acting in behalf of the Partisans of Peace; 2) that the Peace Information Center was subject to control of the Partisans of Peace; 3) that the Partisans of Peace had consented to the fact that the Peace Information Center should act on its behalf; 4) that the Peace Information Center consented to the control of the Partisans of Peace; 5) that the Peace Information Center consented to act for the Partisans of Peace, and 6) that there was a consent on the part of the Peace Information Center to be subject to the control of the Partisans of Peace. "All these are musts; if any one of these fails, the case fails."

The Court brought up the case of interlocking directorate, where, for instance, Dr. Du Bois was a member of the Partisans of Peace, and also a member of the Peace Information Center. The judge admitted that this in itself did not necessarily prove that one was subject to the control of either, but he asked if that wasn't a circumstance which, along with other evidence, might prove it. Marcantonio answered:

> "No, sir. I will tell you why it is not. Because you have no evidence of control. Let me put it this way. All you have here, so far as Dr. Du Bois is concerned, is that he was a member of the Congress of the Defenders of Peace, and that he is president of this organization; period."

He said there was no testimony that the organization of which Dr. Du Bois was a member decided to have an organization over here; nor that there were directions given which Dr. Du Bois had to carry out over here.

The argument went over into the afternoon. The judge intervened with the following analogy, directed to Mr. Maddrix of the Prosecution. He said suppose you were living in Vienna and published a pamphlet on taxation which I liked. I ask your permission to republish your pamphlet in New York at my expense. The Government asks me to register as your agent. I refuse. I maintain that while I agree with your thought I am not your agent and therefore will not register. Is not that right?

Mr. Maddrix replied that the Government insisted that the agency was implied by the similarity of ideas.

Here Mr. Cunningham of the Government prosecution, a lank Texan with a perpetually anxious scowl, came up with the extraordinary plea that no connection need be proven. He maintained that a publicity agent as defined by the law of 1942 was not an agency in the sense of the law of 1938:

> "You have to go further and show, as your Honor points out, that one was doing it for the other, not necessarily by contract, and not necessarily by any agreement at all. The foreign principal may never have heard of the person here, as I have said before. We have to show it was the subjective intent of these people here to disseminate information in the United States, propaganda for and on behalf of, and further the propaganda objectives of the European organization."

The judge leaned forward and asked how a person disseminating propaganda of the type that the statute prohibits could be found guilty of acting for a foreign principal, "if the principal never heard of the disseminator and the disseminator never heard of the principal?" The judge continued, "Your contention is this: that if there is an argument about salt and pepper, Congress, by virtue of its power, said, 'pepper could be salt and salt could be pepper'."

Mr. Cunningham answered, "Yes, sir. That is exactly what is confusing the issue here."

Mr. Marcantonio retorted: "Except that the English language is still the same. Salt is salt and pepper is pepper. Principal is principal and agent is agent."

The court recessed until the afternoon. Mr. Marcantonio then insisted that the Government had not proved its contention of agency.

> "Again, I repeat, repeat, repeat and repeat again there was no evidence of control and direction. Furthermore, even if they went so far (and let's assume for the sake of argument only) that the Stockholm Appeal which we circulated was the propaganda of a foreign organization, we still would not be guilty and there still would be no evidence of our being guilty under this act, unless they showed control, unless they showed relationship. Merely circulating the Stockholm Peace Petition in and of itself is not evidence. It is not any evidence of control. It is not any evidence of consensual relationship. . . . What is more—in the Government's case, we grasp something that is positive. We find in all of the documentary evidence adduced time and time again there appears the affirmative statement that the Peace Information Center is not affiliated with anybody."

Mr. Maddrix of the prosecution followed and stressed the testimony of Rogge; he showed the various things done by the Peace Information Center which corresponded to the actions of the World Defenders of Peace. He referred to Mrs. Moos and Dr. Du Bois and to the fact that while Dr. Du Bois was Chairman of the Peace Information Center, he had been to Paris; he was a member of the World Congress; and had made other trips. He spoke of Abbott Simon's activities. He said:

> ". . . people who represent in the United States foreign interests in the form of disseminating propaganda, do not do so as openly as business contracts are made. There is not available the type of specific agreements which we would ordinarily desire; and the framers of this Act, Congressman McCormick and the rest, knew what they were up against; and so in 1942, they did amend it considerably. I am not going into that. I am saying that to show that under the 1942 Act, less evidence was needed than is needed under the 1938 Act."

Here the arguments ended. The jury had not yet been summoned. Without giving us any chance to offer our testimony or the sworn depositions of the Defenders of Peace; without waiting for the character witnesses, Judge McGuire, sitting at his high rostrum, rendered his verdict. We still were waiting for that overwhelming proof of guilt which for nine months the Department of Justice had promised. It never came. The judge said:

> "Now, we are faced with a situation as it comes in every criminal case, where the responsibility is upon the Court to interpose its ruling in the matter of a determination as to whether the case shall continue and as to whether or not, under those circumstances, the defendants shall be obliged to place defense on the stand as to the charge made against them before the jury.

"I don't know whether or not these individual defendants who sit here at the bar of this court are sincere or misguided, or whether or not they have deliberately and designedly set out to subvert the very liberties under which they live and we live.

"It is an old aphorism, however, that has been more or less channeled by the Supreme Court in the Bennis case, and that is this: I may hate the very things you say, but I respect your right to say them, and as Americans, we have confidence both in our material strength, which is important, and our spiritual strength; that is, in the validity of the institutions in which we live. . . .

"First of all, with reference to the motion for dismissal predicated upon juris-dictional ground, that is denied and the record will so indicate."

We sighed. Here came, we were sure, what we were expecting—denial of our plea and introduction of a misleading interpretation of the evidence. We sat back and listened. The judge continued:

"The Government has alleged that 'Peace Information Center' was the agent of a foreign principal. They proved the existence, in my judgment, of the Peace Infor-mation Center. They certainly proved the existence of the World Council for Peace. Mrs. Moos may very well have gone to Prague, may very well have gone to Moscow. There may have been, and I take it as proven, there were individuals who were officers of both; but, applying the test, as laid down here, in a case which, presum-ably, is the law of the land (because on appeal to the Supreme Court of the United States certiorari was denied in the case)—in this case the Government has failed to support, on the evidence adduced, the allegations laid down in the indictment. So, therefore, the motion, under the circumstances, for a judgment of acquittal will be granted."

For a moment a wave of surprised excitement passed over the audience, which had been listening breathlessly. Applause seemed on the edge of burst-ing out. Behind me, as I afterwards learned, my wife fainted. I, myself, felt slightly numb. Someone on my left kissed my cheek.

But the judge, changing his position slightly, but with no change of tone, quickly warned against any demonstration, and continued to speak. I thought that perhaps I had misunderstood, and that some modification of his words was coming. The judge proceeded:

"The judge's function is exhausted when he determines that the evidence does or does not permit the conclusion of guilt beyond reasonable doubt within a fair operation of a reasonable mind. So, therefore, if the case should go to the jury, I would be permitting the jury to conjecture in a field of conjecture, and, in addition to that, I would have to inform the jury and to instruct them that, if they could resolve the evidence in the case with any reasonable hypothesis looking toward the defendants, then, under the circumstances, they are obliged to do so, and then, as a consequence, they would have to be so instructed.

"So the case goes off, in my view, on a conception of the law.

"The government maintains one point of view and the defense maintains another. I think that the position of the defense is maintained and supported by the opinion mentioned and that opinion is conclusive in my mind; and that is my ruling."

The jury was then brought in, the ruling of the Court explained to them, and they were discharged. We were free for the first time in nine months.

We left Washington as quickly as possible. I was, frankly, bewildered. Of all the results of this fantastic and utterly unfair indictment, this was quite the last which I had awaited. At first I had confidently expected that after conference and explanation, the indictment would be quashed. Then, when it was relentlessly pushed, and the case set for trial, I had expected that after a series of delays and postponements, the actual trial would never take place. This would have been unsatisfactory, and left us long in unease, but it would have been better than a criminal procedure. Then, when the indictment was pushed and the trial opened, our best hope was for a failure to agree on the part of the jury where Negroes outnumbered whites two to one. This would have left a bad taste and brought the charge that narrow race loyalty had defeated Justice—an argument for excluding Negro jurors hereafter. With the acceptance of the jury there could be but one conclusion, and that was that the government thought it had absolute proof to convict us.

Indeed, there is evidence that this is what the highest authorities said, and allowed the public to believe. But we knew that even if the government thought it had such proof, it was either mistaken or the alleged proof was based on a deliberate lie. We had never asked or been offered opportunity to act as agent of any foreign person, organization or government; our organization had never received a cent of money from abroad or from representatives of foreigners for its work, so far as we knew or believed. Indeed, the total amount of our funds was far too modest, and its expenditure too easily proven to indicate any foreign aid. It would have been possible to prove the source of every penny, if we had been pushed to divulge each contributor. But this would have been a betrayal of trust, and grossly unfair to donors, who were often so afraid of the F.B.I. as to refuse to give anything to any cause. But the facts were clear enough without this resort. We had received no large sums; never more than single gifts of a hundred dollars, and very seldom as much as that. We had books and testimony to show receipts and every dollar of expenses.

Of course, there were many who continually intimated that while I or even most of my colleagues knew nothing of treachery and bribery, nevertheless someone in the organization might have been a spy or foreign agent. Anybody can sometimes be deceived, but to those of us who knew this group, such accusation or suspicion was simply silly.

Why, then, had the Department of Justice been so arrogant, determined, and certain? Why did it so impudently brush off my offer to explain our whole work? If, after explanation, the Department had indicated any way in which we had transgressed the law, I was quite ready to change our methods or give up the whole project. But one thing we could not do, and that was to say under oath that we had been and were "agents of a foreign principal." This was a lie that no government could compel us to tell no matter what the penalty.

When, therefore, the Department of Justice refused conference, and insisted on trial, we had to fight, and fight not only with facts and law, but to be ready to meet any deliberate attempt at deception, which we had no means of anticipating.

This was our expectation during every minute of that three weeks trial. I was looking for it down to the very last word of the decision of the judge. It did not come, and that was the basis of my bewilderment as I left the courtroom. I even forgot to call attention to one minor victory of this major case.

One of our chief headaches of this trial was that it must take place in this "Jim Crow" capital of our fatherland, where a Negro could not be sure of hotel accommodations or an opportunity to eat a meal, and sometimes even had difficulty with cabs. Moreover, there was even the more serious problem as to where this racially mixed group of lawyers and defendants, men and women, could meet privately for consultation. These are real problems which most white Americans, and no foreigners, can for a moment envisage. Yet for a white woman to go to a colored hotel; or a colored person to go to a white hotel; for white persons and colored, men and women, to be closeted together, morning, noon or night—such goings on are not only not customary but in at least a third of the states of this union illegal, and would in Alabama, Georgia, or Mississippi lead to arrest if not riot or murder.

Washington is geographically at the edge of the slave South, but has always been Southern in culture. Today its citizens are disfranchised and ruled by an irresponsible Congressional committee, because if Washington had democratic government, Negroes would vote and hold office, go to hotels, and sit in restaurants.

We sought to settle this problem at first by asking change of venue to some more civilized part of the nation. This was promptly denied. Then someone proposed that we hire an apartment and all live together. This I vetoed. It could put us all in jail if the press got wind of it.

At our first arraignment, we tried all stopping at a colored hotel. The accommodations were poor, however, and Mrs. Du Bois and I then procured lodging with a young colored man and his wife, who were not so afraid as their frightened friends. Our white colleagues went to white hotels and the colored attorneys stopped at home. A local trade union furnished us a meeting place for consultation. Thus matters went on for a week. Then one of the white defendants put the case up to the management of the Statler, the newest and best hotel in Washington. They had no space then, but made reservations for the week of the trial, which proved the last. We all stopped there, and were courteously entertained. Indeed, we held our Victory celebration there, in the center of one of their best dining rooms, with white and black persons, lawyers, defendants, and colored newspaper reporters present. Thus we won at least a temporary battle "along the Color Line" just as we won our liberty from a jail sentence.

There remained, however, my quandary. The government not only went to trouble and large expense, risked its own reputation, but also forced us to extraordinary and world-wide effort, to escape punishment. Personally, I had no funds for such a case. I am retired from work, with a pension too small for normal expenses of living. My wife's work and income were seriously curtailed by her complete immersion in this case. We have no rich friends. None of the defendants were able personally to finance this case. Had it not been for the almost miraculous rise of American friends, we would have gone to jail by default. Not a cent of money for the trial came from abroad. Even had this been possible, it would have been used to convict us. But in this nation by popular appeal to poor and middle-class folk, Negroes and white, trade unions and other groups, we raised funds for these purposes:

Legal fees	$18,400
Publicity	5,600
Office	5,250
Salaries	3,600
Travel	2,365

To this should be added additional legal fees of at least $13,000; $3,000 paid to an attorney hired by one of the defendants and not paid for by the Committee, and at least $10,000 which Marcantonio earned but would not accept. This amounts to a total of $40,215. To this should be added at least $2,000 in travel expenses paid by localities. How much the case cost the government we cannot know, but it could not have been less than $100,000, and it might have been much more.

The net result of this extraordinary trial, of wasted time and strength, and at least $150,000 of the earnings of the poor, was neither to prove nor allege that any one of the five defendants had committed any act involving moral turpitude; it did not prove or even allege that the World Peace Council, representing over seventy nations including our own, was guilty of anything but trying to stop war. When the government of the United States alleged that the defendants were agents of the World Peace Council, it was unable with all its power and money to convince one of its own judges that it had sufficient evidence to lay before a jury; and that therefore the demand of the Department of Justice that the defendants register as foreign agents was not sustained.

But of course this unjustified effort to make five persons register as the source of foreign propaganda for peace and particularly to scare fifteen million Negroes from complaint, was not the real object of this long and relentless persecution. The real object was to prevent American citizens of any sort from daring to think or talk against the determination of Big Business to reduce Asia to colonial subserviency to American industry; to reweld the chains on Africa; to consolidate United States control of the Caribbean and South America; and above all to crush Socialism in the Soviet Union and China. That was the object of this case.

This object every intelligent American knew. Our leading thinkers and educators were perfectly aware of this assault on the basis of the democratic process in America. Even if some thought peace at present dangerous and did not believe in socialism, they knew that if democracy was to survive in modern culture and in this vaunted "Land of the Free" and leader of "free nations," the right to think and to speak; the right to know what others were thinking; particularly to know opinion in that Europe which, despite our provincial and vulgar boasting and the golgotha of world wars, is still our main source of science and culture—that this democratic right of freedom of thought and speech must be preserved from Truman and McGrath; McCarran and Smith; from McCarthy and little Georgia Wood leading the reactionary slave South, or America was dead.

Despite this, most Americans of education and stature did not say a word or move a hand. This is the most astonishing and frightening result of this trial. We five are free but America is not. The absence of moral courage and intellectual integrity which our persecution revealed still stands to frighten our own nation and the better world. It is clear still today, that freedom of speech and of thinking can be attacked in the United States without the intellectual and moral leaders of this land raising a hand or saying a word in protest or defense, except in the case of the Saving Few. Their ranks did not include the heads of the great universities, the leaders of religion, or most of the great names in science. Than this fateful silence there is on earth no greater menace to present civilization.

It was the State Department which started this prosecution to quell Communists, and retard the peace movement which was beginning to annoy the Pentagon. The inclusion of myself, a Negro, in the dragnet, was probably at first fortuitous, but quickly backed by the Military as a needed warning to complaining Negroes. When rising public opinion fastened on me as the key figure, the determination of the government to convict me increased, especially when I refused to plead "Nolo Contendere" and my contumacious speeches continued. The continued appeals to Truman and McGrath must have had effect, but were ignored at the insistence of the State Department, until the volume of protest abroad compelled attention, centered emphasis on the Negro question in America, and made even the Catholic Church aware that the growing extent of its proselytizing among Negroes might suffer from the fact that the Attorney-General was a Catholic.

When Marcantonio became our chief counsel, the Catholic hierarchy must also have remembered that around him was a large group of voters with Catholic background. The State Department sent down emissaries to mingle with the audience at the trial, and to make inquiries about me, since apparently they had never heard of me previously.

The Department of Justice evidently put its main faith in Rogge's testimony to secure a conviction, but when the judge excluded testimony about the foreign policy of the Soviet Union, and testimony about the aims and acts of the World Defenders of Peace, demanding first that evidence of our agency of the Defenders of Peace be introduced, the value of Rogge's testimony was very small, and more damning against him than us. Hearing this, the Department of Justice had made a frantic last minute search of all possible sources of information for possible discovery of spies and stoolpigeons. Practically every person who had attended any meetings of the Peace Information Center or been connected in any way was visited by F.B.I. agents, often two or three times, and many of them subpoenaed. So little was discovered, however, that at the last moment most of these witnesses were never summoned.

As public opinion against this prosecution belted the earth and threatened to erupt into the Assembly of the United Nations, and when despite free trips abroad for prominent Negroes, and threats against Negro professionals, civil servants and business men, the volume of Negro protest increased rather than stopped, Truman and the National Democratic Committee began to listen to the warning of the highest placed Negro Democrats, and the pressure for conviction lessened.

There was some indication that an attack on colored jurors might be tried, but that seemed too risky. All Jews on the panel were barred, but Negroes, most of them office-holders and subject to intimidation, were accepted. But any verdict of conviction with a jury of eight Negroes and four whites was hardly probable. A devout Catholic judge, who once faced trouble for refusing to grant any divorces, was assigned to the case.

What turns me cold in all this experience is the certainty that thousands of innocent victims are in jail today because they had neither money, experience nor friends to help them. The eyes of the world were on our trial despite the desperate effort of press and radio to suppress the facts and cloud the real issues; the courage and money of friends and of strangers who dared stand for a principle freed me; but God only knows how many who were as innocent as I and my colleagues are today in hell. They daily stagger out of prison doors embittered, vengeful, hopeless, ruined. And of this army of the wronged, the proportion of Negroes is frightful. We protect and defend sensational cases where Negroes are involved. But the great mass of arrested or accused black folk have no defense. There is desperate need of nation-wide organizations to defense. There is desperate need of nation-wide organizations to oppose this national racket of railroading to jails and chain-gangs the poor, friendless and black.

Only a minority of the business and professional Negroes of Harlem attended my birthday dinner after the indictment was known. Of the fifty presidents of Negro colleges, every one of which I had known and visited—and often many times as speaker and adviser—of these only one, Charles Johnson of Fisk University, publicly professed belief in my integrity before the trial; and only one congratulated me after the acquittal.

The Negro churches varied: the Baptists of Philadelphia strongly supported me, but the National Baptist Convention took no action; several bishops of the A.M.E. and Zion Church connections expressed sympathy, and my undergraduate Negro fraternity, the Alpha Phi Alpha, was divided in opinion. The colored Elks supported me through their chief official, but none of the other colored secret orders did.

Colored public school teachers sat in almost complete silence. All this shows not necessarily lack of sympathy for me in my persecution, but the wide fear and intimidation of the Negro people of America, afraid for jobs, appointments, business opportunities, and even of personal safety.

In contrast to all this lethargy and fright, the mass support which I gained from the Negroes of the nation began slowly as soon as they could understand the facts, and then swelled in astonishing volume as the trial neared. From the beginning of the trial the courtroom was continuously crowded, and largely by out-of-town colored people and white, some of whom came from long distances. The coverage by Negro newspapers attested the nationwide demand for news and sympathy for the accused. The F.B.I. and the Departments of State and Justice had observers seeking information from Negroes present. Republican and Democratic National Committees kept in touch. There is no doubt that increasing apprehension of repercussions of the possible results of this trial on the Negro vote played a great part in its result.

We must admit that the majority of the American Negro intelligentsia, together with much of the West Indian and West African leadership, shows symptoms of following in the footsteps of western acquisitive society, with its exploitation of labor, monopoly of land and its resources, and with private profit for the smart and unscrupulous in a world of poverty, disease and ignorance, as the natural end of human culture. I have long noted and fought this all too evident tendency, and built my faith in its ultimate change on an inner Negro cultural ideal. I thought this ideal would be built on ancient African communism, supported and developed by memory of slavery and experience of caste, which would drive the Negro group into a spiritual unity precluding the development of economic classes and inner class struggle. This was once possible, but it is now improbable. I strove hard to accomplish this while I was yet editor of the *Crisis,* and afterward in my teaching at Atlanta University.

Just before I lost my position there by compulsory age retirement, I had finished plans for uniting all the powerful colored Land Grant colleges into an organization under the leadership of my department in Atlanta University, to pursue co-operative social studies covering the black South. If once this had become established, my guidance of the young Negro intelligentsia might have been increased and implemented, and the science of sociology might have immeasurably benefited by a laboratory test of extraordinary breadth and opportunity. This, as I fondly hoped, might have revived my Atlanta University studies of the late 19th century, which white "philanthropy" starved to untimely death. All this, petty envy killed, just as it was reborn.

The very loosening of outer racial discriminatory pressures has not, as I had once believed, left Negroes free to become a group cemented into a new cultural unity, capable of absorbing socialism, tolerance and democracy, and helping to lead America into a new heaven and new earth. But rather, partial emancipation is freeing some of them to ape the worst of American and Anglo-Saxon chauvinism, luxury, showing-off and "social climbing."

I find, curiously enough then, that my experience in this fantastic accusation and criminal process is tending to free me from that racial provincialism which I always recognized but which I was sure would eventually land me in an upper realm of cultural unity, led by "My People." I have discovered that a large and powerful portion of the educated and well-to-do Negroes are refusing to forge forward in social leadership of anyone, even their own people, but are eager to fight social medicine for sick whites or sicker Negroes; are opposing trade unionism not only for white labor but for the far more helpless black worker; are willing to get "rich quick" not simply by shady business enterprise, but even by organized gambling and the "dope" racket.

On the other hand, I am free from jail today, not only by the efforts of that smaller part of the Negro intelligentsia which has shared my vision, but also by the steadily increasing help of Negro masses and of whites who have risen above race prejudice not by philanthropy but by brotherly and sympathetic sharing of the Negro's burden and identification with it as part of their own. Without the help of the trade unionists, white and black, without the Progressives and radicals, without Socialists and Communists and lovers of peace all over the world, my voice would now be stilled forever.

COMMENT

The end of the trial came with lightning-like suddenness.

With the Prosecution grinding to a close, the Defense was drawing its lines taut, digging into trenches, measuring each position, preparing meticulously for the forward thrust. As chief witness for the defense, W. E. B. spent the weekend carefully checking every moment of the Peace Information Center's existence. Since there was nothing to hide, he demanded that every detail be within his grasp. He was fully aware, however, that here only technicalities would be involved. What really mattered were the circumstances and influences exerted throughout all his eighty-three years which inexorably, step by step, had brought him to the unchallenged leadership of the United States peace movement. Accused of being a foreign agent, a dupe, a liar, *this* proud Negro American whose life had been devoted to the pursuit, not of individual Happiness, but of universal Freedom, whose passion was Truth! He was going on that stand to bear witness for Freedom and Truth. There was to be no compromise in this trial, no excuses made for his "not knowing." He spurned any possible leniency because of his years. This was not bravado on his part nor did it spring from any assurance of what the outcome of the trial would be. He tried to prepare me for the possibility of his going to jail, or being given a suspended sentence—which I think he dreaded even more. He had lost weight and his face was lined. Yet, not for a moment had he considered any other course.

Day after day I had sat in that courtroom waiting. Waiting for the damning proof, the evidence, the incriminating letter, picture, check—the testimony that would show "beyond any reasonable doubt" the guilt of the accused. Since I knew the work of the Peace Information Center as well as anybody concerned, I knew that such "incriminating evidence" would have to be manufactured. Yet, I thought that from some source, in some manner, the Prosecution had secured something. I could not believe that such a serious charge could be brought unless the Department of Justice *believed* it had some evidence—even though that evidence would be proven false when the matter came to trial. But, except for Rogge, whose whole demeanor exuded evil, and a lean, sallow F.B.I. agent who with phonographic rapidity recited every detail of a public meeting held two years before, the Prosecution witnesses were for the most part ordinary, decent folks, not quite sure what they were doing in a witness chair but anxious to do their patriotic duty as loyal citizens.

The judge had been rather short in telling the Prosecution to "produce evidence." Nothing incriminating had been produced, yet the atmosphere in the courtroom that morning when Marc presented his motions was heavy. Lunch at the government cafeteria down the street had been a gloomy affair. And when a group of Howard University law students who had been in court all morning came over to shake hands with Dr. Du Bois they were sober and deferential. They were expressing their sympathy.

The courtroom was already crowded when we returned, but someone got up and gave me my regular seat in the front row. When Judge McGuire entered, I searched his face anxiously. I thought his usually genial, open features had hardened and my heart sank. We had expected denial of the first motion and his reasons were clear and logical. But when he turned to consideration of the second motion—for acquittal—his words were so beautifully sane and impartial that I could not believe my ears. When he pronounced the words "a judgment for acquittal will be granted" my breath stopped and from a whirling distance I saw Bernard Jaffe's face dissolve into a happy glow—then disappear.

I slumped in my seat. Lillian Elkin put her arms around me and we leaned against each other trembling. The quiet, authoritative voice of the judge steadied me.

I remember how Mr. Maddrix stood up uncertainly, looking for all the world as if his pants were falling off, and said plaintively:

"Well, I guess—your Honor—there's nothing more for me to do."

The judge looked down sympathetically and in the kindest possible voice told him:

"No, Mr. Maddrix, I guess there isn't. I am telling the defendants they may go."

Lillian and I were on our feet. The courtroom was a wavering sea of smiling faces. Court was still in session and though Judge McGuire had instructed that there was to be no demonstration he ignored the hugs and kisses and handclasps that greeted the five when they came out of the prisoners' dock.

Newsmen tried to stop us in the lobby but W. E. B. seized my hand and fairly ran down the flight of steps and jumped into a taxi standing at the curb.

"The Statler Hotel!" I had to give instructions. My husband had dropped into the seat, his eyes closed.

There was no need for words between us. Years of normal married life could not have knit us closer together than had the past ten months. There had been no time or place for reticence, no reserves of energies or emotions. Our home had been the whole of the United States: lovely dawn over Lake Michigan, the sun dropping suddenly behind the Rocky Mountains, the sandy wastes of Arizona. We had slept in large and small rooms, on downy mattresses and hard cots; we had dined in banquet halls and from kitchen tables, our family was all the people who so generously had shared our dangers, anxieties, our expenses and hopes— the people who had drawn out this victory. I thought of them now—the thirteen grimy workers, gathered in a room stained with Chicago soot. They had scarcely moved a muscle while I talked to them that hot June afternoon—just listened. Then one of them rose and said, "Thanks for comin', ma'am. We'll tell our men." There were the keen-eyed students at the University of Minnesota, and the tanned, restless co-eds in San Jose, and the Spanish-speaking group outside Denver, Colorado. They all understood that freedom to work for peace was their inalienable right. And how sweet would be the triumph of those spunky Negro women in that clapboard church outside Detroit who defied their deacons by supporting the cause of freedom! "It's time," they declared in no uncertain terms, "for us women to stand together. Our sister's (meaning me) right! It's *our* business!" How right they were.

I laughed aloud as we entered our room at the Statler, he joined me and then we couldn't stop.

The rest of the day and far into the night was a Song of Victory! Friends, reporters, photographers wandered in and out of our room. At six o'clock all our "gang" gathered in the main dining room of the Statler Hotel for a victory dinner. Lillian and I, wives of the late defendants, wore huge corsages; two *Afro-American* press representatives arriving to take pictures were crowded down at the big center table. Other diners must have thought we were a bridal party!

But this was only the beginning. For the Defense Committee had planned a fund-raising affair at a home in a Washington suburb for that Tuesday evening. The acquittal transformed this into a big party attended by people from as far away as Philadelphia. Several carloads came over from Baltimore. People realized that this was their individual and collective victory.

You may not have been there that night, but a toast was drunk to you and you and you—THE PEOPLE WHO THAT DAY WON A VICTORY!

CHAPTER XIV

◆

Interpretations

Blessed are the Peacemakers for they shall be called Communists. Is this shame for the Peacemakers or praise for the Communists? Accursed are the Communists, for they claim to be Peacemakers. Is this shame for the Communists or praise for the Peacemakers? This is the paradox which faces America. What had our trial to do with this paradox?

Looking back over these months of strain and expense, our logical answer could be that it has no connection whatsoever. The government never charged me with being a Communist and it could not, for Communism in this nation is not yet an indictable crime. But my friends insist that the charge of sympathy with Communism, the "Red" smear, while no crime, is a serious handicap, and that our acquittal therefore is a great victory, because it cleared us of any connection with Communism in our work for Peace.

But I am not content to leave the matter here. For whatever the government charged and failed to prove, the real charge in the minds of men was at least sympathy with Communism. This sympathy, in the opinion of our enemies and the fear of our friends, was not proven, or even inquired into; but was it not implicit in the fact that most of our encouragement and congratulation came, as our own story shows, from Communists, Socialists, and adherents of the Left? That is true. It is not the whole story, for many who supported us were liberals, progressives, and even some conservatives who believe in peace and free speech.

If I should put down on a map the geographical sources of all messages received—on the occasion of my birthday dinner, on the announcement of my indictment and trial, and after my acquittal—clearly my support and congratulations came from Eastern European Communists, from western European Socialists, from Communist Asia, from Progressives, Socialists and Communists in the United States, and from the Left in India and South America. To these would be appended the colored peoples of Africa, the Caribbean and the United States, many of whom are conservative.

What now is my attitude toward this Left support? I do not want to avoid this question; on the contrary, I want to make myself perfectly clear: I am thankful for it; I deeply appreciate it, because it strengthens in my mind my belief that much of what they believe corresponds with my belief and with the belief of all honest people.

This runs counter to current American reasoning, and to my mind, current American reasoning on this point is crazy. Suppose that I believe deeply and fervently in Proposition Alpha. I ask support for that belief. Mr. X comes forward and offers me his support. I accept gladly. I accept because I believe in Proposition Alpha. So does X. But he believes also in many other things in which I do not. So, too, I believe in many matters in which he does not. But so long as his other beliefs permit him to support my Proposition Alpha, I welcome his support. If support of my Proposition Alpha interferes with his other beliefs, he need not offer his support. He does offer it and I accept gladly.

But here in America lately we have had seemingly sane citizens, statesmen and thinkers, who loudly and angrily refuse now the support of Communists, Socialists, or Progressives; now of Negroes, Catholics, Jews and the foreign-born; and because they do not believe in everything that these groups do believe in, although these do agree in some matters.

Some men therefore apparently demand complete unity of belief and object as a prerequisite to any co-operation at all. This attitude thwarts democracy and stops progress. This attitude in the United States killed the early moderate Socialist movement; it killed the LaFollette Farmer-Labor movement; it killed the New Deal and now tries to kill the Progressive movement; and it has made any Third Party difficult so long as we are ruled by one party under two names.

I therefore thank all Communists and Socialists who stood out for my right to advocate peace, just as I thank all conservatives and liberals for daring to stand for what they conceived to be right, despite the "Red" smear. I utterly refuse to be stampeded into opposition to my own program by intimations of dire and hidden motives among those who offer me support.

I am perfectly aware that Communists do not believe that the civilized world can survive under Capitalism. But while I have seen Capitalism try to wipe out Communism and Communism point out that Capitalism is bound to commit suicide, I am convinced today that both systems can live together without war and with helpful competition. Stalin has said this, but Truman has not.

But the matter goes further than this. Programs of social reform are never complete or mutually exclusive. They always present wide areas of overlapping. In the 16th century, Catholicism and Protestantism were not absolutely separate realms of God and the Devil. In the early 19th century, Englishmen could believe in some free trade and some tariff protection without being traitors to the Empire. So today there is no path of human progress which a so-called "free democracy" of the West can advocate without adopting at least a part of the program of Socialists and Communists. There is no socialist or communist program which does not advocate use of capital and individual enterprise as freely as is consistent with real social progress. I refuse therefore to be diverted from what I think is right, because someone charges that my program is socialistic or communistic. No program of human progress can escape this charge, for it is true. I do not try to escape. I believe in socialism just as firmly as I believe in democracy. I believe in the right of any people to attempt a communistic state. When John L. Lewis demands federal protection for miners, operators reply: "This is Socialism!" So what?

For this reason I follow a world peace movement which arose in the Soviet Union and today finds there its chief support. By the same token I fight the war movement in the United States which is transforming this traditionally peaceful nation into the greatest warmonger of all history. I deny that this attitude of mine is traitorous.

I am a native-born citizen of the United States as my forefathers on both sides have been for two hundred years. I have in my life loyally done my full duty as a citizen as I saw it. I have obeyed my country's laws even when I thought some of these laws barbarous. I have tried to make this nation a better country for my having lived in it. It would not be true for me to say that I "love my country," for it has enslaved, impoverished, murdered and insulted my people. Despite this I know what America has done for the poor, oppressed and hopeless of many other peoples, and what indeed it has done to contradict and atone for its sins against Negroes. I still believe that some day this nation will become a democracy without a color-line. I work and shall work for an America whose aim is not solely to make a few people rich, but rather to stop War, and abolish Poverty, Disease and Ignorance for all men.

I do not believe that loyalty to the United States involves hatred for other peoples, nor will I promise to support my country "Right or Wrong." I will defend this country when it is right. I will condemn it when it is wrong. If, for instance, during the Civil War, I had lived in Georgia as I did for a quarter of a century after emancipation, and if by law I had been compelled to fight for slavery or die, I would have died.

While, then, I am and expect to be a loyal citizen of the United States, I also respect and admire the Union of Soviet Socialist Republics. I regard that land as today the most hopeful nation on earth, not because of its theory, but because of what it has accomplished. It has in a generation raised hundreds of millions of debased serfs out of illiteracy, superstition and poverty to self-respecting, hard-working manhood. I do not regard the Soviet Union as perfect, but as an historian and sociologist of some training and experience, and as a traveler in many parts of the world, I do not believe the evidence offered charging the Soviets with being a nation of slavery, with being an imperialism exploiting unwilling peoples, or a nation which does not fulfill its commitments to other nations. The crimes of mankind are due to no one religion, system of government or economic doctrine. They will never be corrected by force but by moral character; and what nations today can claim such monopoly of righteousness or wisdom as gives them a right to rule the world?

The greatest single fact about Russia which holds my faith in its future is its system of popular education. There is in the world no system equal to it. If American Negroes had had half the chance of the Russians to learn to read, write and count, there would be no Negro question today. No nation which plans tyranny establishes such public education. Even with propaganda, restrictions on radio and press, and control of the church, no nation which can and does read the vast literature which the Soviet Union prints and distributes, can ever permanently remain subservient or misled people. The greatest proof of the decadence of our own nation is the fact that we are putting into preparation for war today ten times as much as we are spending on education.

As, then, a citizen of the world as well as of the United States of America, I claim the right to know and think and tell the truth as I see it. I believe in Socialism as well as Democracy. I believe in Communism wherever and whenever men are wise and good enough to achieve it; but I do not believe that all nations will achieve it in the same way or at the same time. I despise men and nations which judge human beings by their color, religious beliefs or income. I believe in free enterprise among free men and individual initiative under physical, biological and social law. I hate War.

Under the Truman Doctrine this nation has entered on a path which is bound to lead to disaster. We are set to contain and crush Communism by force, and to do this by inspiring such calculated hatred of the Soviet Union, and of all nations which follow its leadership, as to risk and threaten a Third and final World War. We thus block the path of mankind to social reform which inevitably must lead along many of the same paths followed now by the Soviet Union, Poland, Czechoslovakia, the Balkans and New China.

We defend our awful program by the claim that we alone stand for Freedom, Democracy, efficiency in making and justice in distributing wealth and popular intelligence, as well as science. Let us take each of these categories and examine the evidence.

It is ridiculous today for any nation to call itself "Free." Under the daily unfolding knowledge of the laws of physical nature and of the technique of harnessing physical force; under our increasing understanding of biological development; with our knowledge of psychological behavior; especially with our social organization—inherited and adapted—including intricate industrial technique and organization, domestic and world-wide commerce and finance; with the vast coverage of customary and statute law,—with all this, no man, woman or child today is free or can be. Even the restricted "freedom" of the 12th century traveler; of the 15th century discoverer; of the 17th century "adventurer" in exploitation; or the 19th century pioneer, immigrant and investor,—all of these in the 20th century have yielded to law and regulation and our freedom is progressively narrowed in our ways of making a living but retains or could retain breadth and increase in imagination, science, and expression. Curiously enough it is here in the real realm of freedom that the United States by its war program is limiting liberty.

There cannot survive that "freedom" of business enterprise which in the 19th century made the fortunes of the Vanderbilts, Goulds and Rockefellers. That day is passed and we know it. How much freedom under law and morals we can save is a matter of experiment, thought, and grave scientific research and not of slogans. Every nation today curbs its citizens by law and force. Yet every nation and citizen wants to preserve as large a realm as possible for freedom of imagination, thought and action.

The Soviet Union is trying desperately to evolve a nation working under severe discipline so as to evolve a people as free as abolition of poverty, ignorance and disease makes possible. Most Americans believe Russian discipline is too severe and that complete abolition of poverty is impossible. We have every opportunity to prove this. There is no sense in fighting about it, particularly if that fighting and huge preparation for conquering the world is resulting in curtailment of our own basic freedoms, the ruin of our school system, the encouragement of theft and murder, and the leaving of thousands of hard-working citizens to drown and starve because our making of bombs leaves no money for flood control. Of all areas where men are free to act, that of industry is and ever has been narrowest; because climate, technique and culture patterns leave least leeway for whim and individual choice. But it is precisely in industry that America demands for its owners anarchy of force and chance, while in literature, science, art and expression we curtail creative genius.

We claim that America leads in democracy. This claim is old and has at times approached truth. It is not true today. For democracy, while logical in theory, is difficult to achieve and maintain in practice. There have been times in our history when the public opinion of the mass of citizens largely determined our policies. There have been regions like 19th century New England where the democratic town meeting was an effective tool of local government. But over most of our history, democracy has been strictly limited, now by religion and status, now by race, now by ownership of property, later by the slave system, then by legal disfranchisement, and today by the power of corporate wealth. So true is this that the curve of our faith in the American democratic method of government has risen and fallen: from low esteem in the 18th and early 19th centuries to zenith in the Age of Jackson. It then fell under the domination of the Slave Power, darted aloft during early Reconstruction and then plunged suddenly but surely until now often less than half of the voting population make any effort to cast their ballots.

Since the fall of the slave power which ruled the nation by that ownership of land and labor necessary to the valuable cotton crop, the nation, turning sharply from democratic control by freedmen and immigrants, yielded control gradually but definitely to corporate wealth. Congress lost its representative character by the disfranchisement of voters—Negroes by law, white labor by threat of economic reprisal, and lately enfranchised women by dominant culture patterns. Units of representation became startlingly unequal, so that 5,000 voters in South Carolina had the same political power as 100,000 in New York; and 36,000 votes give the reactionary McCarran of Nevada the same power as the liberal Douglas of Illinois who received two million votes.

In legislation even under these inequalities, Congress and most legislatures further tie their own hands, so that laws can more easily be dictated by special interests and usually by interests which regard the nation as the instrument by which Big Business makes the largest profits. Proposed legislation is referred to committees, presided over by powerful chairmen chosen not by democratic methods but by seniority—that is, assigned to those persons who retain their seats longest by disfranchisement of their constituents or use of patronage or money. Most of the powerful Congressional committees are thus ruled by Southern reactionary politicians whose election for life depends on disfranchised Negroes

and poor whites. And beyond this, by surrendering power to a "rules" committee which can bury any proposal indefinitely, or with a by-law which prevents
even a majority from voting on any proposed legislation which a small minority
opposes, Congress deliberately curtails democracy in its own halls.

With such a background, lobbies representing all the major business interests, manned by well-paid men of high ability and social and business connections, are in constant attendance on sessions and in close personal contact with
members, quite overwhelming the few and intermittent delegations representing from time to time some sections of the nation's electorate. The consequent
cost of promoting legislation has reached such figures that only corporations
can afford them. The cost of campaigns for public office is prohibitive for the
ordinary candidate. Only some person chosen by a huge and well organized
machine, with millions to spend, can think of running for high office.

Even the character of the political campaign has of late totally changed. With
news sources controlled by Big Business, with private control of radio and television and of the larger hotels and meeting halls, it is practically impossible for
the ordinary citizen to gain in any election that understanding of the broad
political questions before the voters which can lead to an intelligent ballot. In
such elections, both Church and University, scientist and poet, are often dumb,
on pain of public condemnation and private loss of income. Add to this the fact
that 150,000,000 people cannot know the personalities of candidates as the members of a town meeting know the candidates for selectmen. The voter can seldom directly see or hear them, nor can he know for what they stand or how they
will vote, save as the kept press tells him. Real political debate and heckling and
open forums are disappearing.

If size of territory and variety of folk is some excuse for our failures in national
democracy, what can we say to the almost total atrophy of local self-rule? Time
was when the village, town and city ruled themselves by democracy; when the
town meeting laid taxes and spent them; selected their rulers, decided policies
as to roads, poor relief, and crime. Today the town and ward and largely the city
is in thrall to state and nation: it elects no officials, adopts no policies, pays taxes
but has no funds to spend; it has no place for a democratic town meeting or
even for adequate discussion. It is ruled by the officials of the county or state
and cannot decide even its street laws and carfare, its sewage system or lights.
It is a pensioner of the state and in turn the state begs alms of the nation. The
nation is ruled by the more or less hidden concentration of power in the hands
of an industrial oligarchy.

Thus the citizen of the United States today has small control over candidates
or over the issues which will be voted on. The main decisions in national policies
will rest in the hands of those business interests which are today in the control
of a huge oligarchy striving to belt the world.

These are the reasons why our claim to champion democracy in the world is
not valid and cannot be proven by honest inquiry. Let us frankly admit that putting of public opinion in control of a modern state, with all the local interests
and personal ambitions in conflict with the public weal, and with so unread and
inexperienced a public mind, is enormously difficult. Admitting this, does it

improve matters to claim success where there is little, and to proclaim to the world a triumph which we do not have? When pressed, we defend our limitation of democracy by the necessity of producing and distributing wealth in sufficient quantity and under the control of such persons as can best use it for the benefit of all. Let us turn to the facts concerning wealth and its ownership in the United States.

Production in fields which are today of dominant importance is not an individual adventure but a vast social undertaking. A large number of persons work together in numberless ways, in widely separated places and for periods varying from a week or less to ten years or more to produce a valuable product. The exact proportion of their contributions to the final result by physical or ethical measure, by kind and efficiency of effort, by length and intensity of labor or by money value, cannot be determined accurately by any mathematical method. The product of modern industry is a social product and belongs to society. It should be distributed in accord with the highest standards of social justice.

Wealth is not and never was entirely the result of individual effort; it always involved some measure of group co-operation. And today more than ever before, wealth is the result of social effort added to the bounty of nature. Property is the legal right to use wealth; the wealth may stem from your own effort or from the effort of others; it may come from seizure of natural resources; it may come from inheritance or gift, from cheating or gambling, from theft. There is nothing sacred about property; everything depends on the social welfare involved in its accumulation and use.

This means that property and its use are proper subjects of political consideration and of democratic decision. There has been in America too much cheating and theft in the acquisition of property, and too much injustice in its use. Huge properties have been accumulated by highway robbery, monopoly of natural resources belonging of right to all, and even by transgressing the very law which protects the rights of the public.

Our present economic problem stems from the fact that while production is increasingly a social process, the distribution of its results still remains largely a matter of the individual judgment of persons who happen to have the power or who seize the power to decide, and on the basis of concepts of property and income which no longer correspond to fact.

The paradox which consequently upsets the labor world is that despite the indispensable co-operation of laborers, managers and capitalists, inventors and thinkers in current industry, when the results and increasingly valuable results are distributed, most of the laborers get less than is necessary for decent life, while many of the capitalists get more than they need or can spend. And particularly, capitalists get the power to direct the use of the residue for any purpose which they choose.

The age-long explanation of this is that goods are so scarce that with the best effort some folk must remain in poverty and need. It is this alleged fact that the 20th century laborer is disputing. He maintains that a more just distribution of the results of industry could eliminate poverty, disease and ignorance among the working class. For this purpose he has been organizing labor unions and trying by appeal, bargaining, and if necessary by strikes, picketing, and law, to raise his standard of living to decency and comfort. He does not want in this contest to deprive manager or owner of his just reward for saving, planning and direction, but he insists that he, the laborer as partner in production, should have some voice in deciding what is just. He rejects certain age-old excuses for present conditions. When the National Association of Manufacturers advertises that "the more we produce the more we will have," he knows full well that this depends on who does the dividing and who gets the shares.

The conventional answer to this contention of labor is that the essential capital to employ labor can only be had if its owners are attracted by large profit to invest their wealth instead of consuming it. Once this was true. In the 17th and 18th centuries most of the rich did not save; they spent conspicuously and extravagantly; and industry could only secure their co-operation by the gambler's bribe of high profit.

Today the situation is far different; there is capital in so great abundance that it begs opportunity for investment and indeed cannot be used in any other way. Also the risk of loss in legitimate industry is small and might be reduced nearly to nil by intelligent and scientific planning. Moreover, most of the current capital comes not from the rich but from the comparatively poor who save for old age and a rainy day.

But the huge profits of industry go not to them but to the financiers who as middle-men handle their funds, giving them 2% in savings banks while this wealth in foreign trade often reaps 50%. Small wonder Big Business fights and schemes and drafts the 18-year-old youth. Profit is thicker than blood.

This has led many a social thinker to point out that capital for all real human want and improvement could easily be taken from production and leave sufficient income for all consumers, provided, of course, that individual consumption was so limited that no man had cake if any man lacked bread; that mink coats for the rich were not allowed if the poor had no shoes. And of course here's the rub. This compulsion, which socialism proposed long before Lenin as the only way to decent human life, raises shrieks of protest if hinted at today in the United States. Remember what happened when Roosevelt proposed to limit incomes to $25,000!

What church of the lowly Jesus, who railed against the rich, would for a moment admit or preach such doctrine? And yet is it strange that the poor and hardworking laborers of the world, without sufficient food, shelter and clothes, fearing old age and sickness more than the flames of hell—is it strange that they by overwhelming majority are demanding this regulation of production and consumption and saying that this is not Russian imperialism but American common sense?

You cannot stop this line of thought from growing in an intelligent world if you kill all the youth and dye the oceans red with blood. Social control of production and distribution of wealth is coming as sure as the rolling of the stars. The whole concept of property is changing and must change. Not even a Harvard School of Business can make greed into a science, nor can the unscrupulous ambition of a Secretary of State forever use atomic energy for Death instead of Life.

Despite every effort in the United States to conceal and deny the facts, all civilized nations have been progressing toward socialism, especially since 1900. They own and run the railways, the telephones and telegraph, street cars, buses and subways; they largely conduct housing, sanitation, insurance and relief; they guarantee employment; they engage in industry, in manufacturing, foreign trade, mining, forestry and river control, in power conversion and control and wide ownership of land. Some nations like Britain go further than this; others like the Scandinavian lands plan less in theory but do ever more in practice; while Communist lands attempt complete social and industrial planning and ownership of all capital.

Here then is a world movement which almost alone the United States is attempting to stem. We are attempting to champion private enterprise when no great industrial effort can possibly be private or carried on primarily for private ends; we stress individual initiative which is laudable when it is for social ends and inadmissable when it leads to anarchy.

Furthermore, we must not imagine that our American economy is not planned, but simply an unplanned individual enterprise. On the contrary, in no modern state is industry more carefully planned and supervised than here. It is in the objects of the planning and not in the fact that we differ from socialist lands. Socialism seeks the public welfare in all its facets. American free enterprise seeks the simpler aim of securing the comfort and control of the state for the present owners of wealth and their successors, arguing that this will result in more for all than the broader object, which they regard as chimerical.

American business has evolved an extraordinary code of morals: the chief object of business is the private profit of the owners; universal selfishness, sometimes called self-interest, results in universal good; business has the right to influence government for its own objects; the chief end of government is freedom for profitable private business; government has no right to take direct part in business or to interfere in business, except to help private enterprise when it ceases to be profitable; cheating in business is wrong, but most cheating corrects itself automatically and some loss is better than government interference. From this code stem some of the worst crimes of private capitalistic enterprise. The question is, can this system of ethics be improved within the capitalist system? This evidently is a question of science and morals. The answer will require peace and sanity, and cannot be found in a war psychology. But American business, convinced that the Soviet Union has in reality the same objects as we have, proposes to answer the problem by military force.

By a propaganda of suspicion and hate, the American public has been driven into war; this war may become total; and if so the whole capitalist structure may be threatened. The planning of American Big Business therefore today faces severe crisis and is threaded with fears of inflation and radical thought. It is here that peace and peace alone can save the capitalist as well as the socialist world.

Let us now consider the effect of our war policy against the Soviet Union on education in the United States. For many years this nation stood foremost in popular education, and until the First World War, in adult education and scientific research. Today this is no longer true. The nations behind the so-called Iron

Curtain have better popular systems of universal popular education than we have, because while their schools have progressed rapidly, ours have steadily retrograded, from poor housing, lack of teachers and lack of proper distribution and planning of curricula. We still have large college and university facilities, but the entering students are poorly equipped and with limited ideals and objectives. The professors are today increasingly afraid to study and teach the social sciences, so that history becomes propaganda; economics hides in higher mathematics and social study is limited by military objectives. In the physical sciences our objects have become limited mainly to weapons of war. Young men are in grave moral quandary as to the decency of such a life object; and if Soviet science is accused of discouraging science for science's sake, America is certainly today encouraging science mainly for private profit, and thus killing future scholarship. As a result our place in science is losing ground and our talent is crowding into business and mechanics.

The cause of this is three-fold: our deliberately narrowed objectives in Negro education which have covered from a fourth to an eighth of our workers; our propaganda against socialism and the Soviet Union; and finally the vast transfer of public funds from social welfare to war preparation.

In the alembic of time, a strange dichotomy has arisen between the long contrasted teachings of Booker T. Washington and myself. He wanted the American Negro taught the technique of modern industry so as to make him the preferred exploited worker of American industry. He put no faith in philanthropy of whites for raising the Negro but only in their economic interest. For my part, I too knew that the salvation of the Negro worker lay in trained technique; but as a worker he would, I argued, need social guidance, and that must come from his own educated leaders if at all. I insisted, therefore, on the education of a Talented Tenth, assuming naively that these trained members of the learned professions would supply leadership for the working classes. This was true, but in much lesser degree than I expected. They naturally tended to become, as Washington hoped, themselves exploiters of the Negro and white workers, as acquisitive and as hard-fisted as the white employers. But, on the other hand, some of them did not. The miracle which I had regarded as probable did come true, but only after long years: this leadership for the workers came mainly from intelligent and better paid workers, trained as workers and not as exploiting aristocrats.

The Booker Washington doctrine of industrial education for Negroes had far more influence on white education than is generally recognized; but there it was rephrased as Education for the benefit of Industry. It lay back of the whole public school system of the South, white and black, where the elementary schools never taught reading, writing and counting as once they had been taught in the North, but went off into sewing, cooking and typewriting; and so on to technical schools and engineering. Northern cities followed this trend which ended in University Schools of Business.

Thus Industry and Big Business, with politics and philanthropic foundations, took over Education as the best path to profits; and when profits in private industry were threatened by Socialism, Business began a system of adult education in the United States unequalled in modern history. Improving on the propaganda technique of Hitler and Goebbels, the National Association of Manufacturers and allied organizations began, after the death of F. D. Roosevelt and the decline of his New Deal, to train the nation to fear government interference with industry, to combat further socialism in the United States, and to hate Communism as a threat to our "Way of Life."

That way of life was not "free enterprise," lack of economic planning and "individual initiative" for all men under democratic control. It was far from this, and all conclusions based on the conception of the United States as a country of free individual capitalism are false. Today Business holds Science and Art in iron bonds. It furnishes the main endowments of universities, or if this money comes from the State, Business runs the State. It endows literature and research under the control of business men. The realm of scientific enquiry is increasingly limited, with economics tabu, sociology limited, and history strictly conventional. In literature, subject and imagination are directed by Chambers of Commerce and ideals are channeled by spies, traitors, liars and informers. In a "Time for Greatness," the great are dead or dumb. With the advent of Harry Truman, a man with no education in economics or social development and too much training in "practical politics," this nation has become a country ruled by an oligarchy of less than 1,000 persons, controlling the largest pool of natural resources, processed goods and finance capital the world ever saw; and devoted today to making the world believe that its greatest danger is Communism and the Soviet Union. By means of a monopoly of news, periodicals and newspapers, by direction of radio and television, by control of schools and colleges, and by domination of the courts and help of secret police, this object has become accomplished in the United States. Before its impact our liberties are falling and our democracy is collapsing.

Last year eleven leaders of the Communist Party were sentenced to jail for long terms. They were not accused of any real crime or conspiring to such action. No testimony on their acts and plans was allowed to be introduced. They lie in jail today because our Supreme Court declared that because at some future time when violent revolution may be imminent they may advocate it, that we were justified in disregarding the intent and plain wording of the Constitution of the United States. Fifty other American citizens are now threatened with the same fate on the same grounds. Such reasoning in the past would have hanged Washington and Jefferson; sent Garrison, Douglass and Phillips to jail for life, and imprisoned Eugene O'Neill and Harry Hopkins.

If, however, the democracy we are losing can be restored and made alive, because of our natural resources, technique, intelligence and science, why are we not undertaking this vast task immediately, instead of trying to murder civilization? In such an effort here and now I long to help. Meantime I watch and am right to watch the strained effort of the Soviet Union to lay foundations of a new democracy where the old has not succeeded; if this effort fails because

"es wär so schön gewesen,
es hat nicht sollen sein,"

at least it was a magnificent effort, using the imperfect men and tools at hand and warding off attack of sixteen invading nations and every kind of disparagement and misrepresentation. But if this effort at Communism fails not of incompetency but because of us, God damn us!

We are rapidly approaching in this nation a point where there is but one crime which brings swift and severe punishment and that is "Communism," which may mean anything from unpopular opinions to revolution. Americans may kill, steal, cheat and gamble with certainty of a fair trial or none at all; they may lie, betray, slander and inform with a chance of money, professorships and Book-of-the-Month Club selection; but let any man study or praise anything connected with the Soviet Union and he may be starved or imprisoned, without facing his accusers, knowing the accusation, or escaping trial by witch-hunt.

As a result of this propaganda we have a national hysteria; citizens dare not think without danger of losing their good character and chance of earning a decent living. Their past lives are dragged up out of all context and misinterpreted with the testimony of confessed traitors and spies. At this time there comes the court case of which I try to tell in this book, and our initial difficulty was a chance to tell the facts which no newspaper would print.

On top of this comes a preparation for war on a scale which is simply inconceivable. The time will come when science will devote long investigation and study to revealing to the world how our present situation developed and became terrible fact. This result was hastened by the sad truth that in a day when as perhaps never before in human history, government calls for broad cultural background and expert knowledge, knowledge of society and technology, we have at the helm of state, with few exceptions, men without broad education, who have not traveled widely and are seldom well-read.

As our chief advisers, ambassadors and administrators, we have military men who got their rank usually by seniority, and whose whole training not only does not fit them for government and science, but absolutely unfits most of them for ordinary human relations. The moral basis of military training and its ethical standards must revolve about murder and destruction and can never normally grasp social uplift and human progress. For this reason all civilizations of the past have sedulously avoided the rule of soldiers save as a last fatal resort. Yet today amid the delicate balance of eternal social decisions, we have generals trained in mathematics and trajectories, in logistics and parade, with no real knowledge of history and sociology, and no dream of economics, set to adjust the relations of socialism and free enterprise, put in absolute rule of colonial peoples, and given charge of the education of our most promising youth.

It could be tragedy to put an Eisenhower in control of our destinies at this critical time, just as Ridgway is the last man to wield power over Europe and the recovery of Germany was immeasurably retarded by Clay. With all good will and basic loyalty, no man trained in current war politics will be able to grasp the meaning of the role of this nation in the reeling world of today; he may easily mistake the *Götterdämmerung* of modern culture for "police action."

It is difficult to follow this reasoning of men who know the increasing horror of war and its threat to all civilization. In our own nation nearly every step toward social progress is stopped today because of the supposed necessity for spending more for murder and destruction than we ever spent for education,

health, better standards of living. Let any man today propose aid to our collapsing school system; to begin social medicine for a people deprived to a frightful
extent of medical care; for a whole system of TVA's to tame the destructive and
wasting rivers of our land, and preserve the dwindling treasure of our forests—
no sooner are such plans advocated than the proponent is faced by two answers:
we have no money for social progress because of all-out preparation for killing
men and destroying property all over the world.

And secondly that anyone advocating such social aid and control is a communist or a socialist, and a traitor or prospective traitor to his country.

Behind our present plight lie a hundred years of teaching of false ideals. We
have envied the might and glory of the British Empire. In my own schooldays
everything Britain did was good; all that she accomplished was better than
what we tried to do. Our democracy stemmed from England; our speech was
hers. At Harvard, Great Britain set the pace and style in all accepted norms. When
in the 20th century Britain declined, we conceived ourselves her natural heirs. Just
as Englishmen once walked the earth as superior beings, now Americans must.
In accord with the best English tradition, we were above "lesser breeds without
the law," even if a tenth of our citizens were of African origin.

All this was fantasy, but hard reality lay in business and industry. British
colonial imperialism must develop into American industrial world rule. We had
experience in South America, which without actual declared war was now
the hewer of wood and drawer of water for the United States Empire. American
investment has put South America at the mercy of a foreign demand for such
products as we have developed in different nations so that the livelihood of
each nation is dependent on us: Cuba on sugar; Chile on copper; Bolivia on tin;
Venezuela on oil; Brazil on coffee; Guatemala on fruit; we hold in power over
many of these lands dictators largely in our pay.

This we proposed to extend over the former British Empire if not over the
world. Russia was lost to this scheme, but we were sure Communism would fail
as an industrial possibility. Russia did not fail; she even stopped our designs in
the Balkans. She was a danger to our profits. She was built up into a danger to
civilization.

Our ideal is wrong and in opposition to the trend of the age. War on the scale
we plan is suicide. It is the duty of all loyal Americans to preach peace.

As one result of this crisis, American Negroes are reaping benefits not due
entirely to more liberal attitudes on the part of the white population, but rather
to increasing sensitiveness of the United States to world criticism of its democracy. The color-line is yielding in the matter of voting and admission to schools.
Negroes have been sent abroad on scholarships and for travel, but always with
the understanding that they will defend or at least not attack the policy of this
nation in regard to Negroes. Thus one Negro alternate to the Assembly of the
United Nations has painted fantastic stories of Negro freedom and prosperity
while another criticized William Patterson's charge of Genocide.

All men at some time are bitterly disappointed at their fellows. Englishmen,
looking on their people as a "happy breed," are shocked to learn how many are
greedy, cruel and dishonest; young Southerners, raised to regard the white South

as chivalrous and brave, must squirm to discover so many lustful scoundrels. So I, having trained myself to think of my race as essentially kindly, loyal and honest, or if selfish and silly to think of this as due to slavery and oppression, have in these last days been astonished to find well-to-do and educated American Negroes cowardly and dishonest. Yet of course this is but natural as human nature goes, and I am strengthened by the knowledge that a larger proportion of intelligent Negroes stood staunch in my defense than of intelligent whites in defense of the Hollywood Ten or other victims of the Un-American Committee.

It has long been the policy of conquerors to let the conquered conquer themselves; thus armies of slaves made slaves of their fellows; mercenary soldiers subdued their peasant brother, and Negroes conquered Africa for Europe, while Chinese and Indians forced China and India to bow to the white race. It was the Negro, Tippo Tib, who organized the African slave trade in the 19th century to benefit the Arabs.

Today France is using the black Senegalese to conquer Viet-Nam, and Britain has used troops of every race and hue to hold the remains of her empire. Perhaps worst of all today is the use of American Negro troops in Korea. Not only is this bound to leave a legacy of hate between yellow nations and black, but the effect on the Negroes of America at being in a sense compelled to murder colored folk who suffer from the same race prejudice that Negroes in the United States have long suffered and still suffer; at being almost forced to be the dumb tools of business corporations seeking to dominate China and Asia—this is bound to result in the exacerbation of prejudice and inner conflict here in America.

Paul Robeson had this in mind when he voiced in Paris the hope that Negroes would never fight Russia, the sole nation on earth which has made race prejudice a crime. His was the far-reaching cry for inter-racial peace, in a war-torn world. For this appeal he has been crucified and characteristically many rich and respectable Negroes have joined the slavery wolf-pack in return for cash and ease. The problem is not ended; it has only begun.

For many years now I have viewed in long procession the pale dreams of men wandering vaguely yet rhythmically down the years. Yet never in any single year has the frustration and paradox of life stood out so clearly as in this year when, having finished 83 years of my life in decency and honor, with something done and something planning, I stepped into the 84th year with handcuffs on my wrists. Like the utter rending of precious fabric I was witnessing the blood-stained collapse of Atlantic culture finding burial on the ancient ruins of the Mediterranean efforts to civilize mankind. I saw this caricature and contradiction of mighty ideals, in frantic dying struggle, trying with lewd incest again to rape the All-Mother Asia from northern Heartland to southern sea, from Russia to India. And when weak and isolated by race I tried to make faint protest against this world suicide, I was slandered and shamed and threatened with five years in prison and $10,000 fine.

Gradually I have come to see the picture of the modern world with more satisfying clarity. Before the First World War, my whole thought and energy was directed toward the victims of race prejudice, which formed the group of persons with which I from birth had been identified. Slowly I came to recognize that the cause of their suffering was not primarily a matter of ethics, but of ease of exploitation; of the larger profit which could be had from low-paid Negro labor, so long as its plight aroused no sympathy or resentment from the community. Thence I fared further to realize that this exploitation of Negroes was more intense than that of white labor, and that white labor despite its own plight joined in the oppression of Negroes and excluded them from their defensive unions. When after the First World War, the C.I.O. began to include black labor in the union movement, I began slowly to emerge from my provincial racialism and to envisage the broader problems of work and income as affecting all men regardless of color or nationality. This I expounded in my *Black Reconstruction* in 1935 and, in 1940, I formulated a thesis of socialism for the American Negro in my *Dusk of Dawn*.

The Second World War sent all my formulations a-whirl. Not from the inner problems of a single social group, no matter how pressing, could the world be guided. I began to enter into a World conception of human uplift, and one centering about the work and income of the working class. I emerge into a World of War, and weep

Hail and Hail again
Uncounted Dead of all the Wars of all the Worlds!
Outnumbering the living
Millions to one.
Hail and farewell!
Brood of blood-clotted babies
Birthed in bitter pain.
Sired of Old Man Murder,
Mothered by the harlot, Gain!
Nursed in the crippled brains of senile Senators
On the milked gold of venal Congressmen.
Trained by Generals, tricked in tawdry tinsel,
Singing to martial music, trumpeting to drum:
March, March, Robots, March!
Kill, kill, ever kill!
Come Deaf, Blind, Dumb!
Die, die, always die!
Rot, rot, ta-ra-ra, rot!

Scream, O silent Dead,
Into whose sad and sightless faces
I stand and stare.
I feel what you felt
When Assyria quenched the first fine flame of Egypt;
I see what you saw when Greeks buried Greece beneath the Parthenon;
I hear what you heard when Rome tore down her towers and fell her
    endless fall.
I know what you know as America murders Asia
As Africa is pain and shame
And Europe rushes down to Hell

Shrieking with candle, book and bell.
I weep the tears you can no longer weep
For you are dead and Death is black
And I am black
And Blacks are red with all the blood
That Whites have shed.

If cowards die let brave men live
To face the sky.
Let all be one and one vast will
Cry: Stop, Halt, Hold!
Awake O Witless, drear and dread
Awake O Mothers of the dead
Save the World!
    Save the children and their dreams
    Save the color and the sound
    Save the form of faiths unfound
Save Civilization, soul and sod,
Save the tattered shreds of God!
War is murder, murder hate
And suicide, stupidity
Incorporate.

Appendix

I represent millions of citizens of the United States who are just as opposed to war as you are. But it is not easy for American citizens either to know the truth about the world or to express it. This is true despite the intelligence and wealth and energy of the United States. Perhaps I can best perform my duty to my country and to the cause of world peace by taking a short time to explain the historic reasons for the part which the United States is playing in the world today. I can do this the more appropriately because I represent that large group of fourteen million Americans, one tenth of the nation, who in a sense explain America's pressing problems.

The two great advantages of the United States have been vast natural resources and effective labor force. The first effective labor force were slaves, at first both white and black, but increasingly as time went on black Africans brought in by an intense effort made by the English especially in the 18th century which succeeded in landing 15 million black laborers in all the Americas from 1500 to 1800, at a cost of 100,000,000 souls to Africa, disrupting its culture and ruining its economy. This labor gave the world tobacco, cotton, sugar and numbers of other crops and opened America to the world. There followed an increasing migration of millions of workers chiefly from Europe who became energetic laborers with initiative and skill encouraged by the large and immediate returns from their efforts. With free land, favorable climate and freedom of trade, the individual laborer could make a living and often become rich without the necessity of any wide social control for the common good. Plenty for most workers, without socialism, marked America from 1800 to 1900.

But this was possible not only because of vast resources but also because of the slavery of the blacks. So long as a depressed class of slaves with no political nor social rights supplied a rich mass of basic materials and a whole area of personal service the share of white capital and white labor was abnormally large. Even when the expanding mass of white labor tried to build a democratic form of government, inspired by the thinkers of the late 18th century, they faced the uncomfortable fact of slavery in the land of liberty. Some wanted to abolish Negro slavery forthwith: but slaves represented too much invested property and income for this to be easy. So in 1787, the United States declared "All men are equal" in the face of the fact that at the time nearly one American in every five was a slave. This was not complete hypocrisy. Most persons believed that Negro slavery could not continue without a slave trade so they arranged to suppress this African trade in 20 years and thus gradually they hoped the slave labor would disappear.

This did not happen, because slave labor in the United States even with a curtailed slave trade began to raise so valuable a cotton crop that this crop by use of newly invented machinery became one of the most profitable investments of the modern world. The spindles for spinning cotton cloth in Europe increased from five million in 1800 to 150 million in 1900 and black labor furnished the raw material. This was the Cotton Kingdom and it represented vast capital and the income of millions of people. Slavery therefore in the United States by 1820, had so firm an economic foundation that emancipation became impossible without cataclysm.

This pressure for social upheaval naturally did not come from the organizers of industry, nor from property owners, nor even at first from the white workers, who had been taught that their high wages depended on the slavery of Negroes. The pressure came primarily from the Negroes; first by their sheer physical expansion from 750,000 in 1790 to 3 million in 1840, of whom nearly 400,000 had gained their freedom by purchase, escape or philanthropy. They organized systematic escape from the territory where the slave system prevailed: they joined with white men in an abolition movement; and their kin in Haiti and other West Indies Islands shook the world with bloody revolt.

But the struggle of the black slave for freedom did not gain the sympathy of the majority of citizens of the United States. This was because a persistent propaganda campaign had been spread as slave labor began to increase in value, to prove by science and religion that black men were not real men; that they were a sub-species fit only for slavery. Consequently the fight for democracy and especially the struggle for a broader social control of wealth and of individual effort was hindered and turned aside by wide-spread contempt for the lowest class of labor and the consequent undue emphasis put on unhampered freedom of individual effort, even at the cost of social loss and degradation. Therefore at the time when socialism and broad social control for the common good should have spread in the United States as it was spreading in Europe there grew on the contrary exaltation of industrial anarchy, tightening of the slave system and belief in individual or group success even at the expense of national welfare.

The catastrophe was precipitated as the workers gradually discovered that slavery of their black fellows was not to their advantage if slave labor spread to the free soil of the West. The nation went to Civil War therefore not to abolish slavery, but to limit it to the cotton states. The South was determined to spread slavery in the North and if not there, into the Caribbean and South America. This would cut Northern capital off from its most valuable market, and the North fought to preserve this market. But the North could not win without the co-operation of the slaves themselves, since the slaves were raising food for the Southern armies. Gradually by a general strike the Negroes began to desert to the Northern armies as laborers, servants and spies, until at last 300,000 of them became armed soldiers while a million more stood ready to fight. Thus American Negroes gained their freedom.

Now came the problem as to what to do with them. They were ignorant, poverty-stricken, sick. The Northerners wanted to let them drift. The freedmen desperately wanted land and education. A plan of socialistic control with schools and land distribution was worked out by philanthropists, but industry rejected it as too costly and as alien to American individualism. Then came a hitch: unless the slaves were given the right to vote, their numerical voting strength would go to their white former masters, who would vote to lower the tariff on which war industry flourished and to scale the war debt owned by Northern banks. Suddenly industry gave the black freedmen the vote, expecting them to fail but meantime to break the power of the planters. The Negroes did not fail; they enfranchised their white fellow workers, established public schools for all and began a modern socialistic legislation for hospitals, prisons and land distribution. Immediately the former slave owners made a deal with the Northern industrial leaders for the disfranchisement of the freedmen. The South would support the tariff and the debt. The freedmen lost the right to vote but retained their schools, poorly supported as they were by their own meager wages and Northern philanthropy.

The history of the United States in the last 75 years has been one of the great series of events in human history. With marvelous technique based on scientific knowledge with organized expert management, vast natural resources and world wide commerce, this country has built the greatest industrial machine in history—still capable of wide expansion. This organization is socialistic in its planning and coordination and methods but it is not under democratic control, nor are its objects those of the welfare state.

Our industry is today controlled, as George Seldes tells us, by 1,000 individuals and is conducted primarily for their profit and power. This does not exclude a great deal which is for the progress of America and the world, but human progress is not its main object nor its sole result. The American philosophy brought over from pioneer days was that individual success was necessarily social uplift, and today large numbers of Americans firmly believe that the success of monopolized industry controlled by an oligarchy is the success of this nation. It is not; and the high standard of living in the United States and its productive capacity is not due to monopoly and private profit, but has come in spite of this and indicates how much higher standards of living might have been reached not only in America but throughout the world, if the bounty of the United States and its industrial planning had been administered for the progress of the masses instead of the power and luxury of the few.

The power of private corporate wealth in the United States has throttled democracy and this was made possible by the color caste which followed Reconstruction after the Civil War. When the Negro was disfranchised in the South, the white South was and is owned increasingly by the industrial North. Thus, caste which deprived the mass of Negroes of political and Civil Rights and compelled them to accept the lowest wage, lay underneath the vast industrial profit of the years 1890 to 1900 when the greatest combinations of capital took place.

The fight of Negroes for democracy in these years was the main movement of the kind in the United States. They began to gain the sympathy and cooperation of those liberal whites who succeeded the abolitionists and who now realized that physical emancipation of a working class must be followed by political and economic emancipation or means nothing. For more than a half century this battle of a group of black and white Americans for the abolition of color caste has gone on and made striking progress: The American Negro is beginning to vote, to be admitted to labor unions and to be granted many Civil Rights. But the mischief and long neglect of democracy has already spread throughout the Nation. A large percentage of eligible voters do not go to the polls. Democracy has no part in industry, save through the violence or threatened violence of the strike. No great American industry admits that it could or should be controlled by those who do its work. But unless democratic methods enter industry, democracy fails to function in other paths of life. Our political life is admittedly under the control of organized wealth and while the socialized organization of all our work proceeds, its management remains under oligarchical control and its objects are what that oligarchy decide. They may be beneficial decisions, they may be detrimental, but in no case are they arrived at by democratic methods.

The claim of the United States that it represents democracy in contrast to fascism or communism is patently false. Fascism is oligarchy in control of a socialized state which is run for the benefit of the oligarchs and their friends. Communism is a socialized state conducted by a group of workers for the benefit of the mass of the people. There may be little difference in the nature of the controls exercised in the United States, fascist Germany and the Soviet republics. There is a world of difference in the objects of that control. In the United States today the object is to center and increase the power of those who control organized wealth and they seek to prove to Americans that no other system is so successful in human progress. But instead of leaving proof of this to the free investigation of science, the reports of a free press, and the discussion of the public platform, today in the United States, organized wealth owns the press and chief news gathering organs and is exercising increased control over the schools and making public discussion and even free thinking difficult and often impossible.

The cure for this and the way to change the socially planned United States into a welfare state is for the American people to take over the control of the nation in industry as well as government. This is proceeding gradually. Many Americans are not aware of this, but it is true: we conduct the post office; we are in the express and banking business; we have built the great Tennessee Valley river control system; we exercise control in varying degrees over railroads, radio, city planning, air and water traffic; in a thousand other ways, social control for general welfare is growing and must grow in our country. But knowledge of this, of its success and of its prevalence in other lands, does not reach the mass of people. They are today being carried away by almost hysterical propaganda that the freedoms which they have and such individual initiative as remains are being threatened and that a third world war is the only remedy.

Not all America has succumbed to this indefensible belief. The Progressive Party . . . has challenged this program; the voters in 1948 declared wide agreement but were induced by fear to vote for a man who has not carried out his promises; the Council of Arts, Sciences and Professions assembled a vast protest against war last year and the religious sect of Quakers have just issued a fine balanced statement in the same line. There are millions of other Americans who agree with these leaders of the Peace Movement. I bring you their greeting.

B. SOME OF THE 83RD BIRTHDAY GREETINGS

ENGLAND:

"Every year of his noble useful life adds to the richness of our generation and helps to break the shackles which still fetter all enslaved and oppressed peoples,"—THE VERY REV. DR. HEWLETT JOHNSON, *Dean of Canterbury.*

"Dr. Du Bois has shown to all the world that the great tradition of American citizenship is still a living and inspiring reality."—JOHN D. BERNAL, *Prof. of Physics, Birkbeck College.*

"I pay tribute to Dr. Du Bois' courage and integrity and congratulate America in possessing so fine a son steeped in its grandest traditions of truth and freedom."—THE HON. IVOR MONTAGU, *chairman, British Peace Society.*

FRANCE:

"Profound admiration your courageous inspiring efforts for a victorious peace."—JOLIOT-CURIE, *president, World Peace Council.*

"At your side, as at the side of all Americans who work to save peace, are all the defenders of peace throughout the world. They assure you of their active support and warm sympathy."—JEAN LAFFITTE, *secretary, World Peace Council.*

SOVIET UNION:

"I congratulate the great friend of peace and of all the peoples who preserving the youthfulnes of his heart battles now for the youth of all countries and all races."—ILYA EHRENBURG, *author.*

"Wish you good health and many years to live to work successfully for cause of peace throughout world for cause of progress and happiness of whole humanity."—DMITRI SHOSTAKOVITCH, *composer.*

"In my name and in name of Soviet Peace Committee we wholeheartedly congratulate you upon your 83rd birthday. We greet you as an ardent and firm fighter for peace in all countries. Wish you health, success in your noble fight for strengthening of ties of friendship between American and Soviet peoples for strengthening of peace throughout whole world."—NIKOLAI TIKHONOV, *chairman, Soviet Peace Committee.*

"Men of Soviet culture highly appreciate services of this noted fighter for the cause of peace for the rights of the Negro people. Wish Dr. Du Bois good health and success in his noble work devoted to defense of peace in the world."—ALEXANDER FADEYEV, *author.*

HUNGARY:

"The Hungarian working people wish you to be able to continue serving the great cause of peace and fighting against the dark forces of tyranny and racial persecution."—HUNGARIAN NATIONAL PEACE COUNCIL.

"To the meritorious veteran fighter for peace, the heartiest congratulations." —GEORG LUKACS, *author.*

ITALY:

"Best wishes for a long life in the service of progress and peace."—PIETRO NENNI, *Member of Parliament.*

"When we think of the real America we see this great country in terms of the moral stature of public figures like Dr. Du Bois."—GINO BARDI, *writer.*

CHINA:

"I wish you a long life and I hope that all your descendants enjoy the same longevity and the fruits of labor."—KUO MO JO, *Vice Premier, Government Administrative Council, People's Republic of China.*

ISRAEL:

"Heartiest greetings birthday brilliant educator Du Bois grand fighter peace liberty."—AVISHAUL, *writer;* EISENSTADT, *professor.*

NEW ZEALAND:

"May your long and useful life be continued in happiness and peace. The world is your debtor."—THE VERY REV. C. W. CHANDLER, *Dean of Hamilton, New Zealand.*

AFRICA:

"It is to the undying honour of Dr. Du Bois that he has devoted his entire life to the struggle for the dignity of the Negro, and has demonstrated the connection between this struggle and that of the workers throughout the world. And this struggle is today bearing its fruit not only in the United States, but in Africa herself, where the Negroes are becoming conscious not only of the oppression from which they are now suffering, but also of their own historical traditions, of the contributions that they have made to universal civilization and of the immense potentialities lying before their peoples."—GABRIEL D'ARBUSSIER, *Deputy from French North Africa in the Assembly of French Union.*

AUSTRIA:

"Dr. Du Bois' steadfast stand is an inspiring example to defenders of peace, not only in America, but throughout the world."—BRUNO FREI, *editor of* Der Abend *and of* Tagebuch.

POLAND:
"Our best wishes and words of solidarity with his inflexible struggle for progress and peace."—*Polish Committee for Cultural Co-operation with Foreign Countries.*

"We are deeply moved, Professor Du Bois, and protest strongly against the ruthless persecution you are suffering for your staunch fight for the world peace."—DR. JAN WASILKOWSKI, *Rector Prof., University of Warsaw.*

"On behalf of the millions of peace fighters in this country the Polish Peace Defenders Committee conveys to you, the persistent selfless fighter for peace and freedom, its sincere and cordial greetings."—HENRYK MALINOWSKI, *secretary, Polish Peace Defenders Committee.*

"Please convey to Dr. Du Bois on the occasion of his 83rd birthday the warmest congratulations of the Union of Polish Writers. His name is honored in all of Poland."—LEON KRUCZKOWSKI, *chairman;* JERZY PUTRAMENT, *secretary-general.*

CZECHOSLOVAKIA:
"All peace loving people and with them all progressive journalists admire in your person one of the greatest living Americans of our time."—JIRI HRONEK, *Secretary-General, International Organization of Journalists.*

"Charles University in Prague, fully appreciative of your personal qualities and your contribution to the great fight against oppression by those who try to mask their violence and terror, sends you its heartful greetings and warmest sympathy."—PROF. J. MUKAROVSKY, *Rector of Charles University.*

"On behalf of three million members, the Central Council of Trade Unions wishes to convey its warmest fraternal greetings to Professor Du Bois, upright fighter for human rights and world peace."—*Central Council of Trade Unions, Prague.*

"On the occasion of a meeting given in your honour we beg to offer our happiest greetings to you, the gallant fighter for the rights of the Negro people and one of the main representatives of the fight for peace in the world."—*Union of Czechoslovak Writers.*

"Czechoslovak historians highly appreciate your example of a scientist having devoted his life and work to the fight for the triumph of justice, progress and peace. They stand firmly with you in your present struggle to avoid a new world war."—PROFESSOR DR. Z. NEJEDLY, *Minister of Education.*

GERMANY:
"Be assured that we are in our thoughts with you with the most sincere peace greetings."—ARNOLD ZWEIG, *president, German Committee for Peace.*

UNITED STATES:
"Congratulations. You have always given hope to our cause."—MARY WHITE OVINGTON, *Founder,* N.A.A.C.P.

"Hearty congratulations upon your life long service to the cause of freedom. None of your friends have any doubt of your loyalty to our country we know you have the inward fortitude and calm for this hour of trial."—LESLIE PINCKNEY HILL, *Principal, Cheyney State College, Pa.*

"I am extending to our great scholar and forthright fighter for democracy and freedom, my fondest congratulations with a hope that many, many years will still be granted him to hold high the torch of free men in the world of peace and brotherhood."—MARY MCLEOD BETHUNE, *Founder, President-Emeritus, National Council of Negro Women, Inc.*

"Many blessings to a most loyal American, great scholar and a staunch friend."—ADA M. YOUNG, *widow of Colonel Charles Young, U.S.A.*

"Your example of steadfastness and courage is an inspiration to all who yearn for peace and the enlightenment of mankind."—DR. and MRS. JOHN ADAMS KINGSBURY.

"Dr. Du Bois is one of the great pioneers of our new civilization and though for the present the day may seem dark—a new day is arising. Thank God for such a man!"—MOST REV. WILLIAM H. FRANCIS, *Archbishop of the Old Catholic Church, Woodstock, N.Y.*

"In honoring Dr. Du Bois you are honoring yourselves. He is the race's greatest scholar and has been a champion of human rights for a half century and has always been in the forefront when the battle was the hottest."—J. FINLEY WILSON, *Grand Exalted Ruler, I.B.P.O.E.W.*

"I shall consider it a great privilege if you will honor me by including me as one of the sponsors of this occasion."—OLIN DOWNES, *writer.*

"My heartiest greetings and best wishes to him on this occasion. His life and work have been an inspiration to all of us."—CHARLES H. THOMPSON, *Dean, Graduate School, Howard University.*

"Greetings and best wishes to Dr. Du Bois, scholar, statesman and crusader for human rights."—BENJAMIN E. MAYS, *president, Morehouse College.*

"Your foresighted, courageous and uncompromising leadership role in racial, national and world affairs has been through the years an inspiration to the alumni and students of Fisk University, your alma mater, which shall ever revere and hold you in high esteem."—T. M. BRUMFIELD, *Acting Alumni Secretary, Fisk University.*

"I am aroused and concerned that the policy of government officials is to initiate this kind of a prosecution against so distinguished an American liberal at a time when Nazi murderers are being released. . . . I salute Dr. Du Bois, a distinguished American who has fought with courage for sixty years in the battle for civil rights for all of the American people."—HUBERT T. DELANY, *Justice, Domestic Relations Court, New York City.*

"Dr. Du Bois, you have kept the faith."—GEORGE A. COE, *Professor of Education (retired), Teachers College, Columbia University.*

"I salute you as one of America's great men and the Dean of Negro writers and scholars."—LANGSTON HUGHES.

"Honor to a venerable pioneer in true meaning of the humanistic tradition as evident in what he has accomplished."—E. A. JONES, *President, College Languages Association, Baltimore.*

". . . We support you and we wholeheartedly join with you in the struggle for freedom, justice and peace."—OLIVER T. PALMER, *business agent, United Cafeteria and Restaurant Workers, Washington, D.C.*

"Every American who believes in liberty and freedom is grateful for the work Dr. Du Bois has done as editor of the *Crisis* and in support of the great work of the National Association for the Advancement of Colored People."—JEROME DAVIS, *author*.

"The contributions you made to the world in literature stand as a monument to you. I count it a privilege to have known you down through the years and wish for many more birthdays."—SADIE P. DELANEY, *Librarian, Veterans Hospital, Tuskegee*.

"I join you all in spirit as you honor our most sterling realist and defender of human decency."—JEFFERSON P. ROGERS, *Secretary for Race Relations, Evangelical & Reformed Church of America, Cleveland, Ohio*.

"We would like to be counted among the millions who are greeting you with love on your 83rd anniversary."—LYDIA *and* ROBERT MINOR, *Croton, N.Y.*

"With pride in you, our people, and our family I send this wish for happiness for your 83rd birthday."—DU BOIS WILLIAMS, *granddaughter of Dr. Du Bois, freshman at Fisk University*.

C. FOLLOWING THE VERDICT

As soon as the trial was finished by a directed acquittal, the press of the nation in small, partially buried accounts, the radio on nation-wide broadcasts, and the Negro press with headlines and pictures, announced the result; and a flood of messages from all over the world poured in.

From white Americans or from organizations in which both white and colored people participated, there came telegrams and letters. Trade unions sent in congratulations from all over the United States and Europe, from Africa and Asia and the West Indies. Many persons sent letters which they had mailed Judge McGuire.

The American Negro press printed some caustic comments. P. L. Prattis in the Pittsburgh *Courier* said:

> "November 20 will undoubtedly become a date long remembered in the history of the American Negro. It will mark the high point, not the low point, of the long career of Dr. Du Bois. When these days shall have passed and 'the terror' shall have vanished upon the return of sanity, the measure of those who truly fought for peace will be taken. In those days to come, future historians will measure off the dimensions of Dr. Du Bois and discover the stature of one of the greatest protagonists of peace, and of the poor, of this and all times.
>
> "This bit of history, denied me, will be the pleasure and inspiration of my children and grandchildren."

One of the most interesting tributes came from Gordon B. Hancock, a conservative colored writer, a graduate of Colgate and Harvard, who has taught sociology thirty years at a Negro college in Virginia. He wrote for the Associated Negro press, in December, 1951:

> "There is a shout in the heart of Negroes everywhere, for Du Bois has long been our symbol of manhood and integrity. He has shown in a thousand ways that he is

the ablest champion of the Negroes' yet unrealized full citizenship. It was a shame that Dr. Du Bois, the Negro champion, almost had to bear his cross alone.

"Negroes who might have helped and held up his hands followed afar off. This writer was humbled to see in a list of Negroes petitioning President Truman for executive help so few influential Negroes. In other words the important Negroes of this country, the headliners, the highly positioned, the degreed Negroes stayed off the petition by droves. Negroes who claim to be race champions and crusaders and fighters and leaders and uncompromisers to the last ditch actually deserted Dr. Du Bois in the hour of his greatest trial."

D. AFTERMATH—A POSTSCRIPT BY SHIRLEY GRAHAM

As we were working on this manuscript, we received in January an invitation to attend the American Intercontinental Peace Conference scheduled for January 22–27, 1952, in Rio de Janeiro. The call said:

"We call to participate in this Conference all those who sincerely want peace, regardless of their political opinions, their religious beliefs or their ideas on the cause of the present crisis; workers and farmers, mothers and youth, intellectuals and churchmen, scientists and technicians, men and students, industrialists and small businessmen, artists and writers—all men and women of good will in all countries of the American continent."

This invitation was signed by 120 leaders of South America.

We could not go because the notice of the meeting was too short. So my husband wrote:

"My personal feeling of loss in not being present today among you is all the greater because I have so long yearned to visit South America—that vast, rich and fateful continent, which carrying as it does in its veins the blood of Latin and African, European and Indian; and whose great cultural gifts, from Spain, Guinea and the Incas, is destined yet to help lead modern civilization. Its major hindrance, as we well know, lies in that very wealth which today should help South America rise from poverty, ignorance and disease—namely, tin, oil, coffee, rubber, nitrates, fruits and meat. The domination of these and other products of Brazil, Chile, Bolivia, Argentina and Venezuela by the monopoly capitalism of North America and western Europe, together with political and land control by native capital, is the almost irresistible force which is driving us, your nation and mine, to renewed colonialism and war. This is why we see in the United Nations a combination of Big Business in all the Americas, united to force the world into war in order to protect the profits of the greedy. This was the reason why only last October I was forced to beg and spend $35,000 in United States courts to secure acquittal from false charges arising from my advocacy of Peace.

Our great and only hope lies in conferences like this to arouse the peacemakers of the world, to arouse the chained workers to ensure peace, reform industry and distribute wealth according to justice and not by cheating, stealing and gambling; so that the better minds and souls of North and South America, together with socialist Europe, the Communist Soviets, and redeemed China, may stand together for a new and just world.

"For these great objectives, I send you greetings and hope."

When we were notified that the Conference had been postponed until March we immediately applied for passports to attend. I had held American passports for 24 years, and my husband for 59 years.

This is February 14, 1952, our wedding anniversary. And this morning the postman brought us a present—a heavy, white square bearing the emblem of the State Department of the land of our birth. On the sheet was written:

"My dear Mr. Du Bois:
    "The Department has received your recent application for a passport for travel to Brazil accompanied by your wife, Shirley Graham Du Bois.
    "The Department has given careful consideration to your request. However, since it appears that your proposed travel would be contrary to the best interests of the United States, a passport is not being issued to you.
    "The sum of $9.00 which accompanied your application, will be returned to you at a later date. The passport which was issued to Mrs. Du Bois on April 5, 1949, is being retained in the Department's files.

> "Sincerely yours,
> (Signed) R. B. Shipley,
> Chief, Passport Division."

My Country, 'tis of Thee
Sweet Land of Liberty
Of Thee, I sing.

William Edward Burghardt Du Bois: A Chronology

Compiled by Henry Louis Gates, Jr. and Terri Hume Oliver

1868	Born William Edward Burghardt Du Bois, 23 February, in Great Barrington, Massachusetts—the only child of Alfred Du Bois and Mary Silvina Burghardt. Mother and child move to family farm owned by Othello Burghardt, Mary Silvina's father, in South Egremont Plain.
1872	Othello Burghardt dies 19 September and family moves back to Great Barrington, where Mary Sylvina finds work as a domestic servant.
1879	Moves with mother to rooms on Railroad Street. Mother suffers stroke, which partially paralyzes her; she continues to work despite her disability.
1883–1885	Writes occasionally for *Springfield Republican*, the most influential newspaper in the region. Reports on local events for the *New York Globe*, a black weekly, and its successor, the *Freeman*.
1884	Graduates from Great Barrington High School. Works as time-keeper on a construction site.
1885	Mother dies 23 March at age 54. A scholarship is arranged by local Congregational churches so Du Bois can attend Fisk University in Nashville. Enters Fisk with sophomore standing. Contracts typhoid and is seriously ill in October; after recovering, resumes studies and becomes editor of the school newspaper, the *Fisk Herald*.
1886–1887	Teaches at a black school near Alexandria, Tennessee, for two summers. Begins singing with the Mozart Society at Fisk.
1888	Receives BA from Fisk. Enters Harvard College as a junior after receiving a Price-Greenleaf grant.
1890	Awarded second prize in Boylston oratorical competition. Receives BA *cum laude* in philosophy on 25 June. Delivers commencement oration on Jefferson Davis, which receives national press attention. Enters Harvard Graduate School in social science.

1891   Awarded MA in history from Harvard. Begins work on doctorate. Presents paper on the suppression of the African slave trade at meeting of American Historical Association in Washington, D.C.

1892   Awarded a Slater Fund grant to study in Germany at Friedrich Wilhelm University in Berlin.

1893   Grant is extended for an additional year.

1894   Denied doctoral degree at Friedrich Wilhelm University due to residency requirements. Denied further aid from Slater Fund; returns to Great Barrington. Receives teaching chair in classics at Wilberforce University in Xenia, Ohio.

1895   Awarded a PhD in history; he is the first black to receive a PhD from Harvard.

1896   Marries Nina Gomer, a student at Wilberforce. His doctoral thesis, *The Suppression of the African Slave-Trade to United States of America, 1638–1870*, is published as the first volume of Harvard's Historical Monograph Series. Hired by the University of Pennsylvania to conduct a sociological study on the black population of Philadelphia's Seventh Ward.

1897   Joins Alexander Crummell and other black intellectuals to found the American Negro Academy, an association dedicated to black scholarly achievement. Appointed professor of history and economics at Atlanta University. Begins editing a series of sociological studies on black life, the *Atlanta University Studies* (1898–1914). First child, Burghardt Comer Du Bois, is born in Great Barrington on 2 October.

1899   *The Philadelphia Negro* is published by the University of Pennsylvania. Burghardt Gomer Du Bois dies on 24 May in Atlanta and is buried in Great Barrington. Publishes articles in *Atlantic Monthly* and *The Independent*.

1900   In July attends first Pan-African Congress in London and is elected secretary. In an address to the congress, he declares that "the problem of the twentieth century is the problem of the color line." Enters an exhibit at Paris Exposition and wins grand prize for his display on black economic development. Daughter Nina Yolande born 21 October in Great Barrington.

1901   Publishes "The Freedman's Bureau" in *Atlantic Monthly*.

1902   Booker T. Washington offers Du Bois a teaching position at Tuskegee Institute, but Du Bois declines.

1903   *The Souls of Black Folk* is published in April. Publishes the essay "The Talented Tenth" in *The Negro Problem*.

1904   Resigns from Washington's Committee of Twelve for the Advancement of the Negro Race due to ideological differences. Publishes "Credo" in *The Independent*.

1905   Holds the first conference of the Niagara Movement and is named general secretary. Founds and edits *The Moon Illustrated Weekly*.

1906	Second meeting of the Niagara Movement. *The Moon* ceases publication. The Atlanta riots, in which white mobs target blacks, occur in September; Du Bois responds by writing his most famous poem, *A Litany of Atlanta*. After the riots Du Bois's wife and daughter move to Great Barrington.
1907	Niagara Movement in disarray due to debt and dissension. Founds and edits *Horizon*, a monthly paper that folds in 1910.
1908	Fourth conference of Niagara Movement; few attend.
1909	The National Negro Committee, an organization dominated by white liberals, is formed (it will later be renamed the National Association for the Advancement of Colored People [NAACP]); Du Bois joins. The fifth and last Niagara Conference is held. *John Brown*, a biography, is published.
1910	Appointed director of publications and research for the NAACP; becomes the only black member of the board of directors. Moves to New York City to found and edit *The Crisis*, the official publication of the NAACP.
1911	Attends Universal Races Conference in London. Publishes his first novel, *The Quest of the Silver Fleece*. Joins the Socialist Party.
1912	Endorses Woodrow Wilson in *The Crisis*. Resigns from Socialist Party.
1913	Writes and presents *The Star of Ethiopia*, a pageant staged to commemorate the fiftieth anniversary of emancipation.
1914	Supports women's suffrage in *The Crisis*. Supports the Allied effort in World War I despite declaring that imperialist rivalries are a cause of the war.
1915	Booker T. Washington dies on 14 November. *The Negro* is published. Protests D. W. Griffith's racist film *The Birth of a Nation*.
1917	Undergoes kidney operations early in the year. Supports the establishment of separate training camps for black officers as the only way to insure black participation in combat.
1918	In his July editorial for *The Crisis*, he publishes "Close Ranks," urging cooperation with white citizens. The War Department offers Du Bois a commission as a captain in the army in an effort to address racial issues, but the offer is withdrawn after controversy. Goes to Europe in December to evaluate the conditions of black troops for the NAACP.
1919	Organizes the first Pan-African Conference in Paris, and is elected executive secretary. Returns to the U.S. in April and writes the editorial "Returning Soldiers," which the U.S. postmaster Albert Burleson tries to suppress; the issue sells 106,000 copies, the most ever for *The Crisis*.
1920	Founds and edits *The Brownies' Book*, a monthly magazine for children. Publishes *Darkwater: Voices from within the Veil*, a collection of essays.

1921	The second Pan-African Conference is held in London, Brussels, and Paris. Du Bois signs group protest against Henry Ford's support of the anti-Semitic forgery, *Protocols of the Elders of Zion*.
1922	Works for passage of the Dyer Anti-Lynching Bill, which is blocked by Senate.
1923	Writes "Back to Africa," an article attacking Garvey for encouraging racial division. Organizes the third Pan-African Conference in London, Paris, and Lisbon; declines to attend Paris session due to disproval of French assimilationists. Receives the Spingarn Medal from the NAACP. Travels to Liberia to represent the United States at the Liberian presidential inauguration.
1924	Publishes *The Gift of Black Folk: The Negroes in the Making of America*.
1925	Contributes "The Negro Mind Reaches Out" to Alain Locke's *The New Negro: An Interpretation*, one of the most influential works of the Harlem Renaissance.
1926	Founds the Krigwa Players, a Harlem theater group. Travels to the Soviet Union to examine life after the Bolshevik Revolution. Praises Soviet achievements in *The Crisis*.
1927	The fourth and last Pan-African Conference is held in New York City.
1928	Daughter Yolande weds the poet Countee Cullen in Harlem; the marriage ends within a year. Du Bois's novel, *Dark Princess, A Romance*, is published.
1929	*The Crisis* faces financial collapse.
1930	Awarded honorary Doctor of Laws degree from Howard University.
1932	Du Bois's daughter Yolande and her second husband, Arnett Williams, have a daughter, Du Bois Williams.
1933	Losing faith in the possibilities of integration, Du Bois begins to publicly examine his position on segregation. Accepts a one-year visiting professorship at Atlanta University. Relinquishes the editorship of *The Crisis* but retains general control of the magazine.
1934	Writes editorials encouraging voluntary segregation and criticizing the integrationist policies of the NAACP. Resigns as editor of *The Crisis* and from the NAACP. Accepts the chairmanship in sociology at Atlanta University. Named the editor in chief of the *Encyclopedia of the Negro*, which is never completed or published.
1935	Publishes the revolutionary historical study, *Black Reconstruction*.
1936	Spends five months in Germany on a grant to study industrial education. Travels through Poland, the Soviet Union, Manchuria, China, and Japan.
1938	Receives honorary Doctor of Laws degree from Atlanta University and honorary Doctor of Letters degree from Fisk.
1939	*Black Folk, Then and Now*, a revised edition of *The Negro* is published.

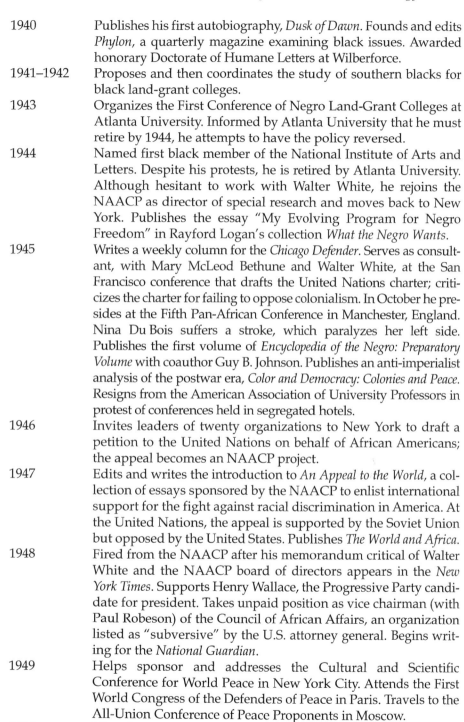

1940   Publishes his first autobiography, *Dusk of Dawn*. Founds and edits
              Phylon, a quarterly magazine examining black issues. Awarded
              honorary Doctorate of Humane Letters at Wilberforce.
1941–1942   Proposes and then coordinates the study of southern blacks for
              black land-grant colleges.
1943   Organizes the First Conference of Negro Land-Grant Colleges at
              Atlanta University. Informed by Atlanta University that he must
              retire by 1944, he attempts to have the policy reversed.
1944   Named first black member of the National Institute of Arts and
              Letters. Despite his protests, he is retired by Atlanta University.
              Although hesitant to work with Walter White, he rejoins the
              NAACP as director of special research and moves back to New
              York. Publishes the essay "My Evolving Program for Negro
              Freedom" in Rayford Logan's collection *What the Negro Wants*.
1945   Writes a weekly column for the *Chicago Defender*. Serves as consult-
              ant, with Mary McLeod Bethune and Walter White, at the San
              Francisco conference that drafts the United Nations charter; criti-
              cizes the charter for failing to oppose colonialism. In October he pre-
              sides at the Fifth Pan-African Conference in Manchester, England.
              Nina Du Bois suffers a stroke, which paralyzes her left side.
              Publishes the first volume of *Encyclopedia of the Negro: Preparatory
              Volume* with coauthor Guy B. Johnson. Publishes an anti-imperialist
              analysis of the postwar era, *Color and Democracy: Colonies and Peace*.
              Resigns from the American Association of University Professors in
              protest of conferences held in segregated hotels.
1946   Invites leaders of twenty organizations to New York to draft a
              petition to the United Nations on behalf of African Americans;
              the appeal becomes an NAACP project.
1947   Edits and writes the introduction to *An Appeal to the World*, a col-
              lection of essays sponsored by the NAACP to enlist international
              support for the fight against racial discrimination in America. At
              the United Nations, the appeal is supported by the Soviet Union
              but opposed by the United States. Publishes *The World and Africa*.
1948   Fired from the NAACP after his memorandum critical of Walter
              White and the NAACP board of directors appears in the *New
              York Times*. Supports Henry Wallace, the Progressive Party candi-
              date for president. Takes unpaid position as vice chairman (with
              Paul Robeson) of the Council of African Affairs, an organization
              listed as "subversive" by the U.S. attorney general. Begins writ-
              ing for the *National Guardian*.
1949   Helps sponsor and addresses the Cultural and Scientific
              Conference for World Peace in New York City. Attends the First
              World Congress of the Defenders of Peace in Paris. Travels to the
              All-Union Conference of Peace Proponents in Moscow.
1950   Nina Gomer Du Bois dies in Baltimore in July; she is buried in
              Great Barrington. Elected chairman of the Peace Information

Center, an organization dedicated to the international peace movement and the banning of nuclear weapons. Organization disbands under pressure from the Department of Justice. Du Bois is nominated by the American Labor Party for U.S. senator from New York. Receives 4 percent of the vote statewide, 15 percent in Harlem.

1951   Secretly marries Shirley Graham, aged 45, a writer, teacher, and civil rights activist, on Valentine's Day. Indicted earlier that month as an "unregistered foreign agent" under the McCormick Act: Du Bois, along with four other officers of the Peace Information Center, is alleged to be agents of foreign interests. He suffers the indignity of being handcuffed, searched, and fingerprinted before being released on bail in Washington, D.C. National lecture tours and a fundraising campaign for his defense expenses raise over $35,000. The five-day trial in Washington ends in acquittal.

1952   Publishes *In Battle for Peace*, an account of the trial. The State Department refuses Du Bois a passport on grounds that his foreign travel is not in the national interest. Later, the State Department demands a statement declaring that he is not a Communist Party member; Du Bois refuses. Advocacy of leftwing political positions widens the distance between Du Bois and the black mainstream.

1953   Prints a eulogy for Stalin in *National Guardian*. Reads 23rd Psalm at the funeral of Julius and Ethel Rosenberg, executed as Soviet spies. Awarded International Peace Prize by the World Peace Council.

1954   Surprised by the Supreme Court decision in *Brown v. Topeka Board of Education*, which outlaws public school segregation, Du Bois declares "I have seen the impossible happen."

1955   Refused a U.S. passport to attend the World Youth Festival in Warsaw, Poland.

1956   Supports Reverend Martin Luther King Jr. during the Montgomery bus boycott. Refused a passport in order to lecture in the People's Republic of China.

1957   Publishes *The Ordeal of Mansart*, the first volume of the *Black Flame*, a trilogy of historical novels chronicling black life from Reconstruction to the mid-twentieth century. A bust of Du Bois is unveiled at the Schomburg Collection of the New York Public Library. Refused a passport to attend independence ceremonies in Ghana. His great-grandson Arthur Edward McFarlane II is born.

1958   A celebration for Du Bois's ninetieth birthday is held at the Roosevelt Hotel in New York City; 2,000 people attend. Begins writing *The Autobiography of W. E. B. Du Bois*, drawing largely from earlier work. A Supreme Court ruling allows Du Bois to obtain a passport. His subsequent world tour includes England, France, Belgium, Holland, Czechoslovakia, East Germany, and the Soviet Union. He receives an honorary doctorate from Humbolt University in East Berlin, known as Friedrich Wilhelm University when Du Bois attended in 1892–1894.

1959   Meets with Nikita Khrushchev. In Beijing, makes broadcast to Africa over Radio Beijing and meets with Mao Zedong and Zhou Enlai. Awarded the International Lenin Prize. Publishes the second volume of the *Black Flame* trilogy, *Mansart Builds a School*.

1960   Participates in the celebration of Ghana's establishment as a republic. Travels to Nigeria for the inauguration of its first African governor-general.

1961   Du Bois's daughter Yolande dies of a heart attack in March. *Worlds of Color*, the final book in the *Black Flame* trilogy, is published. Du Bois accepts the invitation of Kwame Nkrumah to move to Ghana and direct a revival of the *Encyclopedia Africana* project. Before leaving for Africa, Du Bois applies for membership in the Communist Party.

1962   Travels to China. His autobiography is published in the Soviet Union.

1963   Becomes a citizen of Ghana. Turns ninety-five in February. Dies in Accra, Ghana, on 27 August, on the eve of the civil rights march on Washington. W. E. B. Du Bois is buried in a state funeral in Accra on the 29th.

1968   *The Autobiography of W. E. B. Du Bois* is published in the United States.

1992   Honored by the United States Postal Service with a 29-cent commemorative stamp as part of the Black Heritage Series, and again in 1998, with a 32-cent commemorative stamp.

1999   Du Bois's efforts to produce alternately an encyclopedia of the Negro and of Africa and Africans are realized when *Encarta Africana* is published by Microsoft, and *Africana: The Encyclopedia of the African and African American Experience*, edited by Kwame Anthony Appiah and Henry Louis Gates Jr. is published by Basic Civitas Books. In 2005 a second much-expanded edition of *Africana* is published by Oxford University Press.

Selected Bibliography

WORKS OF W. E. B. DU BOIS

The Suppression of the African Slave-Trade to the United States of America, 1638–1870. New York: Longmans, Green, 1896.

Atlanta University Publications on the Study of Negro Problems. Publications of the Atlanta University Conferences, ed. Du Bois (1898–1913).

The Philadelphia Negro: A Social Study. Boston: Ginn and Company, 1899.

The Souls of Black Folk: Essays and Sketches. Chicago: A. C. McClurg, 1911.

John Brown. Philadelphia: George W. Jacobs, 1909.

The Quest of the Silver Fleece: A Novel. Chicago: A. C. McClurg, 1911.

The Negro. New York: Harcourt, Brace, 1928.

Darkwater: Voices from within the Veil. New York: Harcourt, Brace and Howe, 1920.

The Gift of Black Folk: Negroes in the Making of America. Boston: Stratford, 1924.

Dark Princess: A Romance. New York: Harcourt, Brace, 1928.

Africa—Its Place in Modern History. Girard, Kansas: Haldeman-Julius, 1930.

Africa, Its Geography, People, and Products. Girard, Kansas: Haldeman-Julius, 1930.

Black Reconstruction: An Essay toward a History of the Part Which Black Folk Played in the Attempt to Reconstruct Democracy in America, 1860–1880. New York: Harcourt, Brace, 1935.

Black Folk Then and Now: An Essay in the History and Sociology of the Negro Race. New York: Henry Holt, 1939.

Dusk of Dawn: An Essay toward an Autobiography of a Race Concept. New York: Harcourt, Brace, 1940.

Color and Democracy: Colonies and Peace. New York: Harcourt, Brace, 1945.

Du Bois, W. E. B., and Guy B. Johnson. *Encyclopedia of the Negro, Preparatory Volume with Reference Lists and Reports.* New York: Phelps-Stokes Fund, 1946.

The World and Africa: An Inquiry into the Part Which Africa Has Played in World History. New York: Masses & Mainstream, 1947.

I Take My Stand for Peace. New York: Masses & Mainstream, 1951.

The Ordeal of Mansart. New York: Mainstream, 1957.

In Battle for Peace: The Story of My 83rd Birthday. With Comment by Shirley Graham. New York: Masses & Mainstream, 1952.

Fourty-Two Years of the USSR [sic]. Chicago: Baan Books, 1959.

Worlds of Color. New York: Mainstream, 1961.

An ABC of Color: Selections from over a Half Century of the Writings of W. E. B. Du Bois. Berlin: Seven Seas, 1963.

The Autobiography of W. E. B. Du Bois: A Soliloquy on Viewing My Life from the Last Decade of Its First Century, ed. Herbert Aptheker. New York: International Publishers, 1968.

COLLECTIONS

Aptheker, Herbert, ed. *Creative Writings by W. E. B. Du Bois: A Pageant, Poems, Short Stories, and Playlets.* New York: Kraus-Thomson Organization, 1985.

Aptheker, Herbert, ed. *The Complete Published Works of W. E. B. Du Bois.* 35 vols. Millwood, NY: Kraus-Thomson, 1973.

Aptheker, Herbert, ed. *The Correspondence of W. E. B. Du Bois.* 3 vols. Amherst: University of Massachusetts Press, 1973–1978.

Aptheker, Herbert, ed. *Writings by W. E. B. Du Bois in periodicals Edited by Others.* 4 vols. Millwood, NY: Kraus-Thomson, 1982.

Foner, Philip S., ed. *W. E. B. Du Bois Speaks: Speeches and Addresses 1890–1919.* New York: Pathfinder, 1970.

Huggins, Nathan I., ed. *W. E. B. Du Bois: Writings.* New York: Library of America, 1986.

Lewis, David Levering, ed. *W. E. B. Du Bois: A Reader.* New York: Henry Holt, 1985.

Sundquist, Eric J., ed. *The Oxford W. E. B. Du Bois Reader.* New York: Oxford University Press, 1996.

BIBLIOGRAPHIES

Aphtheker, Herbert. *Annotated Bibliography of the Published Writings of W. E. B. Du Bois.* Millwood, NY: Kraus-Thomson, 1973.

McDonnell, Robert W., and Paul C. Partington. *W. E. B. Du Bois: A Bibliography of Writings About Him.* Whittier, CA: Paul C. Partington Book Publisher, 1989.

Partington, Paul C. *W. E. B. Du Bois: A Bibliography of His Published Writings.* Whittier, CA: Paul C. Partington Book Publisher, 1977.

BIOGRAPHIES

Broderick, Francis L. *W. E. B. Du Bois: A Negro Leader in Time of Crisis.* Stanford: Stanford University Press, 1959.

Du Bois, Shirley Graham. *His Day is Marching On: A Memoir of W. E. B. Du Bois.* Philadelphia: Lippincott, 1971.

Lewis, David Levering. *W. E. B. Du Bois: The Fight for Equality and the American Century, 1919–1963.* New York: Henry Holt, 2000.

Marable, Manning. *W. E. B. Du Bois: Black Radical Democrat.* Boston: Twayne, 1986.

Rudwick, Elliot M. *W. E. B. Du Bois: Propagandist of the Negro Protest.* 1960; reprint. New York: Atheneum, 1968.

CRITICAL WORKS

Appiah, Anthony. "The Uncompleted Argument: Du Bois and the Illusion of Race." *Critical Inquiry* 12 (Autumn 1985): 21–37.

Aptheker, Herbert. *The Literary Legacy of W. E. B. Du Bois*. Whit Plains, NY: Kraus International, 1989.

Ashton, Susanna. "Du Bois's 'Horizon': Documenting Movements of the Color Line." *MELUS* 26.4 (2001): 3–23.

Baker, Houston A., Jr. "The Black Man of Culture: W. E. B. Du bois and *The Souls of Black Folk*." In *Long Black Song*. Charlottesville: University of Virginia Press, 1972.

Balfour, Lawrie. "Representative Women: Slavery, Citizenship, and Feminist Theory in Du Bois's 'Damnation of Women.'" *Hypatia: A Journal of Feminist Philosophy* 20.3 (2005): 127–148.

Bauerlein, Mark. "Booker T. Washington and W. E. B. Du Bois: The Origins of a Bitter Intellectual Battle." *Journal of Blacks in Higher Education* 46 (Winter 2004–2005): 106–114.

Bell, Bernard, Emily Grosholz, and James Stewart, eds. *W. E. B. Du Bois on Race and Culture: Philosophy, Politics, and Poetics*. New York: Routledge, Chapman, and Hall, 1996.

Bhabha, Homi K. "The Black Savant and the *Dark Princess*." *ESQ: A Journal of the American Renaissance* 50.1–3 (2004): 137–155.

Blight, David W. "W. E. B. Du Bois and the Struggle for American Historical Memory." In *History and Memory in African-American Culture*, ed. Genevieve Fabre and Robert O'Meally. New York: Oxford University Press, 1994.

Bremen, Brian A. "Du Bois, Emerson, and the 'Fate' of Black Folk." *American Literary Realism* 24 (Spring 1992): 80–88.

Bruce, Dickson D., Jr. "W. E. B. Du Bois and the Idea of Double Consciousness." *American Literature: A Journal of Literary History, Criticism, and Bibliography* 64.2 (June 1992): 299–309.

Byerman, Keith. *Seizing the Word: History, Art, and the Self in the Work of W. E. B. Du Bois*. Athens: University of Georgia Press, 1994.

Castronovo, Russ. "Beauty along the Color Line: Lynching, Aesthetics and the Crisis." *PMLA: Publications of the Modern Language Association of America* 36.2 (2006): 1443–1159.

Crouch, Stanley, and Playthell Benjamin. *Reconsidering the Souls of Black Folk: Thoughts on the Groundbreaking Classic Work of W. E. B. Du Bois*. Philadelphia: Running Press, 2002.

Early, Gerald, ed. *Lure and Loathing: Essays on Race, Identity, and the Ambivalence of Assimilation*. New York: Allen Lane, 1993.

Fisher, Rebecka Rutledge. "Cultural Artifacts and the Narrative of History: W. E. B. Du Bois and the Exhibiting of Culture at the 1900 Paris Exposition Universelle." *MFS: Modern Fiction Studies* 51.4 (2005): 741–774.

Fontenot, Chester J., Mary Alice Morgan, and Sarah Gardner, eds. *W. E. B. Du Bois and Race*. Macon, Georgia: Mercer University Press, 2001.

Frederickson, George. "The Double Life of W. E. B. Du Bois." *New York Review of Books* 48.2 (February 8, 2001): 34–36.

Frederickson, George. *The Black Image in the White Mind: The Debate on Afro-American Character and Destiny, 1817–1914*. New York: Harper and Row, 1971.

Gabiddon, Shaun L. "W. E. B. Du Bois: Pioneering American Criminologist." *Journal of Black Studies* 31.5 (2001): 581–599.

Gooding-Williams, Robert. "Du Bois's Counter-Sublime." *The Massachusetts Review: A Quarterly of Literature, the Arts and Public Affairs* 35.2 (Summer 1994): 202–224.

Herring, Scott. "Du Bois and the Minstrels." *MELUS* 22 (Summer 1997): 3–18.

Hubbard, Dolan, ed. *The Souls of Black Folk One Hundred Years Later*. Columbia, Missouri: University of Missouri Press, 2003.

Jones, Gavin. " 'Whose Line Is It Anyway?' W. E. B. Du Bois and the Language of the Color-Line." In *Race Consciousness: African-American Studies for the New Century*, ed. Judith Jackson Fossett and Jeffrey A. Tucker. New York: New York University Press, 1997.

Judy, Ronald A. T., ed. "Sociology Hesitant: Thinking with W. E. B. Du Bois." Special Issue: *Boundary 2: An International Journal of Literature and Culture* 27.3 (2000).

Juguo, Zhang. *W. E. B. Du Bois and the Quest for the Abolition of the Color Line*. New York: Routledge, 2001.

Kirschke, Amy. "Du Bois, *The Crisis*, and Images of Africa and the Diaspora." In *African Diasporas in the New and Old Worlds: Consciousness and Imagination*, ed. Geneviève Fabre and Benesch Klaus. Amsterdam: Rodopi, 2004. 239–262.

Lemke, Sieglinde. "Transatlantic Relations: The German Du Bois." In *German? American? Literature? New Directions in German-American Studies*, ed. Winfried Fluck and Werner Sollors. New York: Peter Lang, 2002. 207–215.

McCaskill, Barbara, and Caroline Gebhard, eds. and introd. *Post-Bellum, Pre-Harlem: African American Literature and Culture*. New York: New York University Press, 2006.

McKay, Nellie. "W. E. B. Du Bois: The Black Women in His Writings—Selected Fictional and Autobiographical Portraits." In *Critical Essays on W. E. B. Du Bois*, ed. William L. Andrews. Boston: G. K. Hall, 1985.

Meier, August. "The Paradox of W. E. B. Du Bois." In *Negro Thought in America, 1880–1915; Radical Ideologies in the Age of Booker T. Washington*. Ann Arbor: University of Michigan Press, 1963.

Miller, Monica. "W. E. B. Du Bois and the Dandy as Diasporic Race Man." *Callaloo* 26.3 (2003): 738–765.

Mizrunchi, Susan. "Neighbors, Strangers, Corpses: Death and Sympathy in the Early Writings of W. E. B. Du Bois." In *Centuries' Ends, Narrative Means*, ed. Robert Newman. Stanford, CA: Stanford University Press, 1996.

Moses, Wilson Jeremiah. *Creative Conflict in African American Thought: Frederick Douglass, Alexander Crummell, Booker T. Washington, W. E. B. Du Bois, and Marcus Garvey*. Cambridge, England: Cambridge University Press, 2004.

Pauley, Garth E. "W. E. B. Du Bois on Woman Suffrage: A Critical Analysis of His *Crisis* Writings." *Journal of Black Studies* 30.3 (2000): 383–410.

Peterson, Dale. "Notes from the Underworld: Dostoyevsky, Du Bois, and the Discovery of the Ethnic Soul." *Massachusetts Review* 35 (Summer 1994): 225–247.

Posnock, Ross. "The Distinction of Du Bois: Aesthetics, Pragmatism, Politics." *American Literary History* 7 (Fall 1995): 500–524.

Rampersad, Arnold. *The Art and Imagination of W. E. B. Du Bois.* Cambridge, MA: Harvard University Press, 1976.

Rampersad, Arnold, and Deborah E. McDowell, eds. *Slavery and the Literary Imagination: Du Bois's* The Souls of Black Folk. Baltimore: Johns Hopkins University Press, 1989.

Rothberg, Michael. "W. E. B. Du Bois in Warsaw: Holocaust Memory and the Color Line, 1949–1952." *Yale Journal of Criticism* 14.1 (2001): 169–189.

Schneider, Ryan. "Sex and the Race Man: Imagining Interracial Relationships in W. E. B. Du Bois's *Darkwater.*" *Arizona Quarterly: A Journal of American Literature, Culture, and Theory* 59.2 (2003): 59–80.

Schrager, Cynthia D. "Both Sides of the Veil: Race, Science, and Mysticism in W. E. B. Du Bois." *American Quarterly* 48 (December 1996): 551–587.

Siemerling, Winfried. "W. E. B. Du Bois, Hegel, and the Staging of Alterity." *Callaloo* 24.1 (2001): 325–333.

Smith, Shawn Michelle. *Photography on the Color Line: W. E. B. Du Bois, Race, and Visual Culture.* Durham: Duke University Press, 2004.

Sundquist, Eric J. "Swing Low: *The Souls of Black Folk.*" In *To Wake the Nations.* Cambridge, MA: Harvard University Press, 1993.

Temperley, Howard, Michael B. Katz, and Thomas J. Sugrue. "W. E. B. Du Bois, Race, and the City." *The Times Literary Supplement.* No. 4996 (1999).

"The Study of African American Problems: W. E. B. Du Bois's Agenda, Then and Now." *Annals of the American Academy of Political and Social Science* 568 (March 2000): 1–313.

Warren, Kenneth W. "Troubled Black Humanity in *The Souls of Black Folk* and *The Autobiography of an Ex-Colored Man.*" In *The Cambridge Companion to American Realism and Naturalism: Howells to London,* ed. Donald Pizer. Cambridge: Cambridge University Press, 1995.

West, Cornel. "W. E. B. Du Bois: The Jamesian Organic Intellectual." In *The American Evasion of Philosophy: A Genealogy of Pragmatism.* Madison: University of Wisconsin Press, 1989.

Williamson, Joel. *The Crucible of Race: Black-White Relations in the American South Since Emancipation.* New York: Oxford University Press, 1984.

Wolters, Raymond. *Du Bois and His Rivals.* Columbia, Missouri: University of Missouri Press, 2002.

Zamir, Shamoon. *Dark Voices: W. E. B. Du Bois and American Thought, 1888–1903.* Chicago: University of Chicago Press, 1995.

Zamir, Shamoon. "'The Sorrow Songs'/'Song of Myself': Du Bois, the Crisis of Leadership, and Prophetic Imagination." In *The Black Columbiad: Defining Moments in African American Literature and Culture.* Cambridge, MA: Harvard University Press, 1994.

Zwarg, Christina. "Du Bois on Trauma: Psychoanalysis and the Would-Be Black Savant." *Cultural Critique* 51 (2002): 1–39.

Printed and bound by CPI Group (UK) Ltd, Croydon, CR0 4YY